Microaggressions and Modern Racism

Charisse C. Levchak

Microaggressions and Modern Racism

Endurance and Evolution

palgrave
macmillan

Charisse C. Levchak
Department of Sociology
Central Connecticut State University
New Britain, CT, USA

ISBN 978-3-030-09946-6 ISBN 978-3-319-70332-9 (eBook)
https://doi.org/10.1007/978-3-319-70332-9

Printed on acid-free paper

This Palgrave Macmillan imprint is published by Springer Nature
The registered company is Springer International Publishing AG
The registered company address is: Gewerbestrasse 11, 6330 Cham, Switzerland

To my husband and best friend, Philip—growing with you and experiencing your unconditional love and support has been such a wonderful gift. I am grateful that we are able to share this amazing journey together.

To my mother, Marie—thank you for the sacrifices you have made for me and for the love and lessons you have poured into me. I wholeheartedly appreciate everything you've done for me.

To my outstanding mentors, colleagues, friends, and students who have inspired me and who have made this journey brighter—I truly appreciate you.

To the interviewees who courageously shared their experiences—thank you.

To those who have cared for me, inspired me, and stood in solidarity with me—I am eternally grateful.

Preface

> I choose to reflect the times and the situations in which I find myself. That, to me, is my duty…and at this crucial time in our lives, when everything is so desperate, when every day is a matter of survival, I don't think you can help but be involved. Young people, Black and White, know this, that's why they are so involved in politics. We will shape and mold this country or it will not be molded and shaped at all anymore. So, I don't think you have a choice… How can you…not reflect the times?
>
> —Nina Simone

My mother taught me awareness at an early age because awareness is a survival strategy. "Pay attention to your surroundings" is a phrase that my mom constantly told me throughout my childhood. On the surface, her message seems typical of *any* parent who is concerned about protecting their child from the archetypal threats of predators or preventable injuries, but it was her desire that I not only survived but also *thrived* in a world that is oftentimes cruel to Black and Brown children and adults. Her intent was not to instill fear, paranoia, anger, hatred, or respectability politics into my mind. Like most parents, she raised me to believe that I could achieve my dreams and goals through hard work. However, I learned early on, that as a Black girl, obtaining upward mobility and a better quality of life necessitated being aware of race and racism, and how they influenced and impacted much of the social world—from social, academic, and professional interactions to how society was structured.

As I grew, my interest in learning about race and culture also flourished. During my formative years, I lived in Bedford-Stuyvesant, Brooklyn—a predominantly Black neighborhood. It was self-affirming to see beautiful, intelligent, and exquisite people who looked like me throughout the community. I have many fond memories, including experiencing love, warmth, amazing flavorful food, a safe space in my mother's and grandmother's homes, summer block parties with soul-moving music, and regal Black women who worked to protect their children, families, and communities by any means necessary. In many ways, I was insulated and protected from individual acts of racism during those years, albeit reflecting on things now, it's difficult not to see how structural, cultural, and institutional racism impacted Bedford-Stuyvesant in the forms of residential segregation, environmental injustice, underemployment, and drugs.

My mother and I moved to midtown Manhattan in the early 1990s. Growing up in Manhattan exposed me to the beauty, wonders, excitement (and also challenges) of living in a racially and culturally diverse environment. The distinct clothing, food, languages, music, and cultural practices that I experienced in varied places—like classrooms, street fairs, museums, restaurants, and a local after-school program—were fascinating to me. While my neighborhood was diverse, there was still a White majority, which I don't recall experiencing in any capacity prior to leaving Bedford-Stuyvesant. My mom and I have a close relationship, and my earliest memories of her include me following her around and engaging in meaningful discussions about the world and social interactions. Looking back, I love the fact that she had conversations *with* me and asked me probing, analytical questions that sharpened my mind and desire for inquiry.

Early on during my time in Manhattan, as we walked from school, my mom asked me how I felt about living in a predominantly White neighborhood. I replied, "If a White person can live here, so can I." As an adult, I understand why she asked me this important question (a question that any person of color should ask themselves or their loved ones who are people of color if they live in a predominantly White place). It was her subtle, yet protective way of asking if I had experienced overt or covert forms of racism (that could make transitioning into a new neighborhood or environment a nightmare). She didn't ask because of a dislike for White people; she asked because we lived in and continue to live in a world where racism harms people of color who are adults, teens and, yes, even children. My response stemmed from the love, affirmation, and self-confidence that was instilled in me by my mother and the other amazing women who raised me. They taught me that my life has value, that I am worthy of love and respect, that I am worthy of living in a nice and safe neighborhood and that I shouldn't accept or expect less because I am Black in a country that has a legacy of mistreating and debasing Black people.

I continued to live in New York City until I left for graduate school. During high school and college, I'd spend time walking around the city and experiencing the best of New York and the multitude of cultures infused throughout the city. In the classroom, I initially gravitated toward psychology but changed my course of study to sociology after taking a course that focused on ethnographies. The course allowed me to study an individual's narrative and experiences *within* the context of what was occurring in the larger social structure. I was hooked. I loved the idea of learning about the world, society, and people in a methodical and reflective way. Through various classes, and amazing professors, I was exposed to scientific, critical, reflective, and reflexive analyses of racism and race. Thoroughly fascinated with the social sciences, I went on to compete for and win a prestigious undergraduate fellowship that sharpened my social scientific research skills and prepared me for graduate school and a career in academia.

After applying to graduate schools, I was accepted to a good selection of schools, mostly in the Midwest—and ultimately chose to attend a doctoral program in sociology at The University of Iowa. In hindsight, I greatly underestimated how difficult and life-changing my journey from Manhattan to the Midwest would be. Besides candid advice from a successful Black mentor who attended graduate school in the Midwest, and who faced racism there, I had no idea what to expect as it related to race relations and racism in Iowa.

I was taught by my family, teachers, and society that hard work would lead to success, and if graduate school was all about hard work, then as a hard worker I would be fine. Right? Looking back, growing up in Brooklyn and Manhattan was incredibly sheltering. Even though I did experience unfairness, injustice, and outright racism at times, it was certainly not as much racism (in terms of intensity and impact) as I experienced in the Midwest. Whether in personal, academic, or professional spaces, I and people of color who confided in me felt race and experienced racism in ways that were formidable enough to derail our private, scholastic, and professional lives. However, many of us are resilient, and so we survived and thrived, regardless of the covert and overt racist attacks we experienced.

In many ways, those racist experiences helped fuel my academic and professional interests. As I reflected on my life and the lives of others who were impacted by racism, I became enraptured with thinking about potential solutions. I decided to expand my studies beyond sociology because learning about society and social problems wasn't enough anymore; I was compelled to also focus on social solutions. Consequently, I applied and was accepted into the Master of Social Work program at my university and pursued both a sociology doctoral degree and social work master's degree simultaneously. While sociology allowed me to understand social problems, social work became an avenue for me to learn about and imagine individual and institutional level interventions that have the potential to improve our world and social relations.

For my dissertation, I wanted to focus on a social problem that impacted people's daily lives, and I was drawn to racist microaggressions, a covert form of racial aggression. My dissertation *An Examination of Racist and Sexist Microaggressions on College Campuses* (Levchak 2013) focused on the prevalence of race and gender-based aggression on a diverse and predominantly White campus. The project was cathartic and illuminating and eventually became the basis for my current projects.

After graduating from The University of Iowa, I spent time gaining additional social work experience at a local organization before being offered an academic position in Wisconsin, where I taught sociology and social work courses. Again, as I reflect on the past, I was underprepared for the onslaught of racist and sexist experiences that I faced. On the one hand, I was excited to begin my first tenure-track position, and on the other hand, I was still far away from my family and support systems on the East Coast, and I was moving away from the few but meaningful support systems and relationships that I'd developed in Iowa. Fortunately, I was offered and accepted a tenure-track position on the East Coast, and my husband secured a position in a nearby town soon after, placing us closer to family and valuable support systems.

In the end, I was returning to the East Coast a different person. On the surface, I was nearly a decade older, married, more resilient, and more educated about the world because of my experiences inside *and* outside the classroom in the Midwest. I learned firsthand the importance of having mentors and allies from various racial and ethnic backgrounds, the power of cultural competence and awareness education, the liberation in finding my voice and speaking out, and how crucial individual and institutional efforts are in combating racism in all of its forms.

However, I also saw or experienced: race-based differential treatment and disrespect in the classroom, workplace, and social settings; the ugliness of racism, and how it sometimes intersected with sexism to create toxic experiences, environments, and sexualized racial violence and harassment —from business meetings to doctors' examination rooms; the failure of state and local government organizations and collegiate institutions in protecting students and employees of color from covert and overt racism, as well as retaliation from reporting; the emotional, psychological, and verbal hazing that occurred when one chose to resist instead of operating as a compliant token; treatment as though I was invisible, didn't belong, or was a criminal in public spaces; the disrespect of my personal space in public spaces; stares, assumptions, and rude comments associated with being in an interracial relationship; and the manifestation of vertical *and* horizontal oppression in academic, professional, and personal relationships.

The racism that I experienced and the narratives that I was exposed to from other people of color who experienced racism on and off college campuses shaped my desire to continue my research and writing about race and racism. As expressed in the Nina Simone quote above, how could I not reflect the times, when the lives and well-being of many people of color are at stake because of racism? Consequently, I went on to expand the scope of my dissertation, and it eventually developed into this book.

In the end, I have been shaped by positive and negative experiences with race. I have thoroughly enjoyed the solidarity and harmony that I have experienced in many of my interracial and interethnic interactions and friendships, and although unpleasant, I have allowed my experiences with racism to fuel my passion for identifying and ending the various manifestations of racism.

Consequently, essential goals of this book include highlighting the experiences and voices of individuals who have faced overt and covert racism, explaining these phenomena through sociological and social justice frameworks, and contemplating ways that covert and overt racism can be reduced and eliminated. Furthermore, it is my hope, that this book will have a role in improving race relations and generating long-lasting positive social change.

New Britain, USA Charisse C. Levchak

References

Garbus, L. (2015). *What happened, Miss Simone?* United States: Netflix.

Levchak, C. C. (2013). *An examination of racist and sexist microaggressions on college campuses.* Unpublished doctoral dissertation, University of Iowa, Iowa City.

Contents

List of Figures

List of Tables

CHAPTER 1

Introduction

Social problems have social solutions.
—Dr. Charisse Levchak

We Are the Solution

Racism is a social problem, but it has a *social* solution. The solution requires dedication and hard work from individuals and institutions, but it is worth the effort. We all have been socialized and influenced intentionally and unintentionally by our family, friends, the media, schools, and other social institutions to either respect, appreciate, or embrace racial diversity or to hold racial biases. When we learn racial biases (and our prejudices go unchecked and unchallenged), the result is a vile mixture of fear, discomfort, and hatred that we hold against other people and even ourselves. Consequently, for many, reflecting on and talking about race and racism generates feelings of discomfort, trepidation, and distress. Some may even become angry and retaliate against those who *do* want to discuss or address issues related to race and racism. So, whether you want to avoid discussing race, biases, and racism, or whether you find doing so cathartic and useful, there are internal and external obstacles that must be overcome if we will ever heal the wounds of racism, be able to fully enjoy interracial solidarity, and achieve social justice.

C. C. Levchak, *Microaggressions and Modern Racism*,
https://doi.org/10.1007/978-3-319-70332-9_1

We Must Overcome Our Biases, Silence, and Inaction

The good news is that we can overcome our biases, and we can meaningfully contribute to interracial solidarity and racial justice efforts. The biases that we hold have been learned, so we can *unlearn* them by embracing cultural competence and awareness education. Cultural competence and awareness training involve being exposed to social justice ideals and diverse narratives that help us learn how to respectfully live among and interact with people from different racial, ethnic, and cultural backgrounds. Another important step toward racial justice and solidarity is being courageous and speaking up when we see racial injustice or bigotry being directed toward anyone, *regardless of race*. Those of us who are truly interested in peace and racial harmony must be committed to addressing and eradicating race-based aggression and bigotry regardless of whether the target is a person of color *or* White. When we decide that some racial or ethnic groups deserve protection and respect, and others do not, we begin to take on the characteristics of the oppressor. Such biased positions will impede us from attaining true liberation from racial oppression because liberation cannot thrive where oppression is allowed to run rampant. If we will ever achieve peace and healing, we need to work toward these noble goals together and challenge race-based contempt and aggression in all of its forms.

We must also prioritize long-lasting positive social change over our own comfort. This means pushing past short-term discomfort and examining the ways we have been oppressed, the ways that we have contributed to the oppression of others, and the ways that we have been privileged at the expense of others. More importantly, it means finding healing for ourselves, healing for those we have hurt, healing for those who we stand in solidarity with, and ensuring that we do our part to end racism in the United States. It also means questioning and analyzing the intricacies of our social environment, challenging the oppressive behaviors that we see in others, not being defensive when others reveal our transgressions, and checking and challenging ourselves when we are wrong. When our biases start playing in our minds, we have the power to change our course of thinking and action. We can make the active choice to embrace peace and unity by approaching each other with genuine interest, empathy, concern, and respect. Once we have pushed past our biases, apprehension, dread, and, in some cases hatred, we can achieve understanding, awareness, solidarity, and, yes, even love.

We Must Talk About Racism and Do Our Part to Address It

As discussed above, conversations about race can result in a range of emotions that often includes anger, guilt, and avoidance. However, discussing race and racism is inextricably linked to improving race relations in the United States. If we let our emotions deter us from addressing racism, how can our wounded race relations in the United States ever be healed?

Oppression thrives in silence, and if we want to end racism and achieve racial and social justice, silence will not work. Instead, we should seek out educational opportunities to increase our awareness and to learn anti-racism strategies, and once we've gained this knowledge, we should confidently use our voice to speak out against injustice and to engage in anti-racism efforts. However, even with knowledge and empathy, we must still resist the temptation to remain silent because silence about racism can be just as damaging as acts of racism. This sentiment is captured in a quote by Dr. Martin Luther King, Jr.:

> He who passively accepts evil is as much involved in it as he who helps to perpetrate it. He who accepts evil without protesting against it is really cooperating with it. (King 2010: 39)

Benefits for People of Color

I believe that people of color discuss race and racism for three very important reasons that I refer to as the "3Ps"—preparation, protection, and processing. We talk about race and racism in order to *prepare* each other for the harsh realities of being a person of color in a White supremacist society. Such conversations usually center on the racist experiences a person of color has endured, as well as the strategies they used to avoid, challenge, and overcome affronts. The preparation stage helps to *protect* us from victimization because we learn valuable information and strategies through shared narratives. For example, we might learn who our allies are, which spaces are safe, and which spaces are unsafe. During this stage, we might also discover useful strategies such as recording racist incidents or saving racist correspondences so they can be used as evidence when we report aggressors or offenders to authorities or to the police. The *processing* stage involves having an open dialogue about race and racism with a trusted confidant in an effort to heal from the race-based challenges we have faced and so we can further build resilience. The "3Ps" are represented in Fig. 1.1.

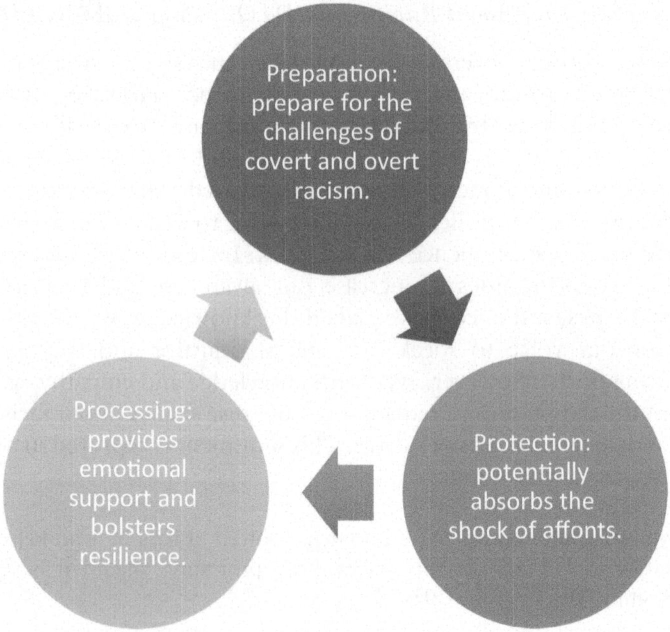

Fig. 1.1 3P's model: Benefits of discussing race for target groups

Benefits for Everyone

Short-term unease related to talking about race is inconsequential compared to enjoying and benefiting from friendships and relationships with people of all racial backgrounds; cultural exchanges where shared knowledge and information can change individuals, communities, and the world for the better; schools and workplaces that are free from racism and where the voices, creativity, and intellect of people of color are no longer suppressed; positive representation in the media where people of color are depicted in positive ways that inspire everyone; and the elimination of racist hate crimes that only increase racial animus and distrust. Overall, it is my hope that this project will encourage *constructive conversations* about modern racism and that it will *inspire interventions* to reduce racism and help targets of racism.

Purpose of Work

When the roots of this project began to develop in 2011, the United States was experiencing a fascinating cultural moment as it related to race. With the election of our first Black president, President Barack Obama, a few years behind us, the anticipation of his reelection in 2012, and the increased visibility of people of color within academia, workplaces, and the media and popular culture, it was easy for some to be hopeful about race relations and racial justice. Some even argued that racism was dead and that we had become a post-racial society because of the publicized advancements and achievements of people of color. However, in actuality, many people of color still experienced racism in their daily lives.

When I casually compared the narratives and experiences of people I knew, many did not involve experiences of blatant and overt racism (although those occurred too). Instead, most of the racist incidents that I learned about were *covert* in nature: the friend who was subtly sabotaged and pushed out of a predominantly White graduate program, the family member whose authority over her non-Black subordinates had constantly been undermined, and the Black mentor who had been unfairly castigated.

I began to wonder if anyone was doing research on *covert forms of racism* in our "post-racial" and "post-racist" society from a sociological and social justice perspective. After beginning a review of the literature on race and racism, and conducting informal inquiries and interviews about modern racism, it became apparent that covert racism was rampant but was rarely talked about in solid, social scientific terms or in a way that was accessible to a wider audience.

As I turned to the literature, I encountered a polarization of views about modern-day racism. On one end of the spectrum, some social critics argued that the election of President Obama meant that we were living in a post-racial and post-racist world, where racism was no longer a major social problem (McWhorter 2008, 2010). On the other end of the spectrum were scholars who argued that racism was not only a chronic issue but that it was becoming more insidious and complex over time. The types of racism that they described included new racism (Bonilla-Silva 2014), Racism 2.0 (Wise 2010), and liquid racism (Weaver 2011); however, when I encountered *microaggressions* (Pierce 1970), it seamlessly described the covert racist experiences that I had become all too familiar with personally and vicariously.

I initially focused on racist microaggressions in academia but later expanded my scope to include a study of microaggressions *and* macroaggressions in the workplace, media, and popular culture. I changed my scope because many believe that representation in these areas means that racism is dead; however, this is not true. Unfortunately, racism in the form of microaggressions and macroaggressions is prevalent throughout the United States.

Microaggressions, originally conceptualized by psychiatrist Chester Pierce, can be defined as covert forms of racial aggression (Pierce 1970: 266–267). In his work *Offensive Mechanisms*, Pierce described microaggressions and their consequences in the following quote:

> Most [racist] offensive actions are not gross and crippling. They are subtle and stunning. The enormity of the complications they cause can be appreciated only when one considers that these subtle blows are delivered incessantly...the cumulative effect to the victim and to the victimizer is of an unimaginable magnitude (266).

Pierce also describes macroaggressions, or overt racism, as "gross, dramatic, obvious" manifestations of racism such as lynching (Pierce 1970: 266). This is an important distinction that has seemingly been lost over time, with some laymen and academics conflating overt and covert forms of racist aggression, combining overt and covert racism under the singular term microaggressions, or making confusing classifications that mystify the concepts of overt and covert racist aggression.

In his work, Pierce (1970) asserted that microaggressions and macroaggressions have the potential to impede the target's mental health—a claim that a growing number of researchers have tested and confirmed about microaggressions (Levchak 2013; Nadal et al. 2014; Torres et al. 2010) as well as macroaggressions (Donovan et al. 2013). Research has also made the connection between race-related stress and the decline of physical health (Utsey et al. 2002).

The connection between racist microaggressions, macroaggressions, and health is key because it highlights the seriousness of racism and its negative impact on targets. The physical, verbal, and behavioral race-based aggression that people of color experience affects them physically, mentally, emotionally, and psychologically which has the potential to negatively impact all aspects of their lives.

Sometimes people hear the "micro" attached to microaggressions and assume they are not an indication of a serious social problem. However, to be clear, microaggressions have major consequences for the individual and for our society. For targeted groups, they can ebb away at one's self-esteem, peace of mind, and well-being, leaving emotional and psychological wounds that may never fully heal. On a larger scale, microaggressions reinforce and support racial oppression, while suppressing the brilliance, creativity, and vision of people of color that would otherwise benefit our world. Moreover, microaggressions are symptomatic of the larger social problem of White supremacy, institutional racism, and hatred that fuels racially motivated macroaggressions, bullying, attacks, murders, and massacres.

By focusing on prominent parts of society, such as academia, workplaces, media, and popular culture, I show that racist microaggressions and macroaggressions continue to be pervasive. In schools, microaggressions and macroaggressions impede scholarly pursuits and academic success; in the workplace, they cause distractions, fuel conflict, obstruct professional aspirations, and cause job instability; and in the media and popular culture, microaggressions and macroaggressions reinforce negative stereotypes, racist beliefs, and racist ideologies about people of color.

To this end, research has inadequately determined the prevalence of microaggressions and macroaggressions within various realms of American society. There is a lack of sociological and social justice scholarship that has examined (1) the experiences of students of color with racist microaggressions at a predominantly White school and a diverse school; (2) the racist microaggressions and macroaggressions that employees of color and White employees experience or witness in the workplace; and (3) the racist microaggressions and macroaggressions present in contemporary media and pop culture.

Therefore, the main objectives of this book include illuminating the causes and consequences of modern racism, racist microaggressions, and racist macroaggressions; expanding related theory; and discussing interventions to reduce race-based aggression. It is my hope that everyone will become more reflective, reflexive, and educated about social problems *and* social solutions. I also hope that we become more intentional about educating ourselves and others about the dangers of racist microaggressions and macroaggressions, and that we embrace the idea of working together so that we can move closer to eliminating racism, fully enjoying interracial solidarity, and healing our strained race relations.

Study Parameters and Methods

The research and anecdotal evidence that were collected for this book came from US citizens and international students attending school in the United States. US social institutions and cultural examples will be used unless otherwise noted. When appropriate, aliases will be used to describe individuals and institutions with the exception of publicized mainstream examples.

All research and the majority of examples used have been collected and cultivated within the last decade, with most being from the last four years. While the book aims to include racism that all people of color experience, at times, it will mainly focus on anti-Black racism in the United States.

I specifically use quantitative data (surveys) and qualitative data (open-ended responses and interviews) that I collected as well as contemporary examples of racist microaggressions and macroaggressions that have been publicized in order to provide the audience with an in-depth look at these phenomena. The theoretical frameworks that I employ include critical race theory as well as a series of social justice theories. Microaggressions, macroaggressions, and modern racism will be examined in chapters on academia, employment and workplaces, and the media and popular culture.

Academia

College campuses and classrooms should be safe spaces for all students; however, racism within academic spaces often prevents students of color from enjoying learning environments that are free from racist microaggressions and macroaggressions. In order to address racism on college campuses, it's important to learn how racism manifests in academia and whether environmental context impacts the prevalence of racism. In this chapter, I specifically examine whether racist microaggressions and macroaggressions manifest differently at a predominantly White institution compared to a racially diverse institution. I define these terms and research parameters in the following ways: (1) a predominantly White institution: the majority of students are White (greater than 50% of student body); (2) a diverse institution: the majority of students are non-White (even if White students are the largest racial group, they do not outnumber minority groups when all minority groups are combined).

I have omitted the names of the schools used in my research to protect study participants. Even though the institutions used in this study differ in a variety of ways, they fit the study parameters very well and are good sites for studying race-based microaggressions and macroaggressions on college campuses. The first school is a Midwestern, predominantly White university, where, at the time of data collection, approximately 77% of the student body was White. The second school is also located in the Midwest but is located in a large, diverse urban area where approximately 60% of the student body was composed of students of color at the time of data collection.

An overarching research question for this chapter is, *will race-based microaggressions and macroaggressions be more prevalent at a predominantly White institution?* To answer this question, I use survey data from a sample of college students at a predominantly White school and a diverse institution to (1) examine the prevalence of racist microaggressions and macroaggressions among college students and develop models of their occurrence by race; (2) test double jeopardy and multiple jeopardy theory by observing if women of color experience racism and sexism more than other groups; (3) examine the prevalence of racist and post-racist beliefs among college students and develop models of their origins by race; (4) examine how environmental context impacts student's experiences and beliefs by comparing college students at a predominantly White institution and at a diverse institution; and (5) examine the relationships between demographic factors (race and gender), institution type, experiences (race-based victimization), and attitudes/outlook (racist, post-racist, campus climate, and stress).

Employment and Workplaces

There is an assumption that across occupations there are basic standards of professionalism, collegiality, and civility that are expected of employees. However, the narratives of people of color reveal that many experience disrespect in the form of racist microaggressions *and* macroaggressions from supervisors, colleagues, and subordinates within the workplace. Many are also racially targeted and disrespected by those they serve, such as customers, clients, patients, and students. To understand how modern racism, microaggressions, and macroaggressions manifest in American workplaces, it was necessary to interview individuals who work in different regions and occupations. The names of employees and their workplaces have been omitted to protect study participants (with the exception of publicized examples). The central research question of this chapter is, *will racist microaggressions and macroaggressions impact workers of color regardless of occupation?* I use interview and survey data from a sample of employed people of color and White people throughout the United States to examine the ways that racist microaggressions and macroaggressions manifest in American workplaces.

The Media and Popular Culture

In my work, I theorize that racist messages precede racist beliefs, and racist beliefs precede racist microaggressions and macroaggressions. Therefore, it is crucial to be diligent about the messages we are consuming if we want to reduce racism. Sociologists generally consider the media to be a major agent of socialization because it presents us with messages that have the power to influence our beliefs and behaviors throughout our lives. The media and popular culture also shape how we think about and treat ourselves and others. While the media can positively impact us, its negative effect is deeply concerning (see Prot et al. 2015 for an exemplary review on the media and its influence on us).

As pointed out by Prot et al. (2015), the media has the power to adversely influence our attitudes, beliefs, and behaviors about racial minorities and particularly Black people. People of color are often underrepresented in the media (Hunt and Ramon 2015; Washington 2014), and when they are portrayed, the depictions are frequently negative (Dixon and Linz 2000; Johnson 2015; Savali 2015). This may result in negative beliefs about people of color (Dixon 2008; Gilliam and Iyengar 2000) and fuel negative attitudes and behaviors toward people of color (Johnson et al. 2009).

Therefore, the central research question of this chapter is, ***how do racist microaggressions, macroaggressions, and modern racism manifest within the media?*** To address this question, I examine the prevalence of racist microaggressions and macroaggressions within the media and popular culture (i.e. music, film, television, the Internet, news stories, and politics), and I explain how they contribute to the persistence of racist ideologies and racial oppression. I provide a wide spectrum of examples to show how prevalent, pervasive, and taken-for-granted racist microaggressions, macroaggressions, and modern racism are.

Chapter Outline

In Chap. 2, I discuss important theoretical frameworks and concepts needed to understand modern racism, microaggressions, and macroaggressions. In Chap. 3, I examine racist beliefs and present my findings on racist beliefs and the importance of cultural competence. In Chap. 4, I examine manifestations of modern racism, microaggressions, and macroaggressions in higher education. I explore microaggressions and macroaggressions in the workplace in Chap. 5, and I examine displays of modern racism, microaggressions, and macroaggressions in the media and popular culture in Chap. 6. In Chap. 7, I discuss the future of race and racism in the United States and present suggestions to reduce and address racist microaggressions and macroaggressions at the individual and institutional levels. I also discuss the importance of self-care, education, organizing, and voting in generating positive social change. In summary, this research will illuminate the topic of modern racism, and it will also add to the bourgeoning areas of racist microaggressions and macroaggressions. Additionally, the knowledge gained through this book has the potential to inform policy, programming, and practice that can impact the lives, well-being, and success of all people.

References

Bonilla-Silva, E. (2014). *Racism without racists: Color-blind racism and the persistence of racial inequality in the United States.* Lanham: Rowman and Littlefield.

Dixon, T. L. (2008). Crime news and racialized beliefs: Understanding the relationship between local news viewing and perceptions of African Americans and crime. *Journal of Communication, 58*, 106–125.

Dixon, T. L., & Linz, D. (2000). Overrepresentation and underrepresentation of African American and Latinos as law breakers on television news. *Journal of Communication, 50*, 131–154.

Donovan, R. A., Galban, D. J., Grace, R. K., Bennett, J. K., & Felicié, S. Z. (2013). Impact of racial macro- and microaggressions in Black women's lives: A preliminary analysis. *Journal of Black Psychology, 39*, 185–196.

Gilliam, F. D., Jr., & Iyengar, S. (2000). Prime suspects: The influence of local television news on the viewing public. *American Journal of Political Science, 44*, 560–574.

Hunt, D., & Ramón, A. C. (2015). *2015 Hollywood diversity report: Flipping the script.* Retrieved from http://www.bunchecenter.ucla.edu/wp-content/uploads/2015/02/2015-Hollywood-Diversity-Report-2-25-15.pdf

Johnson, M. Z. (2015, June 14). 8 ways the media upholds White privilege and demonizes people of color. *Everyday Feminism.* Retrieved from http://everydayfeminism.com/ 2015/07/the-media white privilege/

Johnson, J. D., Olivo, N., Gibson, N., Reed, W., & Ashburn-Nardo, L. (2009). Priming media stereotypes reduces support for social welfare policies: The mediating role of empathy. *Personality and Social Psychology Bulletin, 35*, 463–476.

King, M. L., Jr. (2010). *Stride toward freedom: The Montgomery story*. Boston: Beacon Press.

Levchak, C. C. (2013). *An examination of racist and sexist microaggressions on college campuses* (Unpublished doctoral dissertation). University of Iowa, Iowa City.

McWhorter, J. H. (2008, December 30). Racism in America is over. *Forbes*. Retrieved from http://www.forbes.com/2008/12/30/end-of-racism-oped-cx_jm_1230mcwhorter.html

McWhorter, J. H. (2010, January 14). It's official: America is 'post-racial' in the age of Obama. *The Grio*. Retrieved from http://www.thegrio.com/2010/01/its-official-america-is-postracial-in-the-age-of-obama.php

Nadal, K. L., Griffin, K. E., Wong, Y., Hamit, S., & Rasmus, M. (2014). The impact of racial microaggressions on mental health: Counseling implications for clients of color. *Journal of Counseling & Development, 92*, 57–66.

Pierce, C. (1970). Offensive mechanisms. In F. Barbour (Ed.), *The Black seventies* (pp. 265–282). Boston: Porter Sargent.

Prot, S., Anderson, C. A., Gentile, D. A., Warburton, W., Saleem, M., Groves, C. L., & Brown, S. C. (2015). Media as agents of socialization. In J. E. Grusec & P. D. Hastings (Eds.), *Handbook of socialization* (2nd ed., pp. 276–300). New York: Guilford Press.

Savali, K. W. (2015, June 2). Throw away the script: How media bias is killing Black America. *The Root*. Retrieved from http://www.theroot.com/articles/culture/2015/06/how_media_ bias_is_ killing_black_america/

Torres, L., Driscoll, M. W., & Burrow, A. L. (2010). Racial microaggressions and psychological functioning among highly achieving African Americans: A mixed-methods approach. *Journal of Social & Clinical Psychology, 29*, 1074–1099.

Utsey, S. O., Payne, Y. A., Jackson, E. S., & Jones, A. M. (2002). Race-related stress, quality of life indicators, and life satisfaction among elderly African Americans. *Cultural Diversity and Ethnic Minority Psychology, 8*, 224–233.

Washington, J. (2014, August 9). Less than 5% of actors in top films are Hispanic, new study finds. *Washington Post*. Retrieved from https://www.washingtonpost.com/entertainment/less-than-5percent-of-actors-in-top-films-are-hispanic-new-study-finds/2014/08/06/5be9b224-1be7-11e4-82f9-2cd6fa8da5c4_story.html?utm_term=.0a953b7c89ae

Weaver, S. (2011). Liquid racism and the ambiguity of Ali G. *European Journal of Cultural Studies, 14*, 249–264.

Wise, T. (2010). *Colorblind: The rise of post-racial politics and the retreat from racial equity*. San Francisco: City Lights Books.

CHAPTER 2

Microaggressions, Macroaggressions, and Modern Racism

Offensive mechanisms, the small, continuous bombardments of micro-aggression…is the essential ingredient in race relations and race interactions.
—Chester Pierce (1970: 282)

The State of Contemporary Race Relations in the United States

As I write these words, the Black community and its allies are deeply distressed at the racism in modern-day America. Many are heartbroken, yet empowered to generate positive social change, because we want to end racism, and we desire safety and freedom for ourselves and others. We want to end racist attacks on our bodies and communities—like the massacre at the Mother Emanuel AME Church; the race-based harassment and violence during and after the 2016 election season; the burning of Black churches; racially motivated murders of Black men, women, and children; race-based violence and domestic terrorism committed by White nationalists; and the countless unpublicized narratives of indignity that are directed toward marginalized communities. We are living in a time when people are attacked for wanting justice for all and where virtual and physical spaces aren't safe because of vitriolic speech and hateful behavior. We are certainly living in precarious times, when racial justice seems like a lofty goal and a distant reality.

C. C. Levchak, *Microaggressions and Modern Racism*,
https://doi.org/10.1007/978-3-319-70332-9_2

Personal accounts, news reports, and research reveal how widespread and rampant racist microaggressions and macroaggressions are (Levchak 2013; Donovan et al. 2013). Whether in academic settings, workplaces, or within the media and popular culture, racist biases, stereotypes, and actions abound. For college and graduate students, experiencing racist microaggressions and macroaggressions can compromise their well-being and negatively impact their academic experience (see Chap. 4). Racist aggression can also derail short-term and long-term scholastic and professional goals. For groups who have historically been subjugated, microaggressions and macroaggressions on campus can negatively impact their chances of attaining upward mobility.

Being the recipient of racist microaggressions and macroaggressions in the workplace may result in unemployment, job insecurity, and a decline in one's mental and emotional health (see Chap. 5). Racist aggression in the workplace can create a toxic and hostile work environment that limits the creativity and productivity of employees and may even result in lawsuits or fines for the employer.

In terms of the media and popular culture, research shows that if we are not mindful of the media we are consuming, we can absorb racist messages that adversely affect our perceptions of, and interactions with, targeted group members (Dixon 2008; Gilliam and Iyengar 2000; Greenberg et al. 2002; Johnson et al. 2009; Mastro and Tropp 2004; Prot et al. 2015). We are living in a time when technology, and particularly the Internet, has made the world feel smaller, and one would imagine that online access would provide an opportunity for us to see the humanity in one another. However, instead of fostering unity across racial, social, cultural, and political lines, our online interactions on forums and comment sections operate more like minefields filled with hate speech between *and* within groups, rather than places where we can learn from one another and nurture cultural competence and cultural awareness (see Chap. 6).

The Need for Protections Against Racist Macroaggressions and Microaggressions

Even though there are some laws, policies, and procedures in place to protect targeted group members from macroaggressions or blatant manifestations of racism, the success of such efforts is questionable. The Civil Rights Movement of the 1960s influenced legislation (e.g. The Civil Rights Act of 1964 and The Civil Rights Act of 1968) that was crafted to protect people of color from some forms of overt racism, although it is arguable how effective the corresponding laws and their implementations have been. Although affirmative action policies and programs attempt to level the playing field for individuals by removing racist barriers that would otherwise block people of color from pursuing and achieving upward mobility through higher education and employment, these efforts only address a small portion of diversity-related issues in higher education and workplaces. Creating a diverse student body and workforce is one issue, but *retaining* diverse students and employees and protecting them from racist aggression on campuses and worksites is another issue that has not been adequately addressed. Additionally, while it is extremely important that there are federal and state laws against hate crimes, there has been a growing concern that such laws are not being enforced effectively (Wagner 2015; Cassidy 2016; Jacobson 2016). Protections against microaggressions or covert racism are even more elusive, since it is often difficult to detect and address microaggressions due to their intricate and insidious nature. However, we won't be able to eradicate racism unless we can protect targets from harmful microaggressions and macroaggressions and hold aggressors accountable for their racist actions.

Policies and procedures that combat race-based microaggressions and macroaggressions and that protect targets should be implemented in all schools and workplaces. However, research indicates that we should pay particular attention to racism in predominantly White environments. Levin and McDevitt (1993) explain that most perpetrators of hate crimes engaged in what they call "retaliatory" hate crimes, where aggressors claimed to be "defending their territory" from a wrongful intrusion of racial minorities into traditionally "White" environments. While Levin and McDevitt's work explains the occurrence of macroaggressions in predominantly White environments, the idea of "defending White territory" may also explain the manifestation of *microaggressions* in predominantly White spaces.

The Anti-Defamation League (2008) reports that nearly one third of hate crimes occur on school grounds. In their study, Stotzer and Hossellman (2012) write: "[G]iven that colleges and universities are traditionally White domains, the increase of racial/ethnic minorities could potentially trigger resistance to their increasing presence through race-based hate crimes and other forms of ethnoviolence." Research also shows that the majority of identified perpetrators who committed violence toward minority students were White males, who were oftentimes fraternity members (Ehrlich 1998; Perry 2010). Perpetrators also included faculty members and people without campus affiliations who were connected to White supremacist groups (Ehrlich 1998; Perry 2010). Furthermore, such environments often fail to provide the support and safeguards students of color need to enjoy a successful and safe academic journey free of racial aggression (Price et al. 2009; Wilson and Constantine 1999).

While more research must be done on racist aggression in the workplace, it is clear that racism and racial harassment are present in American workplaces (Tahmincioglu 2008; Vega 2015). Research also shows that Latinos and African Americans experience higher rates of workplace bullying than Whites (Namie 2014).

As for the media, people of color are underrepresented in films and television, and when they are represented, they are often negatively portrayed. Negative representations are incredibly concerning because not only do they influence how we think about and value people of color (Dixon 2008; Gilliam and Iyengar 2000) they also adversely impact how people of color view themselves and can even reduce their self-esteem (Martins and Harrison 2011; Goldberg 2012). Underrepresentation is also troubling because it robs us from seeing, appreciating, and learning about individuals, cultures, and communities of color. The fact that our country is composed of people from a variety of racial, ethnic, and cultural backgrounds should be cause enough to create racially, ethnically, and culturally diverse television shows and films. However, due to the legacy of White supremacy in this country, the narratives of people of color are silenced, and many are disallowed the opportunity to see positive representations of themselves that are brilliant, lovely, complex, and antithetical to the racialized stereotypes that are common in the mainstream media.

Racism is a cancer that harms individuals, institutions, and social relations. We can no longer afford to disregard racism because when racism is ignored it cannot be prevented, reported, or eradicated. Therefore, it is extremely important to evaluate the current manifestations of modern racism, microaggressions, and macroaggressions and to work together to rid them from our lives and our social institutions.

Theoretical Frameworks

> One of the most durable paradoxes of white supremacy—[is] the idea that those who are closest to an experience of oppression... are its least credible witnesses.
>
> —Walter Johnson (1999: 9)

Over time, I have learned that writing about and studying issues related to race and racism is cathartic and liberating. I have also learned that researching and writing about race and racism requires an honesty and authenticity that comes from being reflective and reflexive. I am not just a social scientist; I am a social scientist who is also a Black woman. It would be disingenuous to pretend that my understanding of race and racism solely comes from intellectual exposure and not also from my lived experience as a Black woman who has experienced racist microaggressions and macroaggressions firsthand.

Relatedly, I believe that hearing a variety of narratives from people who have experienced racism is essential to gaining a comprehensive understanding of racism. For too long, the narratives and voices of marginalized people have been suppressed and silenced. While targets and allies understand the value and importance of discussing race and naming racism, aggressors and oppressors embrace a culture of silence regarding race and racism. Moreover, this culture of silence has disastrous consequences for targets of racism and for race relations, because it makes it easy to ignore the narratives of targets, masks the seriousness of racism, and stunts the creation of interventions to address racism and improve race relations.

The importance of telling, owning, and sharing our narrative is wonderfully captured in the following Brené Brown quote:

> When we own our stories, we get to write a brave new ending...[w]hen we push down hurt or pretend that struggle doesn't exist, the hurt and struggle own us...Until we find a way to own our collective stories around racism in this country, our history and the stories of pain will own us...Our collective stories of race in the US are not easy to own. They are stories of slavery, violence, and systemic dehumanization. We will have to choose courage over comfort. We will have to feel our way through the shame and sorrow... We have to keep listening even when we want to scream, "I'm not that way. This isn't my fault!" We have to examine and own stereotypes and prejudices. Every single one of us has them. It will be tough... This means honest conversations about how we were raised and what we need to work on. No blaming or shaming, but truth. It's not productive to deny how hard we all work for what we have, but it's not honest to deny that many of us are afforded privileges based on who we are and what we look like. Will these conversations stop violent hate crimes? No one knows for sure, but we shouldn't underestimate the power of love and truth-telling. (Brown 2015)

Sharing our narratives of oppression and listening to the narratives of others is key in understanding and addressing racial oppression. Aggressors and oppressors will continue their destructive behavior if we fail to raise our voices in objection and resistance to racism and if we fail to make room for the narratives of the oppressed to be heard. In this work, I counter the suppression of voices of color by featuring the voices and experiences of people of color who have experienced microaggressions and macroaggressions.

Critical Race Theory

Critical race theory (CRT) is a framework that helps us understand and address race-based oppression because it centers the voices and experiences of people of color with the expectation that we will use such insights to promote long-lasting positive social change (Ortiz and Jani 2010; Hughes and Giles 2010). As a sociologist, social worker, and professor, I choose to employ CRT in my work because I value and appreciate the narratives and perspectives of individuals (even those that differ from my own and that I don't agree with), since listening can be the start of an amazing learning opportunity that can bridge gaps, create solidarity, and contribute to positive social change. Furthermore, I utilize CRT in my work because it compliments my use of qualitative methodologies like open-ended questions and interviews that provide rich and in-depth information on people's experiences with racism (see Solórzano 1998; Solórzano et al. 2000). CRT has specifically been used to understand racial inequities within academic environments (Solórzano and Yosso 2002; Hughes and Giles 2010). However, in this book, it will also be used to understand racism in the workplace, media, and popular culture. Therefore, I use CRT in this book to (1) understand, document, and analyze how race-based microaggressions and macroaggressions manifest on college campuses, at workplaces, and within the media and pop culture; (2) examine racist microaggressions and macroaggressions throughout society by displaying and elucidating the insight and voices of people of color; and (3) highlight anti-racism efforts aimed at reducing racism, increasing inter- racial solidarity, and generating long-lasting positive social change.

Microaggression and Macroaggression Theory: Classic and Contemporary Frameworks

> Most [racist] offensive actions are not gross and crippling. They are subtle and stunning. The enormity of the complications they cause can be appreciated only when one considers that these subtle blows are delivered inces-

santly...the cumulative effect to the victim and to the victimizer is of an unimaginable magnitude.

—Chester Pierce (1970: 266)

The term microaggression was introduced by psychiatrist Chester Pierce in 1970 to describe covert forms of racist aggression that are "subtle and stunning" yet unimaginably harmful (266–267). As noted in the quote at the beginning of this chapter, Pierce also describes microaggressions as "continuous bombardments" of aggression that negatively impact "race relations" and interactions between racial groups (Pierce 1970: 282). Pierce also presents the concept of macroaggressions or overt forms of racist aggression that are "gross, dramatic, [and] obvious" manifestations of racism such as lynching (Pierce 1970: 266). Pierce (1970) makes a clear distinction between racism that is covert (microaggressions) and overt (macroaggressions). This important distinction has seemingly been lost over time, with some laymen and academics conflating overt and covert forms of racist aggression, combining overt and covert racism under the singular term microaggressions, or making confusing classifications that mystify the concepts. I believe that Pierce's (1970) original distinction provides a clear method of talking about racism in a way that makes sense sociologically and generally.

Understanding Overt and Covert Racism

For people of color, navigating workplaces, campuses, and other social spaces becomes more complicated because of racism. Regardless of social critiques that claim we live in a post-racial and post-racist society, racism *is* alive, and not only is racism alive, it manifests overtly *and* covertly. Overt or blatant forms of racism are acts that are undeniably racist. An example would be the domestic terrorism that occurred at the Mother Emanuel AME Church when a racist murdered the church's pastor and Bible study attendees because they were Black.

Covert racism is more underhanded and subtle, but it is also very insidious. Covert racism often bolsters overt racism and is a building block of White supremacy. It is used to construct barriers that oppress people of color while maintaining privileges that benefit White people. Historically, covert racism has been difficult to define and, therefore, challenge. It flourished in the post-Civil Rights era and during the politically correct movement of the 1990s, when blatantly racist speech and actions were not only morally condemned but could also lead to negative legal, social, academic, and professional consequences. On the surface, it appeared to be a great win that blatant racist behavior was on the decline. However, not only did overt racism *endure*, it mutated into harmful and insidious microaggressions and modern racism.

One of the hallmarks of covert racism is that it is elusive and underhanded, and when it is named, the perpetrator (or those who defend the perpetrator), argue that the statement or behavior was a "joke" or a "misunderstanding" which puts the onus on the target or ally to either challenge the assertion or to ignore the offense. Some common examples of covert racism include telling a racist joke, discouraging interracial relationships and friendships, using dog-whistles, racial profiling, perpetuating racial stereotypes, acting on or holding onto prejudices and race-based fears after being exposed to accurate or bias-challenging information, and appropriating Black culture, as well as the unabashed, brazen display and defense of artifacts of hate like confederate flags.

In this book, I refer to covert racism as "racist microaggressions" (e.g. following a person of color around a store as if they will steal or rudely staring at an interracial couple) and overt racism as "racist macroaggressions" (e.g. physical and verbal attacks on people of color because of their race or racist policing procedures like stop-and-frisk campaigns).

I also conceptualize covert and overt racism as existing on a continuum with varying intensities of racist aggression and violence (see Fig. 2.1). Furthermore, defining a racist act of aggression as a microaggression or macroaggression is both an individual and societal process that is based on the target's perception as well as socially agreed upon understandings of what a serious incident is and what an insignificant incident is.

As seen in Fig. 2.1, I make the distinction between microaggressions (covert, subtle, or underhanded racism) and macroaggressions (overt, blatant, or obvious racism) *as well as* acts of aggression that are intentional and unintentional. Moving horizontally, we see that racism can be displayed covertly or overtly, and moving vertically, we see that racism can be either intentional or unintentional. Examples for each type are given below:

- ***Intentional microaggression***: An employer refuses to hire a person because of the target's race or people staring angrily at an interracial couple.

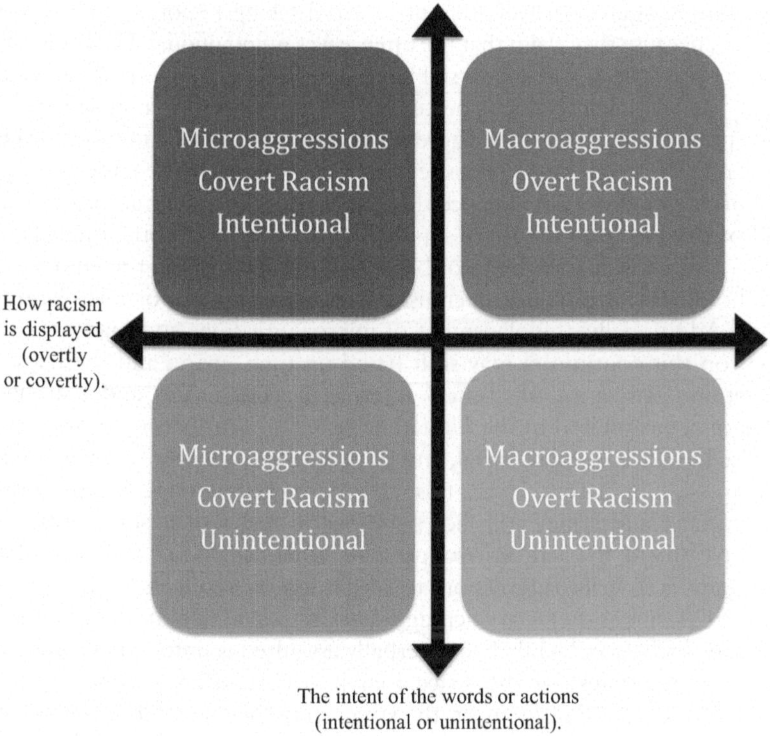

Fig. 2.1 Microaggression and macroaggression continuum

- ***Unintentional microaggression***: A person fails to correctly observe a particular cultural tradition because they haven't been exposed to a given culture or assuming an Asian person is foreign-born.
- ***Intentional macroaggression***: The implementation of Jim Crow Laws and American slavery or physically harming a person of color because of their race.
- ***Unintentional macroaggression***: Carrying out supposedly race-neutral policies that result in disparate outcomes for Blacks and Latinos (e.g. stop-and-frisk policies or sentencing disparities between cocaine users and crack users—although for these examples, it is possible that some policymakers *intended* for these policies to have disparate outcomes).

Regardless of the "intent" of the aggressor, what matters most is the *impact* that racist microaggressions and macroaggressions have on the target.

Oftentimes, aggressors will attempt to avoid taking responsibility for their actions, because they claim that the offense was unintentional. However, that doesn't erase the fact that they still hurt someone and should make amends. In my view, valuing a target's perception of an incident, over an aggressor's perception, helps to hold the aggressor accountable, helps empower the target, and gives credence to the experiences and feelings of the target.

Forms of racism and violence that fall on the covert or microaggressive end of the spectrum are there simply because they are subtle, indirect, or underhanded in nature, and not because I am diminishing the emotional, psychological, or physical repercussions of covert racism or microaggressions. Additionally, the placement of microaggressions and macroaggressions on this continuum may shift based on time, space, and the target's perception. In terms of "time," interracial relationships and marriages were once prohibited in the United States and participating in one often resulted in adverse legal, social, and physical consequences that were *macro*aggressive in nature. Even though interracial marriage is now legal, interracial couples may still face sanctions in terms of looks, stares, and rude treatment that are *micro*aggressive in nature. I will also note that, although racist macroaggressions toward interracial couples have declined, they still occur, as do racial microaggressions that are wounding to targets. In terms of "space," while being verbally assaulted is unfortunate and detrimental (regardless of the space that it occurs in), someone saying a racially motivated comment on the street may have fewer long-term consequences than a coworker or a supervisor saying racist slurs in the workplace (since such comments may adversely impact workplace climate and shape how others view the target as a professional). As for the target's "perception", as explained above, targets have the right to name and label racist incidents as they see fit. While it is common for aggressors, oppressors, and their apologists to victim blame or downplay targets' experiences, as a society, we should learn to respect the perception of targets and offer assistance to them if they want or need support.

Microaggressions and Macroaggressions: Revisiting, Revising, and Creating Concepts

In Chester Pierce's seminal work *Offensive Mechanisms* (1970), he explained that Black people experienced blatant, obvious, and vicious forms of racism called macroaggressions, as well as subtle, underhanded, and elusive forms of racism called microaggressions. Although he problematized both macroaggressions and microaggressions in his work, he spends most of the piece explaining that microaggressions are an especially significant pillar of race relations and racism since they are embedded in everyday interactions. He also explains that microaggressions reinforce the racist message that Black people are inferior and White people are superior.

Derald Wing Sue has also greatly contributed to microaggression theory. Sue et al. (2007: 274–275) theorized that there are three forms of microaggressions: (1) microassaults, (2) microinsults, and (3) microinvalidations. Kevin Nadal has also impressively added to microaggression theory, providing the following explanations. Nadal (2008: 22) notes that microassaults are similar to "old-fashioned" racism, where people behave and speak in blatantly racist ways (e.g. the use of a racial slur to attack someone or striking a person with the intent to harm them because of their race). He also explains that microinsults are "statements or actions that indirectly belittle a person of color and are often unconscious and unintentional." Examples of microinsults include a person being surprised that a person of color is "articulate" or being shocked that they are good at math, because it underscores the racial stereotypes that people of color are not intelligent. Another example of a microinsult includes a student of color being watched on campus as if they are a criminal, a thief, or dangerous (Nadal 2008: 22). Lastly, he explains that microinvalidations "are statements and behaviors that negate or nullify a person of color's experiences or realities" (Nadal 2008: 22). Examples of microinvalidations include a student of color being told that they are "too sensitive about race" or an individual telling a student of color that they "don't see race" (Nadal 2008: 22). Nadal (2008) notes that such declarations are harmful because the perpetrator ignores the target's race-based experiences and reality, and, by ignoring the harm they have done, the perpetrator avoids taking responsibility for their actions and for perpetuating racism.

In my work, for clarity and simplicity, I refer to *microassaults* as *macroaggressions*, and I refer to *microinsults* and *microinvalidations* as *microaggressions*. Additionally, I largely refer to overt racist behaviors *and* speech as macroaggressions and covert racist behavior as microaggressions. As mentioned above, I believe that Pierce's (1970) original classification provides a well-defined way of talking about racism that makes sense sociologically and generally (see Fig. 2.2).

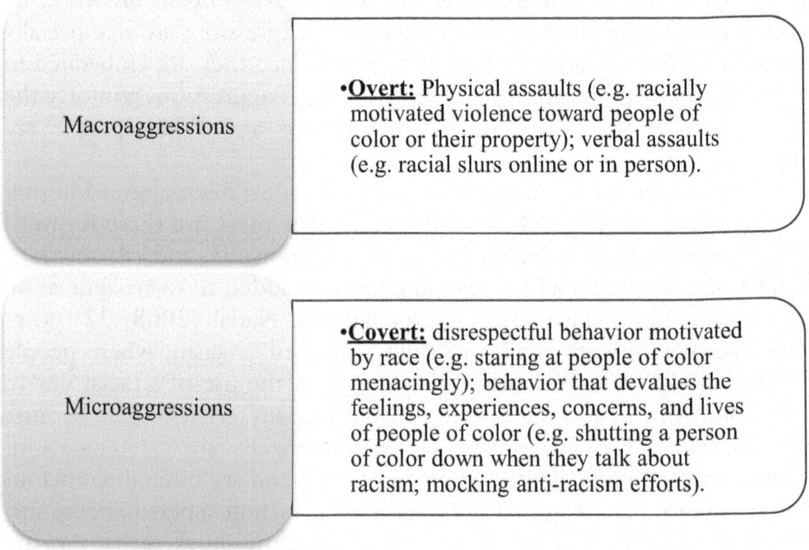

Fig. 2.2 Microaggression and macroaggression classification diagram

Microassaults Are Macroaggressions

Pierce (1970: 266) explained that *macroaggressions* are "gross, dramatic, [and] obvious" forms of racism like lynching, while Sue and others who followed in his tradition labeled such behaviors as *microassaults* (Nadal 2008; Sue et al. 2007). In my view, microassaults *are* macroaggressions and include physical violence, name-calling, mean comments, and threats that occur in person or online and are directed toward a person because of their race.

Macroaggressions have seemingly reduced during the twentieth century as a result of the Civil Rights Movement and the Politically Correct Movement of the 1990s. This resulted in macroaggressors facing social, legal, economic, professional, and academic consequences for their blatantly racist words and actions. Even though there has seemingly been a reduction in overt racist behavior, it is important to note that overt racism still occurs and can increase in prevalence under the right conditions (e.g. when dominant groups feel as though racial minorities are encroaching on their territory [Levin and McDevitt 1993], or when public figures embolden racist behavior). As seen in the prevalence of hate crimes in the United States (Southern Poverty Law Center 2016; Yan et al. 2016; Federal Bureau of Investigation 2015) as well as the following examples from my research on microaggressions and macroaggressions on college campuses (Levchak 2013), it is clear that macroaggressions are very much alive:

> Targets' Experiences
>
> I have been discriminated against a lot. My friends (Black) and I have been harassed by the police many times. I received hate mail for my opinion column about race in the [local paper]. Teachers have harassed me because of my race. I have been judged because I received "a race-card-scholarship (Latina, 22)."
>
> Had people call me nigger (Multiracial man, 21).
>
> Verbal harassment (Multiracial woman, 19).
>
> Being called a spic (Latino man, 20).
>
> Vicarious Experiences and Bystanders' Perceptions
>
> I haven't had any personally, but a group of my friends [were] called niggers when walking to Wal-Mart from [their dorm] (White man, 20).
>
> Person in dorms yelling racial slurs out the window (White man, 20).
>
> I've overheard racist comments while eating or walking (White woman, 19).
>
> I have heard so many racist comments (White woman, 20).
>
> I often hear my peers say extremely derogatory things about individuals from the Black, Hispanic, and especially Asian communities (White woman, 19).
>
> I hear racial slurs all the time (White woman, 18).
>
> My friends have been discriminated against because they were minorities walking home at night. Other friends have not been allowed in bars, because they are minorities (Latina, 21).

Microinsults Are Microaggressions

Microinsults are typically covert and include "statements or actions that indirectly belittle a person of color and are often unconscious and unintentional", although I would stress that based on my observations they are often intentional (Nadal 2008: 22). An example of a microinsult would be when an individual expresses surprise that an Asian person is "articulate" or speaks clear English. This particular stereotype underscores the perpetual foreigner sentiment in which it is assumed that all Asian people are foreign-born and that English is not their first language. Another example would be when an individual expresses surprise that a person of color, and particularly a young person of color, holds a position of power or has a prestigious occupation such as a professor, medical doctor, lawyer, or director of a program. In the autumn of 2016, there was a news story that went viral in which a young Black woman who was also a medical doctor was on a flight and wanted to help another passenger who was having a medical emergency. However, the flight attendant was shocked and didn't believe that the woman was *actually* a doctor and prevented the physician from helping (Hoffman 2016). Many believed that this was a manifestation of racism since the flight attendant couldn't believe that a young Black woman could actually be intelligent and successful enough to be a medical doctor. In response to the story, other Black doctors took to social media using the hashtag #thisiswhatadoctorlookslike in order to demonstrate that there is diversity in the medical profession (Workneh 2016). Research shows that young, Black PhD-holding professors also experience this microinsult (Bailey 2015). Furthermore, this is something that I can attest to experiencing.

The racist harassment associated with "shopping while Black" (which occurs when Black people are followed around stores as if they are going to steal something) is also considered a microinsult (Nadal 2008). Similarly, the race-based vilification that Black students experience when they are watched, followed, or racially profiled by members of the campus community and law enforcement as though they are dangerous or don't belong is also a microinsult. In 2014, a series of microinsults were caught on camera when Rashid Polo, a young Black teenager, filmed himself while being followed by a series of clerks who assumed that he would steal from the store because of his race (Matthews 2014).

Below are examples of microinsults from my research (Levchak 2013):

Targets' Experiences

People are less likely to engage with you because of your race (Latino man, 20).

Having some people fear me or my intentions because I'm Black (Multiracial man, 19).

Stared at; talked to like I'm stupid; avoided; cut off from conversations; ignored (Black man, 19).

I have felt a lot of racism my freshman year here at [my predominantly White school], I have just heard people call me names and just stare at me as [if] I don't belong (Multiracial woman, 19).

Vicarious Experiences and Bystanders' Perceptions

The campus is quite a lot whiter than my home state and so I think most racism I've seen is rooted in awkward exchanges. Not just Black v. White issues, but international student/multiracial and ethnic issues come up a lot. People don't really talk about either in public but there are coded/subtle exchanges. Like White people tell my friends who are international that their English is surprisingly good. Or they ask my friends who are Black "Where are you from?" like they couldn't have grown up here [in a predominantly white, Midwestern state]. I think it's called microaggressions (White woman, 21).

I know some people who are scared of Black men for no reason at all, (when out at night) (White woman, 20).

I have a Black roommate and people are surprised how well we get along with each other (White man, 18).

At night by [the mall near campus], people get scared of the Black people walking around (White woman, 19).

People tell me they don't ride the bus at certain times of day because of Black people (Indian man, 20).

If I am with one of my friends who is colored we are sometimes looked at which makes me feel uncomfortable and I know he feels the same (White woman, 19).

Microinvalidations Are Microaggressions

Microinvalidations are typically covert and include "statements and behaviors that negate or nullify a person of color's experiences or realities" (Nadal 2008: 22). Examples of microinvalidations include a person of color being told that they are "too sensitive about race" or an individual telling a person of color that they "don't see race" (Nadal 2008: 22). Nadal (2008) also explains that such declarations are harmful because the perpetrator ignores the target's racial experiences and reality, and in effect, the perpetrator denies that they are capable of perpetuating racism. Microinvalidations also occur when people of color have their ideas, opinions, and feelings ignored, when they are left out of conversations, or when they are mistaken for someone because they share the same racial or ethnic background.

Below are examples of microinvalidations from my research (Levchak 2013):

> Targets' Experiences
>
> During the group discussion, [a] White guy ignored me while [I was] speaking (Asian woman, 24).
>
> White student[s] sometimes ignored my opinion in discussion section (Asian man, 24).
>
> International Advisors didn't treat me fairly and they ignored my efforts (Asian man, 20).
>
> People [think] if a person is Asian, they are really smart, good at fighting and are good with technology...People often stare at me to try to fit a racial profile on me based on my looks, and they usually guess wrongly, or ask me and look surprised (Multiracial woman, 19).
>
> Bystander's Perception
>
> This might be mixed with other factors other than race, but international students, because they may speak another language or dress differently are not blatantly disrespected, but [are] conveniently ignored (White man, 20).
>
> Microaggressive Perspective
>
> I had one T.A. who ... believed he was still mistreated for being colored (White woman, 21).
>
> There isn't any (racism). People are way too sensitive (White man, 21).
>
> What is race? We are 1 human race! (White man, 18).

Aggressor and Target Relationship

> There is a need to acknowledge each other's pain, even as we attend to our own...The task of resisting our own oppression does not relieve us of the responsibility of acknowledging our complicity in the oppression of others.
>
> —Beverly Daniel Tatum (2013: 9)

Current microaggression and macroaggression theory lacks an in-depth explanation on the relationship between the aggressor (microaggressor/ macroaggressor) and the target. I expand this theory by introducing and explaining the following types of aggressors: (1) intimate microaggressors or macroaggressors, (2) acquaintance microaggressors or macroaggressors, and (3) unknown microaggressors or macroaggressors. However, before delving into these new concepts, it's essential that I first discuss the Oppression Dynamics Conceptual Framework (Hardiman and Jackson 2007). The Oppression Dynamics Conceptual Framework accounts for the behaviors, social identities, social positions, and social locations of both aggressors and targets. The framework provides a comprehensive understanding of how oppressive systems are maintained due to a variety of dynamics both among *and* within advantaged and targeted social groups.

Hardiman and Jackson (2007) explain that while oppression certainly involves advantaged group members (e.g. Whites, men) acting against targeted group members (e.g. people of color, women) oppression includes other noteworthy dynamics as well. The Oppression Dynamics Conceptual Framework highlights the complexity of race relations. There are White people and people of color who are aware and who are doing daily work to reduce racism, and there are also White people and people of color who unintentionally *and* intentionally harm race relations. This framework shows us that regardless of our social position and status, we can be complicit in maintaining oppressive dynamics.

In their work, Hardiman and Jackson (2007) outline three important concepts that are key to this framework: vertical dynamics of oppression, horizontal dynamics of oppression, and internalized dynamics of oppression.

Vertical Dynamics of Oppression According to Hardiman and Jackson (2007) "[v]ertical oppression occurs in interactions between advantaged and targeted groups that maintain and reinforce oppression" (60). Vertical oppression includes advantaged group members acting in ways that negatively impact targeted group members, but it can also include targeted group members behaving in ways that negatively impact advantaged group members. Hardiman and Jackson (2007) go on to explain that actions by targeted group members that negatively impact advantaged group members are "more complicated and are not equivalent to the actions of a member of an advantaged group against a member of a targeted group". They specifically note that:

> [B]oth members of advantaged and targeted groups are capable of prejudice, abuse, violence, and hatred, but only the advantaged groups have the institutional and cultural power to back up their prejudices against targeted groups. For example, individual people of color might feel or express prejudices against white people…but as a group…people of color [don't] hold many positions of power in major institutions in the United States that would enable them to turn their prejudices into widely held institutional and social policy. Claims of "reverse racism" …fail to take this power dynamic into account (61).

Vertically oppressive behaviors conducted by advantaged group members include the following: a White faculty member having low expectations of their students of color, a White employer refusing to hire people of color, or a White political pundit making racist comments. Vertically oppressive behavior conducted by a targeted group member includes a student of color who believes that all White people are racist and avoids associating with White members of the campus community or a mental health practitioner of color who refuses to help White people and refers their White clients on to White practitioners.

Horizontal Dynamics of Oppression Hardiman and Jackson (2007) explain that "…interactions among advantaged group members *as well as* interactions among targeted group members can maintain and reinforce oppression" (61). Although we frequently examine oppressive behaviors between racial groups (vertical oppression), it is important to discuss occasions when members of the *same racial group* or people who share a similar social position (people of color) harm one another. I also want to note that although intraracial crime is usually only talked about in terms of "Black on Black crime," intraracial violence occurs in all communities, which means that "White on White crime," "Asian on Asian crime," "Latino on Latino crime," and other types of intraracial violence exist.

Horizontally oppressive behaviors conducted by advantaged group members include Whites who ridicule, harass, or harm other Whites who support the Movement for Black Lives, or Whites who ridicule, harass, or harm other Whites in interracial relationships. Horizontally oppressive behaviors conducted by targeted group members include Latinos who say negative things about or mistreat Black people, or people of color who physically harm other people of color or their property.

Internalized Dynamics of Oppression Hardiman and Jackson (2007) also explain that internalized oppression "…occurs when members of advantaged and targeted groups adopt the dominant ideology about their own groups that maintains and reinforces oppression (61)." Internalized oppression has two subcategories: internalized domination (behavior exhibited by dominant group members) and internalized subordination (behavior exhibited by targeted or subordinate group members).

Internalized domination occurs when "members of advantaged groups accept their group's socially superior status as normal and deserved (Hardiman and Jackson 2007: 61)." Examples include a White educator who believes White children should be punished less harshly than students of color who commit the same offenses; a White manager who believes that Whites should be promoted before people of color with the same or superior qualifications; and White media executives who devalue the narratives of people of color, while favoring predominantly White stories and hiring predominantly White casts. Internalized subordination occurs when "members of targeted groups internalize dominant social messages of inferiority about their group (Hardiman and Jackson 2007: 61)." Examples include a person of color who believes that White people have a higher sense of morality than people of color, or people of color who believe that European features are superior and who consequently bleach their skin.

Intimate Microaggressors and Macroaggressors Intimate microaggressors or macroaggressors can be family members, close friends, spouses, and anyone with whom an individual has a close relationship. An example of an *intimate microaggressor* would be a family member who speaks negatively of another family member's interracial relationship or slights the interracial couple by not inviting them to holiday celebrations and family gatherings. Hearing negative messages like this from an individual who is close can be very damaging especially since there is an expectation that we should be able to trust and depend on close relationships for support and encouragement. An example of an *intimate macroaggressor* would be a friend or partner in an interracial relationship who is verbally abusive (using racial epithets toward their friend or partner). Another example would be domestic abuse that occurs because the perpetrator believes they are racially superior compared to the victim/survivor.

Acquaintance Microaggressors and Macroaggressors Acquaintance microaggressors or macroaggressors can be classmates, dormmates, coworkers, supervisors, students, or instructors. An example of an acquaintance microaggressor would be an instructor who calls a student of color "too sensitive" when the student tells the instructor that other students are making racially insensitive comments during class discussions. In some cases, it may be difficult or risky to interrupt the microaggressive behaviors of an acquaintance microaggressor, especially if the acquaintance is in a position of power like a supervisor or instructor. In these cases, reporting an incident may lead to revictimization or retaliation that can affect the short-term and long-term quality of life of an individual, as well as their professional and academic goals. An example of an acquaintance macroaggressor would be a classmate who writes a racial epithet on another student's desk, who yells racial slurs at their classmates, or who physically assaults their classmate because of the student's race.

Unknown Microaggressors and Macroaggressors Unknown microaggressors and macroaggressors are individuals the target does not know. An example of an unknown microaggressor would be a stranger who stares at a person of color as though they don't belong in the vicinity or a stranger who laughs at a person of color's ethnic clothing or practices because they believe that their own culture is superior. An example of an unknown macroaggressor would be a stranger who calls a person of color racist names from a moving car or a stranger who stalks and harms a person of color because of their race. I'll also note that microaggressions and macroaggressions from unknown individuals are rampant online, and depending on the level of privacy on the site, the perpetrator can remain anonymous. Additionally, while the advent of the Internet has been beneficial in many cases (specifically in terms of generating awareness and creating community), this technology has also introduced Internet stalking and other forms of harassment that target people and communities of color (Duggan 2014).

Responses to Microaggressions and Macroaggressions: Reactions That Help and Harm Targets

I advance microaggression and macroaggression theory by articulating two overarching responses to racist microaggressions and macroaggressions (as supported by my research and observations): (1) responses that may help or empower the target and (2) responses that are unhelpful to the target.

Helpful responses include (1) interrupting the act of aggression and (2) rectifying the situation. *Interrupting* microaggressive or macroaggressive behavior usually becomes the responsibility of the target, co-victim, or a concerned bystander. However, disrupting racist behavior can be challenging for even the most skilled conflict resolution specialist. Nonetheless, bystander intervention training and de-escalation training provide important and necessary skills that *everyone* should have because *everyone* is responsible for working to combat, reduce, and eradicate social ills like racism. Similar to the way individual citizens adapted to life in the post-9/11 world, where many were committed to reporting suspicious behavior and activity (as encouraged by the "If You See Something, Say Something" campaign) (Department of Homeland Security 2016), interrupting race-based aggression requires a similar effort from individual citizens where they should adopt an "If You See a Racist Microaggression or Macroaggression, Say Something, Do Something, and Help the Target" approach.

Additionally, when institutions become aware of race-based aggression among their students, employees, or the population they are serving, they need to act swiftly to provide assistance to the victim/survivor, and should enforce penalties and implement practices to reduce the likelihood that the racist behavior will occur again. Not only does swift action help the victim/survivor but it also sends a message to the aggressor and "would be" aggressors that racist bullying and aggression will not be tolerated by our institutions and our society, and that such behavior will be met with negative sanctions.

When acts of racial aggression occur, perpetrators should take responsibility for their negative beliefs and actions and should also make *efforts to rectify the situation* (in a way that is appropriate to the circumstance and in a manner that does not further aggravate the victim/survivor). When a target is offended or harmed as the result of racist aggression, the aggressor doesn't have the right to qualify the target's feelings; instead, the aggressor should focus on apologizing, rectifying the situation, and embracing awareness education and unbiased behavior. Even when an aggressor is remorseful, the institution should provide awareness education to assist the aggressor in avoiding improper behavior in the future. In cases where perpetrators show no remorse, refuse to acknowledge their harmful beliefs and actions, and shrug the responsibility of rectifying the situation, institutions should enforce penalties (e.g. suspension, termination) and teachable consequences (e.g. community service, making amends with target) (see Chap. 7 for further information on interventions and solutions).

As seen in online spaces, there has been a trend of microaggressors and macroaggressors being reported to their supervisors or schools to face punishment and admonishment for their racist actions on the Internet. In fact, all institutions should have policies and procedures in place to address instances of racism, penalize perpetrators, and support victims/survivors of racism. Institutions that have disregarded or ignored instances of racism or that operate without a system in place to address racism, should implement anti-racism policies and procedures as soon as possible. As it relates to hate crimes, local and state law enforcement need to have better methods in place to effectively record hate crimes, penalize perpetrators, and support victims (Wagner 2015; Cassidy 2016; Jacobson 2016).

Unhelpful responses include (1) being an inactive bystander, (2) institutional inaction, and (3) excusing or endorsing the negative behavior. *Inactive bystanders* see, hear, or are aware of racist behavior but do not interrupt the behavior because of fear, willful ignorance, a lack of concern, a lack of bystander intervention skills, or a mixture of these reasons. An example of an inactive bystander would be an employee who hears a colleague disparage a customer because of the customer's race but fails to intervene because they are fearful that their colleague may admonish them for intervening. In this case, a procedure should be in place that makes it possible for the employee to report such behavior without fear of retaliation and for the customer to be helped by another representative.

Institutional inaction, as well as disorganized and revictimizing responses to racism, is unacceptable. Our institutions, especially those funded by our taxes, need to be committed to protecting us and improving race relations. When we fail to talk about racism or ignore it when it occurs, we make the situation worse. Our silence becomes a sign of approval, and perpetrators are emboldened to continue their behavior while targets continue to be violated and harmed.

Excusing includes downplaying the magnitude of the event and suggesting that the event or behavior does not require attention or intervention. An example of someone excusing racist behavior would be a coach who hears athletes making racialized comments and "jokes" about a fellow athlete but downplays the behavior by saying that "boys will be boys."

Endorsing the behavior involves supporting or defending the aggressor's behavior. An example of endorsing racist behavior would be a political commentator who staunchly supports and defends a politician who makes racist comments.

In all of these examples, individuals and institutions can improve their responses by embracing awareness training, bystander intervention training, and by committing to developing empathy for targeted groups and individuals.

Victims/survivors of racism can also respond in ways that will either be helpful or harmful to their well-being. *Helpful responses* include (1) collecting and documenting evidence, (2) reporting the incident, (3) seeking physical and/or emotional care, (4) focusing on being empowered, and (5) engaging in community organizing. When possible, a victim/survivor of racial aggression should immediately *collect* and *document* evidence of the racist incident. Saving and storing backup copies may also be useful. The victim/survivor should also find an advocate who believes them and supports them during the reporting and healing process. They should then *report* the incident to relevant authorities (e.g. appropriate institutional offices and officials, local and state law enforcement agencies, or the local FBI field office). The victim/survivor should also *seek physical and/or emotional care* to ensure that they will recover from the incident. Another constructive response to racist aggression includes focusing on becoming *empowered* as well as engaging in self-care, advocacy, activism, and service.

When aggressors vandalize a home or neighborhood because of the race of the residents, *community organizing* can be a useful response. Communities can employ strategies like those outlined by the National Crime Prevention Council's (2017) "Neighborhood Watch" program, where community members are encouraged to work together to protect its members and to report hate crimes and other crimes. By having a united front, participants can enjoy protection and strength in numbers and potential aggressors will learn that their behaviors will not go unnoticed, unchallenged, and unreported.

Unhelpful responses include internalizing racism. *Internalizing* can occur when targets absorb negative messages about themselves, resulting in the target believing that they are inferior. Internalizing may also lead the target to blame themselves for an act of aggression, even though racial aggression is solely the fault of the perpetrator. In these cases, victims/survivors should seek mental health care and engage in empowering responses (like those listed above).

Where Microaggressions and Macroaggressions Occur: Precarious vs. Protective Spaces

Microaggressions and macroaggressions manifest differently and have varying consequences depending on the social context, location, and space where the racist incident occurs. Therefore, I add to microaggression and macroaggression theory by making the distinction between precarious spaces and protective spaces as sites where racism occurs.

In precarious spaces, the person of color may be wary of racism occurring. I theorize that precarious spaces are usually public spaces, but not always. Based on personal or vicarious experiences, an individual may be cautious in going to certain locations, places, or spaces because it is viewed as potentially dangerous, or because they may experience racism from people (e.g. civilians, residents, or law enforcement) in those areas.

Examples of microaggressions in precarious spaces include people of color being avoided out of hatred, fear, or disgust in public; watched as if they are a threat to other people or property in their vicinity; stopped and frisked; or slighted or ignored when they seek help. Macroaggressions in precarious places include people of color being physically and verbally assaulted in public arenas like streets or common areas on college campuses.

Unfortunately for people of color, many public, semipublic, semiprivate, and private places are precarious and unsafe. During the last few years, we have seen the deaths of Black people broadcasted throughout mainstream news media outlets and social media, reinforcing the idea that safety is not guaranteed even on busy streets, in broad daylight. Additionally, our homes and communities can quickly become precarious spaces when strangers, neighbors, or police officers treat us like criminals or intruders if we don't "look" like we "belong" in certain neighborhoods or areas. We not only saw this in the case of Dr. Henry Gates Jr., a prestigious Black professor who was racially profiled and arrested outside his home in a middle-class, predominantly White neighborhood (Thompson 2009), we also saw this in the case of Trayvon Martin who was hunted and murdered for being in an area where he didn't "belong" (Tienabeso et al. 2013).

As for protective spaces, people of color create, seek out, and invest in environments that feel safe and secure from racism. Many protective spaces shelter people of color as well as their loved ones, pets, or possessions. Protective spaces are usually private spaces and are similar to what hooks (1990) theorized as a "homeplace" (see section on Racism and Resilience).

Microaggressions that take place in or near protective spaces can include a neighbor being unfriendly because they don't want to live next to a person of color. Macroaggressions that take place in or near protective spaces include racial or ethnic minorities' homes, dorms, or offices being vandalized with racist words or images.

Microaggressions and macroaggressions can cause stress regardless of where they occur. However, when they occur in protective spaces, individuals may experience a reduced sense of security, which will undoubtedly result in emotional stress and trauma. For instance, experiencing a macroaggression within your dormitory or your home (protective spaces) may have more long-term socio-emotional consequences than a macroaggression that occurs on the street (a precarious space). Relatedly, research shows that after experiencing acts of violence in their homes (presumably protective spaces), victims were more likely to report socio-emotional problems such as feelings of distress, major problems at work or school, and significant problems with family or friends (Langton and Truman 2014).

The Consequences of Racist Microaggressions and Macroaggressions: Stress, Trauma, and Death

> Racism is a mental health and public health disease characterized by perceptual distortion, contagion and fatality. The vehicle for these characteristics is the cumulative effect of offensive mechanisms...
>
> —Chester Pierce (1970: 268)

As a result of the White supremacist social structure that the United States was built upon and operates from, many people of color (and especially African Americans) live their lives in a constant state of awareness and caution since being in the *wrong place*, at the *wrong time*, and around the *wrong people* may result in them being mistreated because of their race and ethnicity. Furthermore, in some spaces, people of color may be completely ignored as if they don't matter or exist, and in other spaces, they may be constantly watched and treated as a threat that needs to be eliminated. While people of color are strong and resilient, it is unsurprising that the constant bombardment of racist microaggressions and macroaggressions causes some to experience emotional stress and psychological trauma.

The Consequences of Racism Across the Life Course Racism negatively impacts the mental health of targets, regardless of age or position in the life course. For instance, it contributes to poor adjustment among children and teenagers of color (Umaña-Taylor 2016); poor performance and stress among African American college students (Greer and Chwalisz 2007); self-consciousness among Black faculty as a result of having their qualifications questioned or challenged by students, faculty, and staff (Constantine et al. 2008); stress, frustration, and diminished self-confidence among Black women in senior positions in corporate America as a result of having their competence, capabilities, and intellect undermined and questioned (Holder et al. 2015); and high levels of race-related stress among elderly Black men (Utsey et al. 2002).

Umaña-Taylor (2016) conducted a review of research and concluded that perceived ethnic-racial discrimination negatively impacts the lives of youth, adjustment to their social environment, and their future. She notes:

> [T]he potential negative consequences of ethnic-racial discrimination for youth adjustment are clear; the deleterious associations emerge across childhood and through adolescence, [and] are evident for youth across all ethnic-racial minority groups, and…are not limited to a single region of the U.S. (114).

The negative consequences that Umaña-Taylor (2016) refers to include post-traumatic stress symptoms, depressive symptoms, low self-esteem, suicidal ideation, poor academic adjustment (e.g. lower grades), and behavioral problems (e.g. substance use, physical aggression, delinquency, and risky sexual behaviors). She also notes that, "…across ethnic-racial minority groups, youths' experiences with perceived ethnic-racial discrimination increase with age (114)," meaning that their experiences with racism are likely to intensify over the course of their lives.

Racism and Stress Racism-related stress can be defined as the emotional and psychological strain that a target or recipient of racism experiences after a racist incident. Research has shown that racism-related stress can impact an individual's well-being (Harrell 2000). In Harrell's (2000) work on racism and stress, she found that experiencing racism can result in severe emotional and psychological reactions in people of color. These include feelings of vulnerability, anger, sadness, and anxiety.

Harrell also outlined six types of racism-related stress: (1) *race-related life events*: significant experiences that have major impacts on the individual's life (e.g. losing one's job because of workplace racism or being racially profiled and arrested); (2) *vicarious racism experiences*: gaining knowledge of racist acts through the reports of others or through observation (e.g. the disseminated video of Philando Castile's death); (3) *daily racism microstressors*: covert microaggressions that accumulate and contribute to the overall stress load of individuals; (4) *chronic contextual stress*: when people of color try to cope with or adapt to challenging social environments (e.g. living in a predominantly White environment where there is a lack of support and protection from racist microaggressions and macroaggressions); (5) *collective experiences*: stress that develops when a person of color perceives their racial or ethnic group to be disadvantaged socially, economically, politically, as well as portrayed negatively in the media; and (6) *transgenerational transmission*: racist historical events and survival strategies that are passed down through the generations by way of storytelling, discussions, and lessons (Harrell 2000: 45–47).

Additionally, research has found that frequent, stressful, racist experiences can result in depression, anxiety, and anger (US Department of Health and Human Services, Surgeon General's Report 2001). I found that experiencing racist macroaggressions produced negative perceptions of campus climate and higher levels of stress for non-White students (Levchak 2013). In their work, Greer and Chwalisz (2007: 399) found that African American students who attended a predominantly White school experienced higher levels of minority status stressors compared to their counterparts at a historically Black college and university. Carter (2007) explains that "many people of color…report that their stress is not because of one event, but [due to] a series of emotional wounds and blows [that] were experienced (91)." Similarly, Diaz et al. (2001) provide support for double and multiple jeopardy theories by showing that individuals who are members of several low social status groups suffer compounded mental and physical health issues.

Racism, Mental Health, and Trauma Too often racism and its consequences are ignored or downplayed even though experiencing racism can be traumatic for people of color. Race-related trauma describes the psychological and physical symptoms that people of color experience following an encounter with racism (Carter 2007). Race-related trauma may include the following emotional, psychological, and physical symptoms: anxiety, anger, rage, depression, lowered self-esteem, shame, guilt, fear, hypervigilance, headaches, insomnia, body aches, memory difficulty, self-blame, and confusion after experiencing racism (Carter 2007; Jernigan et al. 2015).

In a 2015 article, Dr. Monnica Williams explains that race-based trauma can also occur vicariously when people of color learn about racist attacks like the church massacre in Charleston, South Carolina (Corley 2015). In the same article, Dr. Carl Bell explains that feeling helpless, powerless, or vulnerable in the face of the incident is what fuels stress and trauma and causes individuals to feel worried and anxious about things that would normally not be bothersome (Corley 2015). Unfortunately, when people of color seek mental health care, they are sometimes revictimized and experience racist microaggressions from their mental healthcare providers (Constantine 2007). Such poor treatment may reduce future help-seeking and will also result in people of color not receiving much needed care in a timely manner.

Racism, Physical Health, and Death When examining the link between racism and physical health, one might readily think about the physical harm people of color and their allies suffer at the hands of racists. However, it is also important to recognize that racism-related stress and trauma manifest into physical ailments that may contribute to the demise of targets.

Acute stress or sudden emotional stress can potentially cause heart attacks, arrhythmias (abnormal heart rhythms), and even sudden death (Krantz et al. 2011). Unlike acute stress, chronic stress kills people slowly, and oftentimes painfully, by making existing illnesses worse. Chronic stress increases the risk of the following: hypertension, heart attack, heart disease, diabetes, stroke, ulcers, severe stomach pain, diarrhea, constipation, erectile dysfunction, irregular menstrual cycles, painful menstrual cycles, intensified premenstrual cycle symptoms, and a decline in sexual desire (American Psychological Association 2016).

There is also the tragic case of Kalief Browder (1993–2015) who committed suicide after being arrested on false charges and imprisoned for three years without conviction. During his imprisonment at New York City's main jail complex, Rikers Island, Browder endured beatings and harassment from guards and inmates as well as roughly two years in solitary confinement (Gonnerman 2014, 2015). He was arrested because of racial profiling, and his mistreatment in prison was rooted in vertical and horizontal race-based oppression.

Racism and Resilience People of color are resilient, both individually and collectively. Resilience is the ability to successfully adapt to change and to recover from challenging circumstances. We see resilience and strength at work in the way that people of color survive and thrive after enduring personal experiences with overt and covert racism, vicarious racist experiences, and historical trauma that is felt across generations, because of horrors like slavery, genocide, and forced removal from native homelands (Brave Heart and DeBruyn 1998).

For example, in the Black community, there are many extraordinary individuals, groups, and families who support each other, share survival strategies, love each other, and live together within healthy and supportive environments. In her essay *Homeplace (a site of resistance)*, bell hooks explains that Black women have created safe spaces or *homeplaces* in order to ensure the physical and emotional safety of their families and loved ones (1990). In her essay, hooks (1990) writes:

> [B]lack women have resisted white supremacist domination by working to establish [a] homeplace... [they cared] for one another, for children, for black men, in ways that elevated our spirits, that kept us from despair, that taught some of us to be revolutionaries able to struggle for freedom... Those of us who were fortunate enough to receive such care understood its value...Working to create a homeplace that affirmed our beings, our blackness, our love for one another was necessary resistance (385–387).

Aside from the support and protection that people of color receive from their families and homeplaces, it is essential that individuals and institutions throughout society become more culturally competent, aware, and committed to anti-racism efforts to ensure that people of color don't have to experience racism-related stress, trauma, sickness, or death.

Core Concepts of Microaggression and Macroaggression Theory

In the following paragraphs, I present core concepts and propositions that advance and bring clarity to existing microaggression and macroaggression theory. While many of the concepts and propositions have been presented above, I have collected and summarized them below so they can be easily reviewed:

1. *Microaggressions and macroaggressions fall on a continuum* (see Fig. 2.1). The continuum shows that microaggressions manifest covertly and macroaggressions manifest overtly. The diagram also shows that race-based aggression can either be intentional or unintentional.
2. *A single act of aggression can be considered significant to some, but insignificant to others.* While a victim/survivor of racist aggression has the right to define the racist incident as microaggressive, macroaggressive, trivial, or severe (see point 11 below), dominant social groups and oppressive authorities use their power and social influence to set standards about victim worthiness and about what acts of aggression should be taken seriously. Unfortunately, such standards often undermine targets' narratives and dismiss their perceptions (especially when a target is a member of one or more marginalized groups).

   Furthermore, since "slights" are often perceived as a lesser form of aggression, their impact and venom are often ignored. However, slights should be perceived as a cornerstone of racial oppression that more intense forms of verbal and physical aggression are built upon (see Fig. 2.3). Regardless of outside perspectives about the severity of an incident, victims/survivors of racist aggression should be believed, empathized with, and supported if they request or require our help.

Low Intensity → High Intensity

SLIGHTS ***(in person, online, over the phone)***	**VERBAL** ***(in person, online, over the phone)***	**PHYSICAL** ***(in person)***
Based on your race:	**Based on your race:**	**Based on your race:**
Being treated as though you are stupid. **Being treated as though you are suspicious.** **Being treated as though you are unattractive.**	**Being spoken to disrespectfully.** **Hearing racist jokes or comments.** **Being verbally threatened.**	**Being handled aggressively, pushed, shoved, spat on, slapped, punched, or stabbed.** **Experiencing racialized sexual violence.** **Experiencing physically intimidating behavior.**

Fig. 2.3 Intensity of aggression

3. *Negative beliefs often precede microaggressive and macroaggressive behavior*. Therefore, it is likely that persistent and/or emboldened racist beliefs will lead to race-based microaggressions and macroaggressions.
4. *The target may know the aggressor, or the aggressor may be a stranger*. Target and aggressors may have a close relationship, be acquaintances, or be strangers. The type of relationship might determine how the act of aggression is responded to. It may also impact the healing process. If the victim/survivor lives or works with the aggressor, their close proximity may impede the healing process.
5. *Microaggressions and macroaggressions manifest differently* and have varying consequences depending on the social context, location, and space where the racist incident occurs. An act of racist aggression will have negative consequences regardless of where it occurs, but, when it occurs in protective spaces, individuals may experience a reduced sense of security, which will undoubtedly result in emotional distress and pain.
6. *Not all microaggressions are intentional, but perpetrators are still responsible for their words and deeds*. Microaggressions can be the result of a lack of awareness about cultural differences and cultural diversity. For instance, someone might unintentionally commit a microaggression by insulting a cultural practice because they haven't been exposed to a particular culture or custom. However, the onus is on the offender to apologize, make amends, and attain education so they can avoid engaging in microaggressive behavior in the future.
7. *Microaggressions and macroaggressions are experienced by targets and perpetrated by aggressors at all levels of society* (see Fig. 2.4).
8. *Microaggressions and macroaggressions are symptomatic of greater social problems and patterns of injustice*. There is a connection between racist beliefs, words, and actions at the individual level and racist practices, procedures, policies, and patterns at the institutional, cultural, and structural levels. The below quotes show us the connection between racist microaggressions and larger patterns of injustice as it relates to the criminalization and harassment of Black people in public spaces:

Target's Experience

I get followed by cops all the time and get stopped. I was once pulled over while walking out of the library and a group of police got out of the car and asked me a bunch of questions saying I "fit the profile (Black man, 21)."

Individual	Family	Groups	Institutional	Cultural	Structural
An aggressor physically attacks a target who moved into a predominantly White area, because of the target's race.	A person doesn't want to engage with their neighbors because of the neighbor's perceived race or ethnicity, and refuses to let their children play with the neighbor's children.	A group of young men harass and torment students of color because they don't "belong" in a "White school."	Management fails to create or implement policies and procedures to address racist speech and behavior within the workplace.	News outlets choose to regularly present stories where Black people are portrayed as criminals, while omitting the indiscretions of White people.	Employers are less likely to interview applicants with "Black sounding names" resulting in Black people being unemployed at higher rates than White people.

Fig. 2.4 Microaggressions and macroaggressions occur at all levels of society

> Vicarious Experiences and Bystanders' Perceptions
>
> I have seen friends who are Black be singled out by police for nothing other than their race (White man, 19).
>
> Police watching Black people at the mall "[i]f they're wearing hoodies and talk like criminals, they might be criminals (White woman, 20)."
>
> The police here HATE African Americans with a passion (White man, 20).
>
> I've heard Black people may get followed by police for no reason (White woman, 19).

The above quotes capture the criminalization and harassment that individual Black people experience, which reflects larger patterns of racial profiling as well as the over-policing of Black bodies.

9. *Microaggressions and macroaggressions harm targets* (see the section The Consequences of Racist Microaggressions & Macroaggressions: Stress, Trauma, and Death). Microaggressions and macroaggressions negatively impact targets mentally, emotionally, psychologically, professionally, and academically.

10. *Responses to racist aggression may help the target or harm the target.* In the aftermath of an incident, the victim/survivor should focus on healing and self-care, and all other parties involved should avoid revictimizing the target.
11. *Targets have the right to tell their story.* Many aggressors and their apologists endeavor to silence targets, dampen discussions on racism, and ignore how racism harms targets.

In their work, Clark et al. (1999: 808) define perceived racism as the "subjective experience of prejudice or discrimination" and show that the *perception* of racism is the most essential aspect of its impact. Their work is incredibly important because it shows that racism does not need to be "objectively" proven or verified in order for it to cause harm to targets. Similarly, Harrell (2000) elucidated the relationship between the subjective experience of racism and race-related stress, as captured in the quote below:

> The subjective judgment of the individual is the critical point of analysis in understanding the impact of racism on well-being. However, it is not uncommon for experiences of racism to be questioned or challenged by others. Such requests for "proof" can create a my-perception-against-yours dilemma that may include accusations of paranoia, hostility, oversensitivity, manipulation, self-serving motives, or having a chip on one's shoulder (Essed 1991). Thus, *the stress–and potential damage–of racism lies not only in the specific incident, but also in the resistance of others to believing and validating the reality or significance of one's personal experience* (44–45).

The exchanges that occur when individuals perceive racism and when aggressors or the aggressor's sympathizers deny that racism occurred, happen daily but are rarely documented. Occasionally, however, such exchanges are captured, as seen during a CNN 2016 presidential debate commentator panel. Directly after the debate, panelists argued about whether terminology used by the Republican presidential nominee was racist or not. The nominee's supporters argued that their candidate's language was not offensive and that we are simply living in a culture where people become offended easily. However, political commentator and activist Van Jones responded to the denial of racism by saying the following:

> You don't get to determine what offends me, I don't get to determine what offends you...if I say something to you, that you find offensive, it's my job to listen to you and figure out in the name of civility [how to make things right] – we used to call it civility...the basis of civilization, but it became politically correct only when certain other people [oppressed groups] started insisting on civil treatment.

Two of the major challenges in combating modern racism, microaggressions, and macroaggressions are the lack of civility toward targeted groups and the lack of respect for the humanity, feelings, perceptions, and experiences of the targets of racism. Therefore, as we pursue racial justice and strive toward living peacefully together, we need to validate targets' perceptions and stop validating the excuses of aggressors and their apologists. We need to boldly shut down aggressors and their apologists when they try to define what is considered racist, whether targets and their allies should be offended, and when they absurdly call targets and their allies *racist* for calling out racism.

12. *Cultural competence and awareness training may reduce racist beliefs, microaggressions, and macroaggressions.* Cultural competence allows us to work and live effectively with people across cultures. In my research, Levchak (2013), I found that students who had higher levels of cultural competence reported lower levels of racist beliefs. Since I theorize that racist beliefs precede racist microaggressions and macroaggressions, it makes sense that future research and practice should focus on the direct link between racist microaggressions, racist macroaggressions, and cultural competence.

Modern Racism

Systems of oppression and struggles for liberation have been present in the United States since the country's formation. According to Bell et al. (2010), "[r]ace is a sociopolitical [construct], not a biological construct...[that] emerged historically in the United States to justify the dominance that people defined as 'White' held over people defined as 'non-White' (60)."

Furthermore, the country was established and developed because of the coercion, cruelty, tyranny, subjugation, exploitation, repression, and oppression of people of color. We see this in the past and present maltreatment of American Indians and people of African descent within America. For centuries, Americas' First Peoples were dominated, subjugated, and had their land stolen (Roppolo 2010). Similarly, for centuries, Africans and their descendants were enslaved, abused, slaughtered, and forced to provide free labor to ensure the growth and prosperity of this nation (Coates 2014). After slavery was abolished, restrictive laws and practices were enforced to ensure that African Americans remained subjugated and oppressed scholastically, professionally, financially, and socially (Gold 2016). Presently, even with the elimination of such overtly racist laws, people of color are still mistreated and disadvantaged because of racist ideologies and practices throughout society.

Racism Earlier definitions and conceptions of racism have usually focused on overt racism. However, in recent years, scholars have argued that racism has transformed, becoming less overt and more covert, shifting from blatant "old-fashioned racism" to subtle "modern racism" that is frequently exhibited through institutional, cultural, and *especially* interpersonal practices. Considering this shift, I find Bell's (2010) definition of racism to be very useful. Bell defines racism as the "institutional, cultural and *interpersonal* patterns and practices that create advantages for people legally defined and socially constructed as White, and the corollary disadvantages for people defined as 'non-White' in the United States (60)."

As discussed earlier, to truly understand how racism and bigotry manifest and endure, we must consider the Oppression Dynamics Conceptual Framework and recognize that White people and people of color can engage in behaviors that harm other groups, their own groups, and race relations in general. However, to be clear, while *racial bigotry* can be committed by *anyone* regardless of race, *racism* can *only* be committed by those with individual, group, cultural, *and* institutional power and privilege granted on the basis of their race.

Since we live in a White supremacist society, White people are afforded such power and privilege, and must make the decision of whether they will collude with the racist system or use their power and privilege to dismantle racism and improve race relations. Furthermore, because of the White supremacist social structure, people of color do *not* enjoy power and privilege on the basis of their race, and instead are targeted *because* of their race, and experience oppression and injustices on the basis of their race. Therefore, I define racism as the mistreatment and harm that people of color experience throughout the social structure on the basis of their race.

The Covert Nature of Modern Racism There are multiple manifestations of modern racism; however, racist microaggressions deserve special attention since they explicitly focus on covert racial aggression *and* interpersonal interactions. In the past, it has been challenging to expose covert racism because of its underhanded and invisible nature. As briefly described earlier, covert racist beliefs, attitudes, and behaviors flourished in the post-Civil Rights era and during the politically correct movement of the 1990s, when blatantly racist speech and actions not only were morally condemned but could lead to a host of negative consequences (legally, socially, academically, and professionally) that could damage the life and livelihood of the offender. To some, the assumed decline of blatant racist behavior appeared to be a great racial and social justice victory. However, not only did blatant racism endure, it mutated, creating covert strains of racism that are, in many ways, more complex and insidious than its original form. Modern racism, a mutation of flagrant racism, manifests through a variety of contemporary racist attitudes and actions that include: new racism (Bonilla-Silva 2014), laissez faire racism (Bobo et al. 1997), and Racism 2.0 (Wise 2010).

According to Bonilla-Silva (2014), even though new racism is more covert and concealed than earlier forms of racism, it is a powerful force that preserves White privilege while keeping people of color subjugated. To Bonilla-Silva (2014), new racism operates by being more subtle than earlier forms of racism and by hiding in plain sight. For instance, he describes how under the guise of liberalism, individuals "rationalize racially unfair situations" and reject "almost all practical approaches to deal with de facto racial inequality" (Bonilla-Silva 2014: 76). In effect, liberalism serves as a shield that some individuals use to avoid taking responsibility for their role in maintaining the racist status quo.

Laissez faire racism is a contemporary racist attitude where individuals view Black Americans as responsible for their own economic dilemma and are therefore unworthy of any special government support (Bobo et al. 1997: 28). Individuals who hold this attitude disregard the structural and institutional causes of racism and "blame the victims" of racism.

Modern racist attitudes are also captured in the concept of Racism 2.0. Wise (2010) argues that there has been a shift in society from "Racism 1.0

to Racism 2.0, an insidious upgrade that allows millions of Whites to cling to racist stereotypes about people of color, while nonetheless carving out exceptions for those who, like [President] Obama, make us comfortable by seeming so 'different' from what we view as a much less desirable norm." With Racism 2.0, individuals preserve their racist beliefs and attitudes, and even engage in racist behavior, while presenting the image that they are open-minded.

Below, I propose and highlight various examples of speech and behavior related to modern racism, including: obstruction, racist jokes, racist gaslighting, dog-whistles, cultural appropriation, support of bigoted speech and racist artifacts, and expressing disapproval of interracial relationships and friendships.

Obstructive Racism Here, I propose a form of racism called "obstructive racism," in which racists use physical or nonphysical barriers to block the progress of people of color. When obstructive racists are called racist, they often deny allegations or cite other reasons for their uncooperative behavior. Obstructive racism can range from blocking promotions to blocking legislation. An example of obstructive racism is seen in how some Republicans blocked many of President Obama's efforts to generate positive change—change that would have undoubtedly benefited their constituents and the American people as a whole. Without a clear, rational reason of why they were uncooperative, one can assume that some Republican politicians engaged in obstruction because of President Obama's race, given the racism that The First Family experienced before, during, and after their time in the White House. President Obama experienced racism in the form of "birtherism" (D'Antonio 2016), where racists suggested that he was not a natural-born US citizen, and therefore ineligible to be president. Racist vitriol was spewed at Malia Obama and Sasha Obama (D'Onofrio 2016; Guzman 2017). First Lady Michelle Obama has also endured a constant onslaught of racism (Chavez 2017). Obstructive racism has also been used by Republican politicians to placate their racist supporters as illustrated in the following quote:

> Republican lawmakers, fearing pressure and primary challenges from extreme conservatives, refused to engage in anything that might be perceived as cooperating with Obama—and so the legislature ground to a halt. The failure to produce, or to do much to address the nation's economic and security woes, caused more disgust with Washington. This, in turn, allowed the rise of a populist demagogue (Milbank 2016).

Racist Jokes Racist jokes are also referred to as liquid racism. Weaver (2011) uses the term ***liquid racism*** to describe the difficulty of identifying behaviors as racist, particularly when racist behaviors are presented in a so-called humorous way. Weaver (2011) explains that racist humor "… is fluid, difficult to collect or identify because it may escape or dissolve before it can be contained, and is explicitly encouraged or given coverage in mass media (252)."

Additionally, racist jokes are often fueled by hidden intentions. For example, if an individual tells a racist joke or does a racist impersonation *with the intention of being offensive*, if confronted about their behavior, *they can hide their true intentions by saying that they were simply joking*. This fluidity and inability to hold offenders accountable makes racist jokes powerful because it provides the aggressor or antagonist with a way to downplay or conceal their racist behavior by labeling it "harmless" or "a joke." In other words, with this form of racism, aggressors' jokes are similar to a Trojan horse because the offender can present their venom in a seemingly harmless way (via a joke) when in reality the contents of the joke may cause a great deal of embarrassment and pain for the target. As seen in the below comments, it is apparent that racist jokes are commonplace and problematic:

> Vicarious Experiences and Bystanders' Perceptions
>
> I believe that people think it's "funny" to make jokes about other races without realizing the gravity of their words. I also believe that some people truly have a dislike or a hatred for other cultures/races [on] campus. However, I have encountered many open-minded, friendly people on campus [as well] (White woman, 18).
>
> Microaggressions related to race [are] often humor related, or the person defends themselves with "it was a joke, relax" (even if it wasn't) and I'm supposed to hang out there and accept it (White woman, 21).
>
> My roommates often make racist jokes… It pains me and I have asked them to stop numerous times (White man, 20).
>
> Racial jokes are thrown around in a casual manner (Black man, 19).
>
> It's not uncommon to hear racist remarks—although it's uncommon to hear people stand up and say something back when these jokes are made (White woman, 20).
>
> Pretty much only around close friends when people of [color] aren't around racist jokes are made, not much else (White man, 21).

> People make rude comments or jokes/stereotype and people accept it because now it's 'ok' (White woman, 19).

> I've heard a lot of jokes, mainly about African Americans, Arab Americans, and Asian Americans. A lot of these comments are based on … their language, actions, things they eat, facial features etc. People just can't handle anything that is different from themselves (White woman, 20).

> I often hear my peers say extremely derogatory things about individuals from the Black, Hispanic, and especially Asian communities (White woman, 19).

It is clear that racist jokes are one of the most common and stealthy forms of modern racism. Furthermore, they are prevalent not only on campuses but also in our workplaces, media, and throughout the social structure.

Gaslighting Gaslighting, is a term that originated from the play *Gas Light* (Hamilton 1938) and its film version *Gaslight* (1944), in which an abusive husband wants to make his wife question her reality and her perceptions. Over time, the term gaslighting has been used to describe a form of psychological abuse and manipulation in cases of intimate partner violence, where the abuser attempts to make the victim question their reality and sanity. However, gaslighting does not only apply to intimate partner abuse. The tactic can be used by those who aim to be racially oppressive. Therefore, I define racist gaslighting as a tactic that racists use to make targets question their own sanity and perception of a racist incident.

Dog-Whistles Dog-whistles epitomize covert racism. Dog-whistles can be defined as coded language used to stealthily convey racist rhetoric. Dog-whistles are common in American politics, and birtherism is a prominent example of it. For years, racist "birthers" accused President Obama of not being born in the United States in order to disqualify his victory, and for years they relentlessly grumbled that they would "take back *their* country."

While there are countless examples of dog-whistles in American politics, they are also ever-present throughout society, including in workplaces, the media, popular culture, and as seen in the below quotes, they are also present in academic environments. In my research (Levchak 2013), I found that dog-whistles were used when speaking about Asian students on a predominantly White campus. Dog-whistles manifested in comments about Asians "not wanting to acculturate," Asians "setting curves," there being "too many" Asians, and about how Asians "are taking spots away from American students." However, a deeper analysis of these statements reveals that some students did not want Asian and international students in this country and certainly not on "*their*" predominantly White campus:

> Aggressors' Perceptions
>
> There is racism on our campus towards the mass amounts of Asian students on our campus. I don't think they try to get to know *our culture*, but that doesn't mean we should be as harsh to them, I guess. It's just a shame we have *so many Asians going to school here setting our curves* when they have perfectly good schools in Asia and there are American students that don't get to have a college education because they are *taking their spots* because they can afford it. I know that statement sounds racist but it's just unfair (White woman, 20).
>
> A lot [of racism] against Asian students because they make up *a good majority* of the university and *set curves* (White woman, 18).
>
> Bystanders' Perceptions
>
> I've heard comments about the abundance of Asian students here (White woman, 18).
>
> I see racism in the dorms, through comments, and through room changes. Most people want to be with those from their same culture. I have also heard people complain that there are *too many Asians* (White female, 19).
>
> I've heard a number of people comment on all of the Asian students or how they *don't belong in America* (Multiracial woman, age undisclosed).
>
> Most of the racism grows out of the fact that White students are a huge majority on this campus. We must all be more wary of the way we speak about International Students (White man, 21).

The belief that Asians don't belong in the United States and that they shouldn't attend school in the United States is connected to the perpetual foreigner sentiment and stereotype threat. With the perpetual foreigner sentiment, individuals assume that all Asian people are foreign-born, that English is not their first language, and that they will never truly be "Americans."

Additionally, students at the predominantly White school accused Asian students of setting the academic curve or outperforming other students. Students at the same school have also created social media pages devoted to anti-Asian memes, with many of those memes accusing Asian students of setting curves. This preoccupation with Asians outperforming White students can be linked to stereotype threat and the declining power of White privilege in some spaces. Stereotype threat occurs when members of a social group believe that they are at risk of confirming negative stereotypes about their group (Steele and Aronson 1995; Steele 1997). In this case, Asian students are expected to be better students than White students. Therefore, the White students who were reacting negatively may have been doing so because of their perception of *their own* academic inferiority and of Asian students' academic superiority.

Dog-whistles also teach people that the hatred and mistreatment of certain groups is acceptable. The consequences of the dog-whistles are seen below:

> Bystanders' Perceptions
>
> I know a lot of people who talk bad about Asians and say that they've become more racist against Asians being here (Latina, 18).
>
> People making fun of groups—especially Asians, is very popular (White woman, 20).
>
> I know a lot of the international students get weird looks, and jokes are made at their expense, particularly Chinese students (White woman, 19).
>
> Asian international students are separated/isolated by ...other students (White man, 20).
>
> The majority of the racism I see deals with the large Asian population. I have never heard anyone make comments about race to their faces only behind their backs. There are many jokes about Asians, especially with the meme page. I hear jokes about race a lot (White woman, 18).

According to the above comments, it is clear that hatred and mistreatment toward Asians on college campuses are in part fueled by dog-whistles.

Cultural Appropriation Cultural appropriation is a nefarious manifestation of modern-day racism. Cultural appropriation is a "*power dynamic* in which members of a dominant culture take elements from a culture of people who have been systematically oppressed *by that dominant group*" (Johnson 2015). People who engage in cultural appropriation often ignore the history of the targeted culture, and they exploit and misuse creations from that culture (with the creator or originator of a particular artifact, genre, or practice never receiving appropriate credit, respect, or recognition) (Johnson 2015).

Cultural appropriation is related to what I refer to as *faux-awareness*, where some claim that they are culturally aware individuals whose cultural appreciation is being *mistaken* for cultural appropriation. An example of faux-awareness is seen in the case of Rachel Dolezal, a White woman who pretended to be Black (and by some views, performed blackface) (Sanchez and Brumfield 2015). Although Dolezal claims to be pro-Black, some have argued that her behaviors were no more than an attempt to appropriate Black culture and Black womanhood for her own benefit (Gibson 2015). While I applaud cultural competence and cultural *appreciation*, cultural appropriation is harmful to people of color and does not help race relations.

Support of Bigoted Speech and Racist Artifacts Racists and bigots frequently spew hatred under the guise of "free speech." Freedom of speech *is* a right bestowed upon American citizens; however, it is wrong for that right to be interpreted as the freedom to bully, be microaggressive, be macroaggressive, or to use racist speech without consequence. There needs to be repercussions for racist actions *and* speech.

Furthermore, just like racist actions and speech are unacceptable, the flaunting of racist artifacts is also deplorable. Examples include the parading of confederate flags and the display of confederate statues. While some argue that confederate flags and confederate statues do not represent hate, many rightly disagree (Suerth 2017). Let it be clear, confederate flags and statues represent *hate and horror* for many Black people. The flag and statues are inextricably linked to racists who wanted to preserve the institution of slavery, a system that perpetuated horrific atrocities against Black women, men, *and* children. Furthermore, confederate flags and statues (as well as other racist symbols) continue to be brazenly supported by White nationalists and supremacists (as seen in the racist rally in Charlottesville, Virginia in August 2017) (Washington Post Staff 2017).

On another note, speech, artifacts, and symbols that are indicative of Black empowerment, solidarity, power, and love are hated because they are a *threat* to White supremacy. Consider the Black Power salute made famous by John Carlos and Tommie Smith. In a 2016 article, John Carlos explains that while he is proud of performing the Black Power salute with fellow athlete Tommie Smith at the 1968 Olympics, he did not anticipate the backlash that resulted from making the gesture that symbolized the need for *Black rights and equity*. He explains that his family received death threats, and his wife eventually committed suicide because she couldn't bear the stress from being targeted (Matthey 2016). As seen in this tragic example, Black empowerment, liberation, and power have been and continue to be portrayed as deviant and wrong because they are a *threat* to the White supremacist power structure.

As it stands, hate and symbols of hate are commonplace throughout society and even plague educational institutions where understanding and cultural awareness should be rampant, as shown in the examples below:

Target's Perception and Bystander's Experience

> My second week at [school] during my freshman year, someone spray painted a swastika on my dorm room door. I didn't socialize with my floor so I was stunned that someone knew I was Jewish first of all. When I spoke to campus police all I got was a police report and nothing else. [My school] prides itself on "acceptance" and "diversity" ... [but] the university and campus police [should] have done more (Multiracial, Jewish woman, 21).
>
> I've seen some racist vandalism ... Nazi stuff (Latino man, 18).

While champions for racial justice work to expose and end covert and overt racism, bigots are also working to create environments where racist speech and racist artifacts can be celebrated without consequence. At the time of this writing, bigots have seemingly been emboldened by the racism spewed during in the 2016 presidential election season. Therefore, we must continue our anti-racism efforts wholeheartedly and make it clear that racism in all of its forms (i.e. words, actions, symbols, and artifacts) is disgraceful, intolerable, and unacceptable.

Expressing Disapproval of Interracial Relationships and Friendships Even though interracial relationships and friendships have become increasingly common over the last few decades, hatred is still directed at those who choose spouses, partners, and friends from different racial backgrounds. While family, friends, and acquaintances may object to interracial relationships and friendships, strangers also expose their racist beliefs through blatant and underhanded objections, as seen in the below comments:

Vicarious and Border Identity Experiences

> Going to the bars I had noticed racism, like trying to get in with my boyfriend who is African American. The security guy wouldn't even take our ID's and just stared at us (Multiracial woman, 19).
>
> [I] faced some [racism] since my girlfriend is Black (White man, 18).
>
> Occasionally someone will holler (scream) at me and my boyfriend. I'm always cautious of it because he's Black (White woman, 20).

I'll also add that bigots who are opposed to interracial relationships can be from *any* racial background. Such aggressors engage in verbal and nonverbal sanctions (e.g. rude looks, comments, and actions) because they want to share their disdain for such pairings in the hope that the pairings will dissolve. However, while negative sanctions and a lack of support may cause some issues and tension, in the end, interracial couples and friendships that are successful can attribute their success to honesty, open communication, commitment, awareness, support, and allyship.

Next, I propose a number of attitudes and characteristics associated with modern racism. The following categories are not mutually exclusive. An individual may embody one or multiple attitudes and characteristics listed below.

The Ambiguous Ally For this particular group, *appearing* aware and unbiased is seemingly more important than *being* aware and unbiased. Ambiguous allies also brag about their interracial friendships, relationships, and in-laws while still holding onto prejudices and behaving in bigoted ways. The frustration of not seeing real positive change and awareness among White "friends" and "allies" is felt in the comment below:

> White people don't even know how racist they are. They don't have a fucking clue as to what's really going on in regards to cultural diversity (e.g. "you're my awesome Black friend (Black woman, 20)."

At the institutional level, some organizations claim to be committed to fostering diversity and providing a safe space for people of color, but their eloquent mission statements and publicized declarations often fail to translate into reality. Sometimes, institutions may offer, (and in some cases, require) short-term or day-long "diversity training" to combat racism and racial biases. However, research shows that in some cases, prepackaged, short-term diversity training does not have a positive long-lasting effect on individuals, and therefore, they fail at helping individuals increase cultural competence and decrease their racist biases and actions (Kalev and Dobbin 2015).

Specifically, colleges and universities may tout how culturally diverse they are, but they may not be engaged in efforts to effectively reduce racism, bridge cultural gaps, and create a sense of community on their campuses, as seen in the below examples:

> We find our own communities, but do not believe the University truly cares about culturally diverse groups outside of "appearances (Black woman, 20)."

> My concern is the University's false diversity advertising (White woman, 19).

> There could be more of an effort to integrate the different cultural groups (White woman, 20).

> No, I rarely see different groups of races co-mingle, [no] opportunities to meet another race. [The school] pride[s] themselves on having many races of people, but no sense of community is visible. Asians hang [out] with other Asians, Latinos with other Latinos. Still tension [and] not knowing how to converse with other groups; I [try] to be open but I [am] shunned when I attempt to try to say hi. (Latino man, 26).

It is apparent that racism at the individual and institutional levels must be addressed if *real* change will ever be achieved. Individuals must be committed to addressing racism at all levels of society, ***and*** within themselves, and institutions must be ***actively*** engaged in creating a climate that is welcoming, inclusive, and safe for all people. In organizations with a lack of racial diversity, recruitment and retention efforts should be prioritized, and exit interviews should be implemented so that the organizations can make necessary changes that might benefit people of color who are connected to the organization.

Apathy About Racism Some individuals are apathetic and disengaged when it comes to racism in modern-day America. These individuals don't take advantage of opportunities to learn about racism and to become culturally competent. Apathy toward racism, in itself, can be considered racist because silence can mean collusion with the oppressive system. Furthermore, within the contexts of intimate and close relationships, showing a lack of concern about the race-based struggles that a "loved one" (spouse, partner, family member, or close friend) experiences is a form of emotional neglect.

Apathy toward racism is also present within institutions. In recent years, there has been a move toward hiring "diversity officers" in various organizations (but particularly in colleges and universities). Many of these individuals are expected to coordinate diversity trainings and investigate and resolve race-related issues. However, there is a huge disparity in the level of preparedness and effectiveness of diversity officers across institutions. While some are very engaged, impassioned, and effective at providing learning opportunities, addressing racism, and creating a welcoming climate for people of color, others are sorely ineffective, imprudent, and essentially apathetic figureheads.

Apathy about racism and Black lives is also seen in the lack of media coverage on missing Black people compared to the coverage on missing White people. The website *Black and Missing, but Not Forgotten* (founded by Deidra Robey) is dedicated to bringing light to this issue and finding the missing individuals.

Ignorance Many people of color are raised to understand their culture *and* the dominant White culture in order to survive and thrive. Many people of color are therefore adept at code switching or changing between their culture and White culture out of necessity. Unfortunately, many White people don't *have* to learn about other cultures, because they can rely on White privilege to help them succeed within American society and beyond. As seen in the below comments from college students, racism fueled by ignorance is common:

> I think there are often off-color comments that people don't fully understand are racist. People say things about every racial group that goes to this school and so I guess racial ignorance is a large problem (Native American man, 18).

> I [was] born and raised in Asia. [There] are too many ignorant [people]… Americans need to be educated more about the world (Asian woman, 21).

> To me, there's too many ignorant White people. Things seem to be good … in groups of culturally diverse people, but [we] still have to interact with ignorant people (Latina, 20).

> Ignorance [of] racial issues outside [of] social science majors; much racism [and] White superiority on campus (White woman, 22).

White supremacy and ignorance reigns, in part, because many people are not expected to do the intellectual and emotional work required to challenge and change their *own* bigotry and ignorance. However, in order to dismantle racism, people everywhere need to take responsibility for their own attitudes, words, and actions, and should embrace social justice education and anti-racism efforts.

Willful Ignorance As it relates to racism, the willfully ignorant are fully aware that racism exists, but they refuse to acknowledge racism and refuse to admit that their words and behaviors are racist. Those who are willfully ignorant may express their "anger" at the phrase "Black Lives Matter" even though they know that the expression really means "Black Lives Matter *Too*" and is a response to the violence inflicted on Black bodies. President Barack Obama has even addressed the criticism of the phrase during an ABC town hall on race relations titled "The President and the People: A National Conversation":

> I know that there are some who have criticized even the phrase 'black lives matter,' as if the notion is… that other lives don't matter. And so, you get

> 'all lives matter' or 'blue lives matter.' I understand the point they're trying to make. I think it's important for us to also understand that the phrase 'black lives matter' simply refers to the notion that there's a specific vulnerability for African Americans that needs to be addressed. It's not meant to suggest that other lives don't matter. It's to suggest that other folks aren't experiencing this particular vulnerability and so we shouldn't get too caught up in this notion that somehow people who are asking for fair treatment are somehow, automatically, anti-police, are trying to only look out for black lives as opposed to others. I think we have to be careful about playing that game, just because that's not obviously what is intended.

One must reflect on why word expressions that are meant to empower and encourage Black people like "Black Lives Matter [Too]," "Black Power," and "Black is Beautiful" are so offensive to some non-Black people. Furthermore, education, awareness, and honesty are key in combating willful ignorance. The more people are educated, the more ridiculous willful racists will appear and the less likely it will be for them to ignore the truth that racism is prevalent and that they have a responsibility to do their part to help end it.

The "Race Card" Sentiment Relatedly, there are individuals who subscribe to the "race card" sentiment. These individuals acknowledge that racism exists, but they choose to dismiss the lived experiences and pain of targets by *accusing* them of trying to manipulate others. Individuals who hold this sentiment do so because they don't care about the impact of racism, don't want their racial privilege questioned, or because they want to relinquish their responsibility for perpetuating racism.

Post-racism Individuals who hold post-racism beliefs think racism is no longer a major social problem. They may also believe that those who discuss race are rabble-rousers and are discussing outdated issues. People of color who hold this sentiment may want to *imagine* that racism is dead and that race is no longer important because doing so allows them to detach themselves from the negativity that is unfairly associated with being non-White. They seemingly believe that the low social status attached to their race can be removed if they imagine racism away. Dominant racial group members also benefit from post-racial and post-racist thought because it relinquishes them from the responsibility of doing their part to end racism. Examples of students making arguments aligned with post-racism and post-racial thought are below:

I don't think it's a problem. Minorities make it a bigger deal than it is. It's B/S (White man, age unknown).

I believe certain races are too sensitive. I am a hard-working student with my high scholastic achievements ...On the other hand, I know some minorities and women that do not have nearly the same scholastic achievements I have yet, they receive substantial tuition assistance based on race/sex. This is not fair and I believe the call of racism and sexism no longer has the same meaning as it did in the past. I believe today, people use those words to their own advantage to get ahead (White man, 22).

With the recent highly publicized murders of Black people, the subsequent protests, and the increase in hate crimes during and following the 2016 presidential election season, it is illogical for anyone to claim that the United States is a post-racial or post-racism society. However, some still embrace post-racism beliefs and insist that racism does not exist and that any harm done to people of color is their own fault.

The Fearful Racist Fearful racists choose to embrace fear and overblown stereotypes about people of color. Additionally, they are fueled by the threat of their White dominance ending. By believing that Black and Brown people are violent and dangerous, they are able to justify segregation, a fixation on guns and loose gun laws, and the over-policing and police brutality directed toward people of color and their neighborhoods. Fearful racists embrace the "angry Black woman," "angry Black man," and "dangerous Black youth" stereotypes. They are susceptible to dog-whistles, and watch news pundits and social critics who continuously fuel racial animus, prejudice, and race-based fear. These are the people who justify shootings of unarmed Black people. These are the police and security guards who follow Black people around unjustifiably and unreasonably. These are the journalists and writers who disproportionately report Black crime. These are the individuals who say that they are "threatened" by Black people or that Black people are "aggressive" when such claims are unfounded. Furthermore, these types of people are *dangerous* because fear is irrational and contagious. When such negative messages about Black and Brown people are shared, other White people *and* some people of color start believing the lies too.

People with this mind-set, unjustly view Black men as deviants who should be feared and criminalized and Black women as hostile, unfriendly, and intimidating. Racist messages, kindled by fear, are still prevalent throughout the social structure and in social institutions, with examples from college campuses seen below:

> People fear the different races due to the stereotypes that they have (Indian woman, 21).
>
> At times, others are intimidated until they get to know me (Black man, 37).
>
> People tell me they don't ride the bus at certain times of day because of Black people (Indian man, 20).
>
> Having some people fear me or my intentions because I'm Black (Multiracial man, 19).
>
> [W]omen…who I know, have been scared of seeing a Black or Latino man [at night] (White woman, 18).
>
> Depending on how wealthy the suburb is that they came from, people are generally intimidated. Or generally befriend me quickly if they don't judge my appearance; people also act surprised when I tell them my major, electrical engineering (Black man, 20).

Again, fear is contagious, and it breeds ignorance, discrimination, and violence toward people of color. The hypocrisy is that, even though there has been more publicity involving the mistreatment, abuse, rape, and murder of Black women, men, and children, fearful racists, and those they infect, *still* believe that Black people are violent and that the behavior of civilians and authority figures who harm Black people are justified. Until the unfair representation and fear of people of color stops, racism will continue to flourish.

"Oppression Olympics" Claims I was inspired to create the term "oppression manifestation" after an unfortunate encounter with an individual who claimed to be a champion of social justice. It is important to note that not all social justice workers are created equal. Some are interested in working toward equity and fairness for *all* people while others are only interested in serving *their own* agenda. The individual wanted a platform to speak about how gender-based oppression impacted *them*, but when I asked them to also share their opinions on race-based oppression, they shut me down, arguing that they didn't want to engage in a discussion about race and racism because they wanted to avoid participating in "Oppression Olympics." Oppression Olympics is the idea that different forms of oppression are "competing" or "contending" for the spotlight or attention.

For Black women, having a conversation *solely* about gender does not fully explain *how we are impacted by oppression*. So, I am always wary when people begin using the term Oppression Olympics because they often do so in an attempt to shut down narratives that don't support *their agenda*. Also, such attitudes continue to marginalize people with multiple low social statuses and people with border identities. For instance, as a result of this thinking, Black women were marginalized during the First and Second waves of feminism when White feminists argued that it wasn't appropriate to discuss race and racism and during the Civil Rights Movement when Black men argued that it wasn't appropriate to discuss gender and sexism.

The reality is that we all balance multiple identities linked to our race, gender, age, class, sexuality, skin color, education, and a variety of other identities, and we all experience both privilege *and* oppression. Therefore, I prefer my concept of "oppression manifestation" to explain the intricacies of oppression: who you are or how you are perceived (e.g. Black woman), the time period or social climate you are living in (e.g. 1962 vs. 2017), where you are (e.g. your workplace or the grocery store), and who is around you (e.g. close friends or strangers) determine how you will experience oppression in its various forms (e.g. racism, sexism).

Oppression manifestation challenges the notion that privilege and oppression are static. More specifically, depending on the variables described above, one form of oppression (e.g. racism) may be more pronounced, while other forms of oppression you experience (e.g. sexism, classism) will be more recessed. For instance, a woman of color is more likely to experience racism on a predominantly White, all-female campus and less likely to experience sexism. That same woman of color may be more likely to experience sexism on a racially diverse male-dominated campus and less likely to experience racism. The same argument can be made for privilege. For instance, a White woman may receive privileges as a result of her "whiteness" in some arenas but may experience sexism in other areas.

The interaction of our privilege and oppression also impacts our actions. For instance, a White man may actively fight against class-based oppression, but he might not want to check his White and male privilege and may even perpetuate racism and sexism. Therefore, we cannot be imprudent and assume that awareness in one area generates awareness in other areas. The reality is that our social identities are complex, and we are constantly contending with our privilege and oppression depending on who we are, the time period or social climate we are living in, where we are, and who is around us. Therefore, it is possible for a White woman to engage in racism while protesting sexist policies, and for a Black man to engage in sexism while working to dismantle racism.

As we make efforts to understand and dismantle modern racism, we have to remember a few key points: (1) modern racism is largely covert, and is strengthened by silence and invisibility; therefore, we must become familiar with covert racism in all of its forms and address racist beliefs, behaviors, and actions as they arise; (2) modern racism is complex and multifaceted; therefore, we must engage in critical thinking about race, racism, and racial privilege; and (3) we must be willing to self-reflect, take constructive criticism, and address our own shortcomings as they relate to racial justice because being "a good person" or "progressive" is not enough (and effectively meaningless) if we are not checking all of our privileges, if we are not actively engaged in generating positive social change, and especially if we are perpetuating any form of racial oppression.

References

American Psychological Association. (2016). *Stress effects on the body*. Retrieved from http://www.apa.org/helpcenter/stress-body.aspx

Anti-Defamation League. (2008, March 6). *White supremacists on campus: Unprecedented recruitment efforts underway*. Retrieved from https://www.adl.org/blog/white-supremacists-on-campus-unprecedented-recruitment-efforts-underway?_ga=1. 259652554.1593255127.1485308910

Bailey, S. (2015, January 24). Young, gifted, and Black: Facing microaggressions as a young college professor. *For Harriet*. Retrieved from http://www.forharriet.com/2015/01/young -gifted-and-black-facing.html#ixzz4NohKownn

Bell, L. A., Castaneda, C., & Zuniga, X. (2010). Racism. In M. Adams, W. J. Blumenfeld, C. Castaneda, H. W. Hackman, M. L. Peters, & X. Zuniga (Eds.), *Readings for diversity and social justice* (pp. 57–64). New York: Routledge.

Bobo, L., Kluegel, J. R., & Smith, R. A. (1997). Laissez-faire racism: The crystallization of a kinder, gentler, antiblack ideology. In S. A. Tuch & J. K. Martin (Eds.), *Racial attitudes in the 1990s: Continuity and change* (pp. 15–42). Westport: Greenwood Publishing Group.

Bonilla-Silva, E. (2014). *Racism without racists: Color-blind racism and the persistence of racial inequality in the United States*. Lanham: Rowman and Littlefield.

Brave Heart, M. Y. H., & DeBruyn, L. M. (1998). The American Indian Holocaust: Healing historical unresolved grief. *American Indian and Alaska Native Mental Health Research, 10*, 56–78.

Brown, B. (2015). *Own our history: Change the story.* Retrieved from http://brenebrown.com/ 2015/06/18/own-our-history-change-the-story/

Carter, R. T. (2007). Racism and psychological and emotional injury: Recognizing and assessing race-based traumatic stress. *The Counseling Psychologist, 35*, 13–105.

Cassidy, C. A. (2016, June 6). Patchy reporting undercuts national hate crimes count. *Associated Press.* Retrieved from http://bigstory.ap.org/article/13412889b85640cfb0 adcd3c28 ad 0093/ap-patchy-reporting-undercuts-national-hate-crimes-count

Chavez, A. (2017, July 26). Michelle Obama opens up about racism she faced as First Lady. *The Hill.* Retrieved from http://thehill.com/blogs/blog-briefing-room/news/343913-michelle-obama-opens-up-about-racism-she-faced-as-first-lady

Clark, R., Anderson, N. B., Clark, V. R., & Williams, D. R. (1999). Racism as a stressor for African Americans: A biopsychosocial model. *American Psychologist, 54*, 805–816.

Coates, T. (2014, June 24). Slavery made America. The case for reparations: A narrative bibliography. *The Atlantic.* Retrieved from https://www.theatlantic.com/business/archive /2014/06/slavery-made-america/373288/

Constantine, M. G. (2007). Racial microaggressions against African American clients in cross-racial counseling relationships. *Journal of Counseling Psychology, 54*, 1–16.

Constantine, M. G., Smith, L., Redington, R. M., & Owens, D. (2008). Racial micro-aggressions against Black counseling and counseling psychology faculty: A central challenge in the multicultural counseling movement. *Journal of Counseling & Development, 86*, 348–355.

Corley, C. (2015, July 2). Coping while black: A season of traumatic news takes a psychological toll. *National Public Radio.* Retrieved from http://www.npr.org/sections/codeswitch/ 2015/07/02/419462959/coping-while-black-a-season-of-traumatic-news-takes-a-psychological-toll

D'Antonio, M. (2016, September 16). The real reason Trump clings to birtherism. *CNN.* Retrieved from http://www.cnn.com/2016/09/10/opinions/why-trump-clings-to-birtherism-dantonio/index.html

D'Onofrio, K. (2016, May 3). Fox news readers bash Obama's daughter with racial slurs, 'ape,' 'monkey'. *DiversityInc.* Retrieved from http://www.diversityinc.com/news/malia-obama-fox-news/

Department of Homeland Security. (2016). *If you see something, say something: About the campaign.* Retrieved from https://www.dhs.gov/see-something-say-something/about-campaign

Diaz, R. M., Ayala, G., Bein, E., Henne, J., & Marin, B. V. (2001). The impact of homophobia, poverty, and racism on the mental health of gay and bisexual Latino men: Findings from 3 US cities. *American Journal of Public Health, 91*, 927–932.

Dixon, T. L. (2008). Crime news and racialized beliefs: Understanding the relationship between local news viewing and perceptions of African Americans and crime. *Journal of Communication, 58*, 106–125.

Donovan, R. A., Galban, D. J., Grace, R. K., Bennett, J. K., & Felicié, S. Z. (2013). Impact of racial macro- and microaggressions in Black women's lives: A preliminary analysis. *Journal of Black Psychology, 39*, 185–196.

Duggan, M. (2014). Online harassment, part 5: Witnessing harassment online. *Pew Research Center*. Retrieved from http://www.pewinternet.org/2014/10/22/part-5-witnessing-harassment-online/

Ehrlich, H. (1998). Prejudice and ethnoviolence on campus. *Higher Education Extension Service Review, 6*, 1–13.

Federal Bureau of Investigation. (2015). *Latest hate crime statistics available: Report contains info on offenses, victims, and offenders*. Retrieved from https://www.fbi.gov/news/ stories/latest-hate-crime-statistics-available

Gibson, A. (2015, June 15). On being #transracial, or the arrogance of white privilege and cultural appropriation. *For Harriet*. Retrieved from http://www.forharriet.com/2015/06/on-being-transracial-or-arrogance-of.html#ixzz4qnzpKTp7

Gilliam, F. D., Jr., & Iyengar, S. (2000). Prime suspects: The influence of local television news on the viewing public. *American Journal of Political Science, 44*, 560–574.

Goldberg, S. (2012, June 1). TV is good for self-esteem if you are a white male. *CNN*. Retrieved from http://www.cnn.com/2012/06/01/showbiz/tv/tv-kids-self-esteem/

Gonnerman, J. (2014, October 6). Before the law. *The New Yorker*. Retrieved from http://www.newyorker.com/magazine/2014/10/06/before-the-law

Gonnerman, J. (2015, June 7). Kalief Browder, 1993–2015. *The New Yorker*. Retrieved from http://www.newyorker.com/news/news-desk/kalief-browder-1993-2015

Greer, T. M., & Chwalisz, K. (2007). Minority-related stressors and coping processes among African American college students. *Journal of College Student Development, 48*, 388–404.

Guzman, N. (2017, August 8). Sasha & Malia Obama are facing backlash for being … regular teenagers. *Bustle*. Retrieved from https://www.bustle.com/p/sasha-malia-obama-are-facing-backlash-for-being-regular-teenagers-75277

Hamilton, P. (1938). *Gas Light*. London: Constable.

Hardiman, M., & Jackson, B. (2007). Conceptual foundations for social justice courses. In M. Adams, L. A. Bell, & P. Griffin (Eds.), *Teaching for diversity and social justice*. New York: Routledge.

Harrell, S. P. (2000). A multidimensional conceptualization of racism-related stress: Implications for the well-being of people of color. *American Journal of Orthopsychiatry, 70*, 42–57.

Hoffman, A. (2016, October 17). Black doctor who said flight attendant stopped her from helping passenger: 'We still have so much further to go'. *Time*. Retrieved from http://time.com/4534080/black-doctor-tamika-cross-delta-flight/

Holder, A. M. B., Jackson, M. A., & Ponterotto, J. G. (2015). Racial microaggression experiences and coping strategies of Black women in corporate leadership. *Qualitative Psychology, 2*, 164–180.

hooks, b. (1990). *Yearning: Race, gender, and cultural politics*. Boston: South End Press.

Hornblow, A., Jr. (Producer), & Cukor, G. (Director). (1944). *Gaslight* [Motion picture]. Los Angeles: Metro-Goldwyn-Mayer.

Hughes, R. L., & Giles, M. (2010). CRiT walking in higher education: Activating critical race theory in the academy. *Race Ethnicity and Education, 13*, 41–57.

Jacobson, B. (2016, June 6). AP study: Inconsistent reporting creates difficulty in evaluating prevalence of hate crimes. *Telegraph Herald*. Retrieved from http://www.telegraphherald.com/news/dubuque/article_b63951b6-d570-5e30-85e2-9c3d4b56a9a9.html

Jernigan M. M., Green, C. E., Liu, M. M., Henze, K. T., Chen, C., & Helms, J. E. (2015). *#racialtraumaisreal*. Chestnut Hill: Institute for the Study and Promotion of Race and Culture. Retrieved from; http://www.bc.edu/schools/lsoe/isprc/manuscript415.html

Johnson, M. Z. (2015, June 14). What's wrong with cultural appropriation? These 9 answers reveal its harm. *Everyday Feminism*. Retrieved from http://everydayfeminism.com/2015/ 06/cultural-appropriation-wrong/

Johnson, J. D., Olivo, N., Gibson, N., Reed, W., & Ashburn-Nardo, L. (2009). Priming media stereotypes reduces support for social welfare policies: The mediating role of empathy. *Personality and Social Psychology Bulletin, 35*, 463–476.

Kalev, A., & Dobbin, F. (2015, March 16). *Try and make me!: Why corporate diversity training fails*. Retrieved from http://mitsloan.mit.edu/iwer/wpcontent/uploads/2015/04 /AA Training-3-16-2015-clean.pdf

Krantz, D. S., Whittaker, K. S., & Sheps, D. S. (2011). Psychological risk factors for coronary artery disease: Pathophysiologic mechanisms. In R. Allan & J. Fisher (Eds.), *In heart and mind: Evolution of cardiac psychology* (pp. 91–113). Washington, DC: APA.

Langton, L., & Truman, J. (2014). *Socio-emotional impact of violent crime*. United States Department of Justice: Bureau of Justice Statistics. Retrieved from http://www.bjs.gov/ content/pub/pdf/sivc.pdf

Levchak, C. C. (2013). *An examination of racist and sexist microaggressions on college campuses* (Unpublished doctoral dissertation). University of Iowa, Iowa City.

Levin, J., & McDevitt, J. (1993). *Hate crimes: The rising tide of bigotry and bloodshed*. New York: Plenum.

Martins, N., & Harrison, K. (2011). Racial and gender differences in the relationship between children's television use and self-esteem. *Communication Research, 39*, 338–357.

Mastro, D. E., & Tropp, L. R. (2004). The effects of interracial contact, attitudes, and stereotypical portrayals on evaluations of Black television sitcom characters. *Communication Research Reports, 21*, 119–129.

Matthews, C. (2014, July 22). Vine user blasts employees following him around stores in best possible way. *Huffington Post.* Retrieved from http://www.huffingtonpost.com/2014/07/22/rashid-polo-shopping-while-black-vine_n_5610667.html

Matthey, J. (2016, April 3). *John Carlos has one regret over his famous Black Power salute.* Retrieved from http://www.news.com.au/sport/sports-life/john-carlos-has-one-regret-over-his-famous-black-power-salute/news-story/17ed6d7c13fec04c74c40eed8bac991c

Nadal, K. L. (2008). Preventing racial, ethnic, gender, sexual minority, disability, and religious microaggressions: Recommendations for promoting positive mental health. *Prevention in Counseling Psychology: Theory, Research, Practice and Training, 2*, 22–27.

Namie, G. (2014). *U.S. workplace bullying survey.* Retrieved from http://workplacebullying.org/multi/pdf/WBI-2014-US-Survey.pdf

National Crime Prevention Council. (2017). *Neighborhood watch.* Retrieved from http://www.ncpc.org/topics/home-and-neighborhood-safety/neighborhood-watch

Ortiz, L., & Jani, J. (2010). Critical race theory: A transformational model for teaching diversity. *Journal of Social Work Education, 46*, 175–193.

Perry, B. (2010). 'No biggie': The denial of oppression on campus. *Education, Citizenship and Social Justice, 5*, 265–279.

Pierce, C. (1970). Offensive mechanisms. In F. Barbour (Ed.), *The Black seventies* (pp. 265–282). Boston: Porter Sargent.

Price, D. B., Hyle, A. E., & Jordan, K. V. (2009). Ties that blind: Perpetuation of racial comfort and discomfort at a community college. *Community College Review, 37*, 3–33.

Prot, S., Anderson, C. A., Gentile, D. A., Warburton, W., Saleem, M., Groves, C. L., & Brown, S. C. (2015). Media as agents of socialization. In J. E. Grusec & P. D. Hastings (Eds.), *Handbook of socialization* (2nd ed., pp. 276–300). New York: Guilford Press.

Sanchez, R., & Brumfield, B. (2015, June 15). Rachel Dolezal's appearance is 'blackface,' brother says. *CNN.* Retrieved from http://www.cnn.com/2015/06/13/us/washington-rachel-dolezal-adopted-brother/index.html

Solórzano, D. (1998). Critical race theory, racial and gender microaggressions, and the experiences of Chicana and Chicano scholars. *International Journal of Qualitative Studies in Education, 11*, 121–136.

Solórzano, D., & Yosso, T. J. (2002). Critical race methodology: Counter-storytelling as an analytical framework for education research. *Qualitative Inquiry, 8*, 23–44.

Solorzano, D., Ceja, M., & Yosso, T. (2000). Critical race theory, racial microaggressions, and campus racial climate: The experiences of African American college students. *Journal of Negro Education, 69*, 60–73.

Southern Poverty Law Center. (2016). *Update: Incidents of hateful harassment since election now number 701.* Retrieved from https://www.splcenter.org/hatewatch/2016/11/18/update-incidents-hateful-harassment-election-day-now-number-701

Steele, C. M. (1997). A threat in the air: How stereotypes shape intellectual identity and performance. *American Psychologist, 52*, 613–629.

Steele, C. M., & Aronson, J. (1995). Stereotype threat and the intellectual test performance of African Americans. *Journal of Personality and Social Psychology, 69*, 797–811.

Stotzer, R. L., & Hossellman, E. (2012). Hate crimes on campus: Racial/ethnic diversity and campus safety. *Journal of Interpersonal Violence, 27*, 644–661.

Sue, D. W., Capodilupo, C. M., Torino, G. C., Bucceri, J. M., Holder, A. M. B., Nadal, K. L., & Esquilin, M. (2007). Racial microaggressions in everyday life: Implications for clinical practice. *American Psychologist, 62*, 271–286.

Suerth, J. (2017, August 22). Here are the Confederate memorials that will be removed after Charlottesville. *CNN.* Retrieved from http://www.cnn.com/2017/08/15/us/confederate-memorial-removal-us-trnd/index.html

Tahmincioglu, E. (2008). Racial harassment still infecting the workplace: Despite decades of civil-rights progress, workers' complaints are rising. *NBS News.* Retrieved from http://www.nbcnews.com/id/22575581/ns/business-careers/t/racial-harassment-still-infecting-workplace/#.WIgQc7GZPGI

Tatum, B. D. (2013). The complexity of identity: "Who Am I?". In M. Adams, W. J. Blumenfeld, C. Castaneda, H. W. Hackman, M. L. Peters, & X. Zuniga (Eds.), *Readings for Diversity and Social Justice* (pp. 6–9). New York: Routledge.

Thompson, K. (2009, July 22). Scholar says arrest will lead him to explore race in criminal justice. *The Washington Post.* Retrieved from http://www.washingtonpost.com/wp-dyn/content/article/2009/07/21/AR2009072101771.html

Tienabeso, S., Gutman, M., & Wash, S. (2013). George Zimmerman found not guilty and goes free. *ABC.* Retrieved from http://abcnews.go.com/US/george-zimmerman-found-guilty-free/story?id=19653300

U.S. Department of Health and Human Services. (2001). *Mental health: Culture, race and ethnicity. A supplement to mental health: A report of the Surgeon General.* Rockville.

Umaña-Taylor, A. J. (2016). A post-racial society in which ethnic-racial discrimination still exists and has significant consequences for youths' adjustment. *Current Directions in Psychological Science, 25*, 111–118.

Utsey, S. O., Payne, Y. A., Jackson, E. S., & Jones, A. M. (2002). Race-related stress, quality of life indicators, and life satisfaction among elderly African Americans. *Cultural Diversity and Ethnic Minority Psychology, 8*, 224–233.

Vega, T. (2015). Working while brown: What discrimination looks like now. *CNN.* Retrieved from http://money.cnn.com/2015/11/25/news/economy/racial-discrimination-work/index.html

Wagner, B. (2015). *Civil rights prosecutions: Hate crimes.* Washington, DC: Office of the United States Attorneys.

Washington Post Staff. (2017, August 18). Deconstructing the symbols and slogans spotted in Charlottesville. *The Washington Post.* Retrieved from https://www.washingtonpost.com/ graphics/2017/local/charlottesville-videos/

Wilson, J. W., & Constantine, M. G. (1999). Racial attitudes, self-concept, and perceived family cohesion in Black college students. *Journal of Black Studies, 29*, 354–366.

Wise, T. (2010). *Colorblind: The rise of post-racial politics and the retreat from racial equity.* San Francisco: City Lights Books.

Workneh, L. (2016). Black women are speaking out to show the world #WhatADoctorLooks Like. *Huffington Post.* Retrieved from http://www.huffingtonpost.com/entry/black-women-are-speaking-out-to-show-the-world-whatadoctorlookslike_us_5801004ae4b 06e047594630e

Yan, H., Squeglia, K., & Walker, K. (2016) 'Make America White Again': Hate speech and crimes post-election. *CNN.* Retrieved from http://www.cnn.com/2016/11/10/us/post-election-hate-crimes-and-fears-trnd/

CHAPTER 3

Racist Beliefs and the Importance of Cultural Competence

Racist and post-racist beliefs often precede racist microaggressions and macroaggressions.
—Dr. Charisse Levchak

Understanding Racist Beliefs

Racist beliefs greatly influence racist microaggressions, macroaggressions, and modern racism. A *racist belief* is a view that a particular race is superior or inferior to another. This definition is reflected in a childhood experience. I traveled to the South to visit my extended family members one summer. My grandmother lived in a beautiful home, in a picturesque community. However, under the surface of prettiness and the "American Dream" was the ugliness of racism. I remember my grandmother giving my cousins and I frozen treats before we went out to ride our bikes around the neighborhood. Soon after we left, we encountered our neighbor's son, a child who we had spent our time playing with throughout the summer. He was a skinny, blonde, White boy—about six years old. After a short exchange, he asked if he could have a frozen treat as well. One of my cousins, about the same age as the boy, explained that there were none left. After hearing my cousin's response, the boy insisted that my cousin give him *his* treat. I asked the boy why he felt that way. He replied, very matter-of-factly, "Because I'm White. You're Black and that makes me better than you."

C. C. Levchak, *Microaggressions and Modern Racism*,
https://doi.org/10.1007/978-3-319-70332-9_3

The encounter was and still is shocking because, even after he'd spent time with us, laughing, playing, and enjoying the summer, he did not see us as friends or equals. He considered my cousins and I inferior because of our blackness and deemed himself superior because of his whiteness. It is also upsetting because my cousins and I were young kids subjected to the betrayal of someone we viewed as a friend, and he was a young kid already flaunting his racist beliefs and attitudes and claiming racial superiority over Black people.

It disturbs me to think of who he has become and the harm he has done if his beliefs were never checked, challenged, and changed. It is unlikely that his sense of racial superiority was limited to our exchange because individuals who hold racist beliefs or stereotypes about a group may *act* in racist ways toward members of that group. Racist beliefs are rarely restricted to one's mind and oftentimes escape through one's words and actions. For example, a person who holds racist beliefs about Black Americans (e.g. all Black Americans are violent) may be more likely to speak or behave in racist ways toward Black Americans (e.g. avoid Black people or "preemptively" harm Black people because they are "violent"). In short, such beliefs perpetuate racism and racial oppression within our society. Therefore, to understand the complex nature of racist microaggressions, macroaggressions, and modern racism, we must first understand racist beliefs.

Biases

There are *social identity categories* like race and gender, and there are *social groups* that are connected to each of those categories. For instance, with race, corresponding groups would include Black, White, and Asian. According to Hardiman and Jackson (2007), such groups "share a range of physical, cultural, or social characteristics (57)." When we encounter an individual, we notice their physical characteristics, like their skin color and facial features, and we instantaneously associate them with a social group and label them (Ito and Urland 2003; Staats 2014). Even though we may have the best intentions, we are still susceptible to developing implicit biases, or attitudes and stereotypes that we hold unconsciously and that impact our "understanding, actions, and decisions" (Staats 2014: 73). In her detailed review on implicit bias, Staats (2014) shared that most Americans "display a pro-White/anti-Black bias" (73) and that implicit biases have been documented in children as young as six. However, I reason that, just like we learn biases and stereotypes, we can *unlearn* them and replace them with positive and accurate information. It is possible. Research supports my assertion and reveals that implicit biases are *malleable* and can change (Dasgupta 2013). The possibility of improvement is why individuals and institutions should invest in awareness training, cultural competence training, and difficult dialogues since they provide unbiased information and promote solidarity which I believe is key to changing our biases.

Post-racist Beliefs

I define post-racist beliefs as the minimization or denial of present-day racism. It is also a perception that racism existed in the United States during a *past period* but does not exist in contemporary America. Furthermore, there isn't a clear-cut time of when post-racism emerged. For example, some social commentators, television reporters, and pundits claim that these kinds of beliefs came into being after Barack Obama was elected president. Others assert that they began after the Civil Rights era. It is out of the scope of the present analysis to discern exactly when post-racism became part of American culture. However, I will assume that these beliefs are present now and are based on vague notions of "sometime past" when it would be perceived that racism existed and also perceived that it does not exist today. Lastly, post-racism is not a term typically used and defined by social scientists; however, I find this concept useful in illuminating modern forms of racism and contemporary racist beliefs.

On the surface, the concepts "post-racism" and "post-racist" appear innocuous. The concepts suggest that racism is no longer a major social problem and that racial equality is a present-day reality. However, the terms are problematic because they discredit the legacy and continued presence of racism in our society. Furthermore, denying the existence of racism is itself an act of oppression because it silences the voices of the oppressed and ignores the plight of those who are targeted by racism.

Although there have been periods in US history when civil rights and social justice efforts resulted in a reduction of prejudice and discrimination, racism still remains a major social problem in the country. The existence of racism is apparent when we consider the following racial disparities (where people of color are disadvantaged in comparison to White individuals): the racial income and wealth gap (Oliver and Shapiro 2006); college completion rates (Knapp et al. 2012); residential segregation (Denton 2006); unemployment rates (Ritter and Taylor 2011);

incarceration rates (Carson and Sabol 2012); and the existence of the school-to-prison pipeline that "push[es] our nation's…most at-risk children into the juvenile and criminal justice systems" (American Civil Liberties Union 2015).

Even though it is clear that racism still exists, there are individuals, notably, social and political commentators who have argued that racism is no longer a major social problem. Daniel Schorr (2008) argued that the ascendance of Barack Obama as a presidential candidate meant that the United States had entered a post-racial era. Schorr's commentary proved to be inaccurate and unrealistic. Pettigrew (2009) explained that racism erupted and intensified during Barack Obama's campaign. Racist acts included physical assaults, threats, intimidation, cross burnings, and racist graffiti. The presence of racism throughout the campaign alone proved that Schorr's argument about post-racism was inaccurate. McWhorter (2008, 2010) also argued that racism had ended in the United States and that America had become "post-racial" after the election of President Obama. McWhorter (2010) specifically contended that the contemporary treatment of Black people is not "grievously biased and unjust." He also argued that racism is not one of Black America's most urgent problems and that "[t]his is a time when we can afford to let the past be the past" (McWhorter 2008). Even though McWhorter is a Black male, his comments reflect a lack of understanding and scrutiny about individual, institutional, cultural, and structural dynamics that intentionally and unintentionally harm Black people and Black communities.

Additionally, the belief that racism is dead is connected to laissez-faire racism and color-blind racism and color-blind racism. According to Bobo et al. (1997), "[l]aissez-faire racism involves persistent negative stereotyping of African Americans, a tendency to blame [B]lacks themselves for the Black-White gap in socioeconomic standing, and resistance to meaningful policy efforts to ameliorate U.S. racist social conditions and institutions (16)." In other words, laissez-faire racism suggests that there is no such thing as racism, only poor individual choices made by people of color—who are therefore undeserving of any federal, state, or institutional assistance. Color-blind racism can manifest when people view "racial inequality as the outcome of nonracial dynamics… [and] minorities' contemporary status as the product of market dynamics, naturally occurring phenomena, and [B]lack's imputed cultural limitations (Bonilla-Silva 2014: 2)." This form of racism essentially involves ignoring the presence of racial biases, bigotry, and discrimination as the causes of racial inequities. When held by institutional leaders, political leaders, and voters, post-racist beliefs, laissez-faire racist beliefs, and color-blind racist beliefs may result in a lack of support for equitable policies designed to help people of color in the United States.

Cultural Competence

Some would argue that cultural competence is the antithesis of racist and post-racist beliefs because it indicates an awareness of and a respect for cultures that differ from one's own. Cultural competence begins with understanding culture. Culture includes learned beliefs, traditions, language, communication styles, customs, values, and practices of a given social group. Cultural competence is not a destination but rather an ongoing process that requires a commitment to individual and institutional growth—particularly since culture is constantly evolving and changing.

Cultural competence involves demonstrating cultural awareness and working respectfully and effectively across cultures. At the individual level, cultural competence includes learning about other cultures and engaging in respectful communication and collaboration with people from different cultures. At the institutional level, cultural competence means creating and implementing practices, programs, and policies that are useful and appropriate for people from a variety of cultures as well as working to create an environment that is welcoming and safe for people of all backgrounds and that holds racist microaggressors and macroaggressors accountable for their harmful behaviors.

In order to fully understand cultural competence, it's useful to become familiar with the cultural competence continuum as presented by Cross et al. (1989). The continuum highlights ways that we should behave and behaviors that we should avoid as we strive toward cultural competence and, ideally, cultural proficiency (responding positively toward other cultures, engaging with other cultures, and even adapting to other cultures). There are six points along the continuum that indicate ways of perceiving and responding to differences. They include cultural destructiveness, cultural incapacity, cultural blindness, cultural pre-competence, cultural competence, and cultural proficiency. In the following section, for each point on the continuum, I note ways that microaggressive and macroaggressive behaviors can reflect a lack of cultural competence, and I also note behaviors that reflect cultural awareness, competence, and proficiency.

Cross et al. (1989) note that cultural destructiveness is the most negative element on the cultural competence continuum. They explain that cultural destructiveness occurs when "[b]igotry coupled with vast power differentials allows the dominant group to disenfranchise, control, exploit, or systematically destroy the minority population (14)." In other words, cultural destructiveness involves viewing one's culture as superior and using one's power to harm, exclude, remove, castigate, or eliminate another culture. An example of a microaggression that is culturally destructive would be an employer who defines "professional dress" based on European standards and castigates employees of color for being "unprofessional" when they wear ethnic clothing or hairstyles. Examples of macroaggressions that are culturally destructive include exclusionary laws and practices like Jim Crow Laws that enforced segregation and excluded Black people from fully participating in American society; the enslavement of African people and the replacement of their languages, religions, and practices with those associated with White culture; and the forced acculturation of Native American children through government-run boarding schools, the government-sanctioned massacre of Native American people, and the ongoing theft and mistreatment of Native lands and water supplies.

Cultural incapacity occurs when individuals and institutions "do not intentionally seek to be culturally destructive…[but] may act as agents of oppression by enforcing racist policies and maintaining stereotypes" (Cross et al. 1989: 15). Such individuals and institutions tend to harbor beliefs about White "superiority" as well as the "inferiority" of people of color. This makes them ineffective in working with individuals and communities of color. Cultural incapacity also involves the disempowerment of people of color and includes an expectation that they will disregard their cultural practices, traditions, and worldview and instead embrace whiteness and the dominant culture. An example of cultural incapacity that is microaggressive in nature would be an employer who demands that English be the only language spoken by employees—even during breaks at work. An example of cultural incapacity that is macroaggressive in nature would be law enforcement officers who hold stereotypes about Black people, have groundless fears about Black people, and subsequently over-police Black communities and bodies.

Cultural blindness is very similar to the concept of color blindness. Such individuals and institutions "function with the belief that color or culture make no difference and that all people are the same" (Cross et al.

1989: 15). Although cultural blindness is rooted in the idea that there is no difference between cultures, and that we all share one culture, individuals and institutions with such beliefs fail to acknowledge that our "common culture" is predicated on the dominant White culture. An example of a microaggression that reflects cultural blindness is an individual who undermines a person of color's lived experience by arguing that "race doesn't matter" and "we are all treated the same way." An example of a macroaggression that reflects cultural blindness is a political leader who asserts that Black people have the same social and economic opportunities as White people, and who then proceeds to make racist comments about Black people's work ethic and intelligence as a rationale of why they are disadvantaged compared to White people.

The next three points on the continuum represent responses to diversity that reflect a greater sense of awareness and usefulness in terms of healing race relations. Consequently, instead of focusing on specific examples of microaggressive and macroaggressive behavior, I will highlight behaviors that reflect varying degrees of cultural awareness and competency.

Cultural pre-competence can be considered a step in the right direction. Culturally pre-competent individuals and institutions have "begun the process of becoming culturally competent and often only lack information on what is possible and how to proceed" (Cross et al. 1989: 17). Examples of individual-level behavior that reflect cultural pre-competence include an individual who can identify racially microaggressive behavior (but who lacks the skills needed to interrupt the behavior) and a person who is making strides to increase their cultural awareness (but who still lacks knowledge about culturally insensitive terms and occasionally offends people from different cultures). An example of institutional-level behavior that reflects cultural pre-competence would be an organization that schedules a "Diversity Day" once a year. While there is nothing wrong with celebrating diversity, this approach is shortsighted. It focuses on issues associated with diversity only one day a year and fails to address such issues the rest of the year.

Cultural competence involves embracing cultural awareness, being respectful to members of other cultures, and not engaging in horizontally or vertically oppressive behaviors. Cultural competence in institutions and individuals is "characterized by acceptance and respect for difference, continuing self-assessment regarding culture, careful attention to the dynamics of difference, [and a] continuous expansion of cultural knowledge and resources" (Cross et al. 1989: 17). For institutions, it also means making a variety of "adaptations to service models in order to better meet the needs of minority populations" who are associated with the institution (Cross et al. 1989: 17). An example of individual-level behavior that reflects cultural competence includes a person dedicated to expanding their cultural awareness and anti-racism skills and who stands in solidarity with people of color who are protesting against racist policies and practices. Examples of institutional-level behavior that reflect cultural competence include "agencies that work to hire unbiased employees, seek advice and consultation from the minority community, …seek minority staff…[and] provide support for staff to become comfortable working in cross-cultural situations" (Cross et al. 1989: 17) and institutions that understand the overt and covert nature of modern-day racism and take efforts to protect people of color who work for their organization and the people of color they serve.

Cultural proficiency is also referred to as "advanced cultural competence" and is the most positive point on the continuum (Cross et al. 1989: 17). It involves having a high regard for culture, responding positively to cultural differences, and having a willingness to *meaningfully engage* with other cultures. Cultural proficiency includes acclimating to other cultures in a way that reflects genuine cultural appreciation that is free of cultural appropriation and the exoticization of members of targeted racial, ethnic, or cultural groups. An example of individual-level behavior that reflects cultural proficiency includes an individual who readily engages in cultural immersion experiences where they adapt to the ways of life of other cultures and where they forge healthy relationships with members of other cultural groups that are based on mutual respect and solidarity. Examples of institutional-level behavior that reflect cultural proficiency include hiring staff who are "specialists in culturally competent practice" (Cross et al. 1989: 17), investing in their employee's development of cultural competence skills, and genuinely being invested in celebrating marginalized cultures and healing race relations within their organization and beyond.

Taking the above information into account, cultural competence training could be very helpful in institutions where there are low retention rates of employees, students, or clients of color, where acts of violence have been committed against members of targeted groups, where institutional leaders practice racial tokenism, and where there are a lack of mentors who are equipped to help employees and students who are members of targeted groups. In such institutions, cultural competence training may also help combat biases, stereotypes, discrimination, microaggressions, and macroaggressions that create an unwelcoming and unsafe environment for people of color and their allies.

In my work on microaggressions, I (Levchak 2013) found that individuals who score higher on cultural competence measures are *less likely* to hold racist and post-racist beliefs. This is one of the most exciting, beneficial, and applicable findings of that study because it means that individuals and institutions should fervently and continuously pursue cultural competence education if they are truly interested in reducing racist and post-racist beliefs and, by extension, racist microaggressions and macroaggressions.

Research Findings on Racist Beliefs

Racist Beliefs

By using the Modern Racism Scale (see McConahay 1986) (a scale that primarily focuses on racism toward Black Americans), I (Levchak 2013) found that racist beliefs were prevalent at *both* a predominantly White Midwestern school and a diverse school in an urban area. *In all racial groups surveyed, there were some individuls who* held anti-Black sentiments and racist beliefs. This supports the Oppression Dynamics Conceptual Framework (see Chap. 2), which proposes that there are a variety of dynamics occurring among *and* within advantaged and targeted social groups that maintain oppressive systems (Hardiman and Jackson 2007). More specifically, I found that White students held more racist beliefs than Black students, but Asian and Latino students held *more* racist beliefs than White students.

This finding may be surprising for a few reasons. First, one might think that sharing a "co-minority" status would create increased awareness and solidarity among racial and ethnic minorities. Second, due to the legacy of racism and White supremacy in this country, one would think that White people would score higher than Asians and Latinos in terms of holding anti-Black racist beliefs. However, Asians and Latinos *are* susceptible to believing in stereotypes and holding racist beliefs about Black Americans *regardless* of their co-minority status. Consequently, the data support the concept of horizontal oppression, where members of targeted groups maintain and reinforce oppression (Hardiman and Jackson 2007) (by verbalizing or acting on their racist beliefs). Furthermore, some people of color may intentionally distance themselves from blackness or Black people, hold anti-Black racist beliefs, and perpetuate anti-Black racism in anticipation that they will be rewarded by individuals and institutions who have power within the White supremacist social structure. Some may also be motivated by the desire to avoid "mistreatment by association" and by a desire to receive approval, high appraisal, and better treatment than Black people. While there are many co-minorities who are allies to the Black community, it is clear that we need to further examine why non-Black people of color hold racist beliefs toward Black people, and we need to ascertain what they gain from holding such beliefs. In 2012, a Black teenager named Travyon Martin was murdered by a Latino man named George Zimmerman. In a *Colorlines* article (Hing 2013) on George Zimmerman's racial identity, sociologist Tamara Nopper argues:

> [w]e really have not developed a vocabulary around talking about Latinos as a racial group in terms of their relative relationship to [B]lacks...it would make us confront some really uncomfortable possibilities, that a Latino person could get away with murdering a [B]lack person, and get support from [W]hite people for doing so.

In the same article, editor and publisher of the *OC Weekly*, Gustavo Arellano argued that "[w]e finally know how know-nothings will accept Latinos—we have to kill an unarmed [B]lack teenager, then they'll accept us." In the end, by engaging in horizontal racism, some non-Black people of color may be attempting to be accepted by the dominant White culture, and they may be trying to decrease their chances of experiencing racism by showing that it is Blacks (not them) who are at the bottom of the racial hierarchy and who deserve the worst treatment.

Post-racist Beliefs

I measured post-racist beliefs by gauging participants' agreement with two statements that I created based on relevant literature. The first statement examines whether students believe that the election of President Obama indicates racism is no longer a problem—"the election of President Obama is proof that racism is not a major social issue anymore." The second statement examines whether students believe that racism is no longer as bad as it was in the past—"racism is not as bad as it was in the past." The two items measure similar but distinct concepts. For instance, an individual can understand that racism exists (item 2) but not think that it is currently a major social problem (item 1).

Compared to White students, Asian and Latino students were more likely to believe that racism is no longer a major social issue. About 17.9% of Latino students and 24.4% of Asian students believed that the election of Barack Obama was proof of this. In comparison, 13.66% of White students and 13.04% of Black students believed that the election of Barack Obama was proof of this. Unsurprisingly, students who scored higher on the modern racism scale (i.e. those who held more racist beliefs) were also more likely to agree with the statement. As mentioned in the previous section on racist beliefs, we must further explore why some people lack awareness and empathy regarding the racial oppression that Black Americans face in modern-day America.

Individuals who scored high on the Modern Racism Scale were also more likely to believe that racism is not as bad now as it was in the past. This supports my argument that racist beliefs and post-racist beliefs *are* connected. Some people benefit from post-racist beliefs because it relinquishes them from doing their part to end racism. Individuals who hold racist beliefs may also subscribe to the notion of a post-racist society in an attempt to convince themselves that they are not racist. Instead of reflecting on how their behavior is racist, how it reflects racial privilege, and how to avoid such behaviors in the future, many follow the illogical premise that "racism does not exist; therefore, my beliefs and actions are not racist." Additionally, participants who experience race-based microaggressions (in the form of microinsults) believe that racism *is not* better than it was in the past. It is unsurprising that participants who have experienced racism firsthand would understand that racism is still a major issue in contemporary society.

Cultural Competency

Cultural competence was measured by using the six-item Respect for Cultural Differences subscale from the Intercultural Sensitivity Scale (Chen and Starosta 2000). This scale gauged participant's respect for other cultures, which is integral to being culturally competent and proficient. It asked respondents to agree or disagree with the following statements: (1) I think people from other cultures are narrow-minded; (2) I don't like to be with people from different cultures; (3) I respect the values of people from different cultures; (4) I respect the ways people from different cultures behave; (5) I would not accept the opinions of people from different cultures; and (6) I think my culture is better than other cultures.

Results show that students who score higher on the cultural competence scale hold fewer racist beliefs and that they are also less likely to believe in a post-racist society. This is a powerful finding because it indicates a possible solution to reducing racist and post-racist beliefs as well as subsequent microaggressions and macroaggressions.

References

American Civil Liberties Union. (2015). *Locating the school-to-prison pipeline.* Retrieved from https://www.aclu.org/node/29079

Bobo, L., Kluegel, J. R., & Smith, R. A. (1997). Laissez-faire racism: The crystallization of a kinder, gentler, antiblack ideology. In S. A. Tuch & J. K. Martin (Eds.), *Racial attitudes in the 1990s: Continuity and change* (pp. 15–42). Westport: Greenwood Publishing Group.

Bonilla-Silva, E. (2014). *Racism without racists: Color-blind racism and the persistence of racial inequality in the United States.* Lanham: Rowman and Littlefield.

Carson, E., & Sabol, W. J. (2012). *Prisoners in 2011.* Washington, DC: United States Department of Justice. Retrieved from http://www.bjs.gov/index.cfm?ty=pbdetail&iid= 4559

Chen, G., & Starosta, W. J. (2000, November). *The development and validation of the intercultural sensitivity scale.* Paper presented at the Annual Meeting of the National Communication Association, Seattle.

Cross, T., Bazron, B., Dennis, K., & Isaacs, M. (1989). *Toward a culturally competent system of care.* Washington, DC: CASSP Technical Assistance Center, Center for Child Health and Mental Health Policy, Georgetown University Child Development Center.

Dasgupta, N. (2013). Implicit attitudes and beliefs adapt to situations: A decade of research on the malleability of implicit prejudice, stereotypes, and the self-concept. In P. Devine & A. Plant (Eds.), *Advances in experimental social psychology* (Vol. 47, pp. 233–280). San Diego: Elsevier.

Denton, N. A. (2006). Segregation and discrimination in housing. In R. G. Bratt, M. E. Stone, & C. Hartman (Eds.), *A right to housing: Foundations for a new social agenda* (pp. 61–81). Philadelphia: Temple University Press.

Hardiman, M., & Jackson, B. (2007). Conceptual foundations for social justice courses. In M. Adams, L. A. Bell, & P. Griffin (Eds.), *Teaching for Diversity and Social Justice.* New York: Routledge.

Hing, J. (2013, July 22). The curious case of George Zimmerman's race. *Colorlines*. Retrieved from https://www.colorlines.com/articles/curious-case-george-zimmermans-race

Ito, T. A., & Urland, G. R. (2003). Race and gender on the brain: Electrocortical measures of attention to the race and gender of multiply categorizable individuals. *Journal of Personality and Social Psychology, 85*, 616.

Knapp, L. G., Kelly-Reid, J. E., & Ginder, S. A. (2012). *Enrollment in postsecondary institutions, fall 2010; financial statistics, fiscal year 2010; and graduation rates, selected cohorts, 2002–07*. Washington, DC: United States Department of Education.

Levchak, C. C. (2013). *An examination of racist and sexist microaggressions on college campuses* (Unpublished doctoral dissertation). University of Iowa, Iowa City.

McConahay, J. B. (1986). Modern racism, ambivalence, and the modern racism scale. In J. Dovidio & S. Gaertner (Eds.), *Prejudice, discrimination, and racism* (pp. 91–126). Orlando: Academic Press.

McWhorter, J. H. (2008, December 30). Racism in America is over. *Forbes*. Retrieved from http://www.forbes.com/2008/12/30/end-of-racism-oped-cx_jm_1230mcwhorter.html

McWhorter, J. H. (2010, January 14). It's official: America is 'post-racial' in the age of Obama. *The Grio*. Retrieved from http://www.thegrio.com/2010/01/its-official-america-is-postracial-in-the-age-of-obama.php

Oliver, M., & Shapiro, T. M. (2006). *Black wealth/white wealth: A new perspective on racial inequality*. New York: Routledge.

Pettigrew, T. F. (2009). Post-racism?: Putting President Obama's victory in perspective. *Du Bois Review: Social Science Research on Race, 6*, 279–292.

Ritter, J., & Taylor, L. (2011). Racial disparity in unemployment. *The Review of Economics and Statistics, 93*, 30–42.

Schorr, D. (2008, January 28). A new, 'post-racial' political era in America. *National Public Radio*. Retrieved from http://www.npr.org/templates/story/story.php?storyId=18489466

Staats, C. (2014). *State of the science: Implicit bias review 2014*. Columbus: Kirwan Institute.

Check for updates

CHAPTER 4

Microaggressions, Macroaggressions, and Modern Racism in Higher Education

What I have experienced as far as racism goes, can't be summed up in a single paragraph. Generally, I feel that racism on this campus is subtle, from the looks you get from people or the feeling you get when walking into a room. However, I have had people straight up call me the n-word or tell me that they don't like people of my race.
—Black man, 21, at predominantly White school

Racism in School

Racism is rampant in our nation's schools. In our primary and secondary schools, "[B]lack preschoolers…make up almost half of all out-of-school suspensions for preschoolers" (Smith 2014); "[B]lack students as young as 4 years old… [face] unequal treatment from school administrators" (Hsieh 2014). Compared to White students, Black and Latino students are less likely to have access to veteran instructors and are more likely to have support staff dedicated to discipline at their schools (Black et al. 2016). According to the Office for Civil Rights (2014), "Black students are suspended and expelled at a rate three times greater than [W]hite students…[and] while [B]lack students represent 16% of student enrollment, they represent 27% of students referred to law enforcement and 31% of students subjected to a school-related arrest." Students who have experienced a suspension or an expulsion are at an increased risk of coming into contact with the juvenile justice system. Oftentimes, school officials will seek to have students arrested. In some cases, students may

C. C. Levchak, *Microaggressions and Modern Racism*,
https://doi.org/10.1007/978-3-319-70332-9_4

even be arrested while at school (Nelson and Lind 2015). This drives the school-to-prison pipeline.

In our nation's colleges and universities, "race-related hate crimes accounted for 41 percent of reported vandalisms classified as hate crimes, 37 percent of reported intimidations, and 38 percent of reported simple assaults in 2013 (Zhang et al. 2016: ix)"; and "the number of racial harassment complaints relating to postsecondary institutions more than doubled during the eight years of the Obama administration (Lhamon 2016)." From September 2016 to March 2017, "there [were] 107 White supremacist fliering incidents on American college campuses (Anti-Defamation League 2017)"; and in doctoral programs, some African American students are treated like criminals and second-class citizens (Torres et al. 2010).

While we must focus our attention on all levels of education, higher education deserves special attention. Higher education has been linked to upward mobility in recent decades. Higher education has particularly served as a road to upward mobility for disadvantaged racial groups. Although some US colleges and universities strive to make their institutions, programs, and departments more diverse, there is still much work to be done to ensure that students of color feel welcome, and to reduce the likelihood that they will experience racism on college campuses. Colleges and universities are often considered bastions of progressive liberalism that challenge racism. However, the seeds of American racism that were planted at the country's inception, and were sustained by the blatant subjugation of people of color, continue to generate race-based oppression throughout American society, including academic institutions. Therefore, it is important to explore racist microaggressions, macroaggressions, and modern racism in higher education since their presence in educational institutions serves to perpetuate race-based differences in achievement and well-being.

Race-based "Tests" in Addition to Academic Tests

Black and White students have vastly different educational experiences even when they are in the same institution, program, and classroom. In addition to experiencing the academic demands and related stressors that their White counterparts experience, students of color also experience pervasive racism both off ***and*** on campus, which presents additional challenges and distractions that no student should have to deal with.

Encountering racism in school, as a student, can be a nightmare—especially when bigotry is perpetuated by an educator who has the ability to sabotage students' progress both academically and professionally.

However, racism in schools can also be perpetuated by other students, staff, and even visitors. This creates a toxic environment for targets and their allies. Therefore, academic policy should account for overt *and* covert forms of racism, and it should be implemented in a way that protects students from race-based attacks that could be perpetrated by people associated with the school as well as visitors.

As explained in the preface, I have experienced race-based challenges on my academic journey. Even though nostalgia oftentimes paints our past in brighter and more vivid colors than it actually was, I truly loved school. I benefited from a mother who challenged and encouraged me intellectually, as well as teachers who genuinely cared about my growth. I remember, at times, feeling an unbridled enthusiasm and motivation to excel at school, whether it was explaining a concept in class or striving for the highest score on an exam. I also remember the first time my excitement for school was dampened.

I had amazing teachers during my primary education. They were intelligent, welcoming, encouraging, and they helped me develop into a serious-minded scholar. One teacher not only believed in me but also recommended that I be transferred to a class for the gifted and talented. I was truly excited and proud. However, my new teacher was cold, unapproachable, unkind, and unwelcoming—essentially the antithesis of my previous teachers. She treated me differently than she treated the White students. She made me feel as though she hated me and did not want me there. Her behavior created a chilly climate that stifled my academic growth and passion. Soon after I joined her class, I remember *dreading* going to school, and my grades briefly suffered. In hindsight, this was the first time that I experienced racism and suffered because of it. Over the course of my academic career, from preschool to graduate school, while I had amazing teachers, I had some, both White and non-White, who behaved in vertically and horizontally oppressive ways. During those encounters, it felt as though there were additional "tests" related to my race that I had to master and associated stress that I had to manage. This was in addition to the actual responsibilities and stressors of being a student.

Challenges Unique to Predominantly White Institutions

Holmes et al. (2000) argued that, compared to students of other racial groups, African Americans at predominantly White institutions are doubly burdened. They specifically argue that African American students have to

(1) cope with the "normal concerns" of being students (such as "being away from home" and familiar support systems for the first time, possibly "sharing a room with a stranger, establishing new relationships", and managing academic pressures), and (2) "adjust in an intellectual and social community that is unprepared to accept their cultural differences" (Holmes et al. 2000: 44). They also assert that some predominantly White institutions are negligent in cultivating campus communities that are "welcoming and conducive to the learning styles of culturally and ethnically diverse student groups" (Holmes et al. 2000: 44). Moreover, the consequences of not improving campus climates at predominantly White institutions include lower rates of retention and lower rates of degree completion among people of color. This will undoubtedly reinforce existing economic and educational disparities.

Similarly, Greer and Chwalisz (2007: 399) found that African American students who attended a predominantly White school experienced "significantly higher levels of environmental, interpersonal, and intragroup stressors" compared to their counterparts at a historically Black institution, showing that the racial composition of institutions matters when examining racism in schools. Price et al. (2009) explain that racial tension and racism were largely ignored at the predominantly White school featured in their study. They assert that racial discomfort, tension, and invisibility have long been problems on many college campuses, and they challenge institutions of higher education to assess their impact on race relations: "[i]f education is critical to a democracy and if racially diverse campus communities better prepare students for participation in a democratic society, higher education needs to evaluate its role in perpetuating race-related inequities" (2009: 4).

Research Findings on Racism in School: Qualitative Data

Here, I present and discuss qualitative data from the research I conducted about racism on college campuses (Levchak 2013). As outlined in the *Introduction*, this data comes from a predominantly White Midwestern school and a racially diverse school in an urban area. The intent of these questions was to generate in-depth responses about participant's experiences with racism on campus as well as their view of their campuses' racial climate. Respondents were asked the following questions: (1) Please describe your experiences with racism on your campus; and (2) Do you think that your school provides a comfortable environment for culturally diverse groups? The following themes emerged: anti-Black racism, anti-Asian racism, segregation, "reverse" discrimination, and racist jokes.

Anti-Black Racist Microaggressions and Macroaggressions

Anti-Black racism was a key issue that arose in the open-ended responses and was common at both schools. The following related themes also emerged: Black people being avoided or excluded from activities; the perception of Black inferiority; racist verbal attacks directed toward Black people; the perception of Black criminality; and anti-Black stereotypes.

Anti-Black Racism

> What I have experienced as far as racism goes, can't be summed up in a single paragraph. Generally, I feel that racism on this campus is subtle, from the looks you get from people or the feeling you get when walking into a room. However, I have had people straight up call me the n-word or tell me that they don't like people of my race (Black man, 21, at a predominantly White school).

> Most racism involves African Americans (Latino man, 20, at a predominantly White school).

> I have never been assaulted because of my race; however, I have seen a lot of racism towards African Americans (White woman, 18, at a racially diverse school).

> Racism is expressed by people of my culture and others, toward African Americans (White woman, 20, at a racially diverse school).

While anti-Black racism can manifest in specific instances, it also operates as persistent background noise that broadcasts the message that Black people are not wanted, don't belong, are substandard, are bad, or are dangerous. For some, it is subtle and easy to overlook. For others, it is palpable and profoundly impacts them and those around them. Anti-Black racism can make simple tasks like walking across campus, engaging with a professor, or participating in group work a nightmare. Black students must have safe spaces to turn to on campus, where there are professionals who are trained to help targets of racism and who are committed to employing anti-racism strategies in their work. There is much work to be done, and it must be done swiftly and thoroughly to protect the lives and academic aspirations of Black students.

Avoiding and Excluding Black People

> The people here have a certain vibe, where they have to accept your presence, but they don't like you at the same time. [For example], on the [college-operated shuttle bus], there will be an open seat next to me and people will look at the seat and rather stand up and try to balance themselves, than sit next to me (Black woman, 20, at a predominantly White school).
>
> People tell me they don't ride the bus at certain times of day because of Black people. (Race undisclosed, man, 20, at a predominantly White school).
>
> A lot of Whites tend not to socialize with Blacks (Black woman, 18, at a predominantly White school).

While some schools are truly committed to increasing diversity and ensuring that their campus climate is welcoming and safe for all students, others have much work to do. In general, schools have to do more than make claims about respecting diversity and inclusivity in their mission statements. Instead, they must fiercely and persistently work toward inclusion and combat racism so that students never feel as though their race is a burden or disadvantage while they are pursuing their education. A school's commitment to diversity and anti-racism efforts not only helps all students but it also helps ensure the prosperity and growth of the school and nearby neighborhoods for years to come.

The Belief in Black Inferiority

> [Racism is] both overt and…undercover. From profiling, discrimination, and name-calling to other students having lower expectations (Black woman, 20, at a predominantly White school).
>
> People are often surprised by my accomplishments and/or who I am, where I come from. I am not looked at equally as my peers are (Black woman, 21, at a predominantly White school).
>
> I always get the feeling from…students that Black men are seen as inferior. I've had students avoid me simply because I was casually approaching them (Black man, 30, at a racially diverse school).

> I'm Black; people always see me as inferior (Black woman, 19, at a racially diverse school).
>
> There are a lot of Black people. A lot of people wonder how some got in because they're "ghetto" (White woman, 18, at a racially diverse school).

Individuals who believe in Black inferiority may have lowered expectations for Black students, ignore the accomplishments of Black students, or convey shock at Black students' academic success. Lowered expectations and shock about Black students' achievements are rooted in the stereotype that Black students (and particularly African Americans) aren't equipped to attend college because they are not intelligent and do not work hard. In the end, such stereotypes make it easier for racism to persist in our schools and for Black excellence, intelligence, ingenuity, hard work, and success to be overlooked.

Anti-Black, Macroaggressive Verbal Attacks

> My friends were called the n-word last year outside their residence hall (Black woman, 19, at a predominantly White school).
>
> I have been called [the] n-word on campus. People won't sit by me on the [college-operated shuttle bus]. I hear comments in situation[s] that [are] racist. Asked how I got here. And whether or not I comb my hair (Black woman, 19, at a predominantly White school).
>
> Other Whites using the n-word (White man, 19, at a predominantly White school).
>
> I haven't had any personally, but a group of my friends [were] called niggers when walking to [the store] from [their dorms] (Black man, 20, at a predominantly White school).
>
> A drunk, White male yelled racial slurs at a group of Black men causing a physical fight (White woman, 20, at a predominantly White school).
>
> People bad-mouthing Blacks. Using the n-word. Derogatory remarks to minorities (Black woman, 18, at a racially diverse school).
>
> People definitely judge me b/c of my color. They make rude comments and it hurts my feelings (Black woman, 21, at a racially diverse school).

It is a myth that racist hate speech is obsolete and *only* used by uneducated, social outcasts. As seen in the above comments, anti-Black, macroaggressive hate speech occurs on both predominantly White and racially diverse campuses. In a time where public figures unabashedly engage in harmful hate speech, we need individuals and institutions to support anti-racism efforts as well as encourage respectful and civil interactions so that people are better protected from racist macroaggressions.

Anti-Black Stereotypes

> I feel there is a lack of Black students here. Also, a lot of stereotypes are spoken about Black people (White woman, 20, at a predominantly White school).
>
> I hear stereotypes about Blacks all the time (White woman, 19, at a predominantly White school).
>
> A lot of stereotypes facing African Americans (White woman, 22, at a predominantly White school).

As discussed in Chap. 3, cultural competence and awareness training are key in reducing racist beliefs, stereotypes, and prejudices. Students who displayed higher levels of cultural competence held fewer racist beliefs. Therefore, all agents of socialization, and particularly families and schools, should be committed to the development of culturally competent, productive members of society who do not engage in racist behavior or speech. Just like there are major and minor requirements that must be fulfilled before graduation, there should be required anti-racism seminars *and* well-promoted, optional anti-racism seminars available to all members of a given academic community. This will allow them to unlearn their biases and learn how to effectively communicate, interact, and live with people of all racial and ethnic groups. With such efforts, we will be moving in the right direction to reduce racism on campuses and throughout society.

Black Criminality

> I have seen friends who are Black be[ing] singled out by police for nothing other than their race (White man, 19, at a predominantly White school).
>
> [My school] is very accepting of all races on campus, but I know certain students who become afraid when someone Black passes by at night (White woman, 20, at a racially diverse school).
>
> People avoiding eye contact and physical contact due to the fact they think a crime will occur (Black man, 18, at a racially diverse school).

Taking such examples into account, it is unsurprising that some Black students don't feel like welcomed and accepted members of their campus communities. As a result of their mistreatment, some may not feel confident enough to develop professional and supportive relationships with other members of the campus community; or, they may not feel safe or worthy enough to seek help from campus police, counselors, or officials because in many cases, they are viewed and treated like deviants and criminals who have no business being on college campuses.

Anti-Asian and Anti-International Racist Sentiments, Microaggressions, and Macroaggressions

Anti-Asian sentiments, microaggressions, and macroaggressions were common at both schools. Asian students at both schools (and particularly the predominantly White school) endured anti-Asian racism, verbal harassment, liquid racism, anti-international antagonism, racist retaliation as a response to the critical mass of Asian students, and being blamed for White students' underperformance.

Anti-Asian Racism

> People hate Asians (White woman, 18, at a predominantly White school).
>
> People are most racist to Asians (White woman, 19, at a predominantly White school).
>
> People dislike Asians the most out of every race. People telling Asians to go home/making fun of their customs and speech (White man, 19, at a predominantly White school).

Although one of the shortest comments, the first quote is one of the most profound in the study. It is a simple and declarative statement that captures the climate of race relations on the predominantly White campus. In this section, I unpack various forms of anti-Asian sentiments, microaggressions, and macroaggressions, and I demystify anti-Asian racism.

Although anti-Asian racism has been present in the United States since the early waves of Asian immigration in the 1800s, the model minority myth obscures the fact that Asians have been, and continue to be, the targets of racism and racial hatred. The model minority myth is the idea that as a group, Asian Americans are successful, well-off, and extremely "educated people who do not suffer from the problems usually associated with minority group status" (Healey 2011: 362). In reality, while some Asians do enjoy economic and educational success, they also experience struggles and anti-Asian racism. Therefore, we must work to identify, name, and eradicate anti-Asian racism in all of its forms because it will otherwise go unchecked, unchallenged, and will remain harmful to Asians.

Anti-Asian Racist Comments and Verbal Harassment

> A week does not go by where I don't hear something negative about my race. There are comments made every day…about the international kids. The way they eat, talk, smell, stick together, and other cliché generalizations of Asians. I've heard many comments about Blacks too, from mostly Whites. Rarely so [do] I ever hear negative comments about Whites. When I do, it's about blondes (Asian woman, 21, at a predominantly White school).

> I've heard people make comments about other races. My friends are somewhat racist. I've had experiences where Asians were made fun of in front of me (they didn't know I was Asian) (Asian woman, 18, at a predominantly White school).

> I get called bad names, and it hurts my feelings (Asian man, 18, at a racially diverse school).

> People usually call Black people the n-word and Asian people chinks (Asian male, 20, at a racially diverse school).

The first comment is incredibly disturbing but is unsurprising given the intense anti-Asian sentiment at the predominantly White school. *At least once a week*, the participant heard "something negative" about her race. Moreover, her experience was not uncommon. Asian students on both campuses were inundated with verbal harassment and racist comments that were dehumanizing, humiliating, and embarrassing. Such comments not only impacted the target's mental and emotional health (as seen in the third comment), it fostered a climate that was generally hostile toward Asians.

Anti-Asian Liquid Racism

> I notice a ton of racism towards Asians. Jokes which people know they will not respond to; stereotypes; rude comments; all around I feel that Asians are most targeted and that is not because I have [an] Asian background (many people do not even know I am) (Asian man, 18, at a predominantly White school).

> I've received racial slurs [from] White people before with no reasoning. People tend to make many Asian jokes but always claim I'm not Asian because I'm Filipino (Asian woman, 20, at a predominantly White school).

> I hear friends and people on the street downtown making racial jokes towards Blacks and Asians <u>ALL</u> the time (White woman, 19, at a predominantly White school).

As explained in Chap. 2, liquid racism is one of the most common and insidious forms of modern racism. "Jokes" are used to dispense racism in a way that allows the offender to hide their true intentions by saying they were simply being playful. Attempts to hold the offender accountable for their words and actions often result in targets, allies, and those investigating such incidents being charged with the difficult task of proving *intent*. However, I believe that regardless of supposed intent, we need to focus on the *impact* of the "joke." If the joke offended the target, or anyone who overheard it, then the offender should be held accountable. While that may sound unreasonable to some, I believe that ignoring racism in favor of supposed humor is not only unreasonable but unacceptable.

Anti-International Antagonism

> Most people are bad to the international students (Asian woman, 19, at a predominantly White school).

> The only racism I have encountered was what I have seen others do and say to the foreign students usually from China (White woman, 18, at a predominantly White school).

> I observe a lot of racism aimed at Asian international students on campus (White man, 20, at a predominantly White school).

> Derogatory slurs about Asian exchange students (White woman, 20, at a predominantly White school).

> Some students in my class don't want to discuss with me, I felt (because I'm Asian) (South Korean woman and international student, 21, at a predominantly White school).

Regardless of their country of origin, international students have many obstacles to overcome. Difficulties come in various forms like language barriers, cultural differences, and homesickness. Aside from such challenges, international students, and particularly Asian international students at the predominantly White school, encountered a hostile and unwelcoming environment. While it is often difficult for US-born students to come forward to report racism and bullying, international students may find it particularly challenging to navigate a foreign school system and to find allies and support systems that can help them document, report, and overcome the challenges of racism. We need to protect all students from racism, but we must pay special attention to the unique challenges and vulnerabilities that international students face.

Defending "White Territory" from Asians

> The Asians are taking over this fucking school and can't even speak English (White man, 21, at a predominantly White school).

> Chinese and Koreans come and don't speak a word of English. They do not learn the language or customs because they make little or no effort to interact with Americans (White man, 22, at a racially diverse school).

The above comments are very hostile and aggressive toward Asian students. It is clear from the comments that these White students believe that there is a wrongful intrusion of Asians onto *their* "White" campuses and, in an attempt to preserve their territory, they are responding with hostility (Levin and McDevitt 1993). Furthermore, since there is a critical mass of Asian students at both schools, their visibility makes them clear targets for retaliatory hostility, microaggressions, and macroaggressions (Levin and McDevitt 1993; Stotzer and Hossellman 2012). Protections for targeted groups as well as cultural competence, awareness, and anti-racism training are needed in such situations where racial hostility is present.

Curve Setting

> Asians are categorized as smart and throwing off our grade curves (White woman, 20, at a predominantly White school).

> A lot [of racism] against Asian students because they make up a good majority of the university and set curves (White woman, 18, at a predominantly White school).

Asian students were accused of "setting the curve" or outperforming other students on exams and assignments. However, it is outlandish for any student to blame someone else for their academic performance.

Unfortunately, for some students, scapegoating, bullying, and engaging in anti-Asian microaggressions and macroaggressions are more appealing than taking responsibility for their own academic performance.

Racial Segregation on College Campuses

Students at both the predominantly White school *and* the diverse school cited racial segregation as a major problem on their respective campuses. I think there is an assumption that a diverse school would be more integrated and that there would be a higher degree of interracial solidarity and positive interactions between racial groups, however as expressed below, this is not the case.

Segregation at the Predominantly White School

> I rarely see different [racial] groups comingle... [The school] prides themselves on having many races of people, but no sense of community is visible. Asians hang [out] with other Asians, Latinos with other Latinos...I tried to be open, but I was shunned when I attempt[ed] to try to say "hi" (Latino man, 26, at a predominantly White school).

> [On] campus, I feel [like] people [are] divided by race, Asian with Asian, White with White (Asian woman, 20, at a predominantly White school).

> [It] just [feels] hard to step into the circle of Whites (Asian woman, 21, at a predominantly White school).

> I see a lot of discrimination and people choosing to be friends with people of the same race (White woman, 22, at a predominantly White school).

Segregation at the Racially Diverse School

> We are a diverse campus, but there is still stereotyping, and races tend to group together (White woman, 20, at a racially diverse school).

> Many races seclude/exclude themselves from others. Sometimes they hang out with the same type of people (Asian woman, 20, at a racially diverse school).

> Even though our campus promotes diversity, I feel that everyone is racially separated (Asian woman, 18, at a racially diverse school).

> I think the problem at [my school] is less about racism and more about the lack of culture mixing. We, as students, tend to stay in our race- or ethnic-based circles of friends. I don't see much racism anymore, but [I do see] ethnocentrism (White woman, 27, at a racially diverse school).

> This school is diverse, but there is plenty of segregation present (Latino man, 21, at a racially diverse school).

> This campus is noticeably racially segregated. I think it's great [to] learn about one's own culture and racial identity, but at the same time the critical learning that emerges through intercultural interaction is transformational… I have been part of projects aimed at providing more opportunities for student dialogue on issues of race, gender, class, etc. (Asian woman, 20, at a racially diverse school).

> [My school] is very diverse, but racial groups tend to stay together, very segregated (White woman, 22, at a racially diverse school).

Ideally, students would interact in meaningful ways and forge positive academic, social, and professional relationships. However, self-segregation and isolation operate on college campuses for three main reasons. First, self-segregation and isolation serve as protective mechanisms for students of color. Some students of color feel that it is safer (physically, emotionally, and psychologically) to separate themselves from the dominant group because of personal experiences, vicarious experiences, and the legacy of racism in America. Second, segregation can be a response to a lack of cultural competence and cultural humility needed to effectively interact and communicate with people from different cultural backgrounds. Last, self-segregation can be the result of a deliberate and intentional attempt to avoid people from different racial backgrounds.

Claims of Reverse Racism and People of Color Receiving Preferential Treatment

Although race relations are complicated (see the discussion on vertical dynamics of oppression in Chap. 2), our world is structured in a way that largely benefits White people over people of color. Furthermore, since White supremacy exists, reverse racism cannot exist. Hardiman and Jackson (2007) explain:

> Actions by members of a targeted group against a member of an advantaged group…are more complicated and are not equivalent to the actions of a member of an advantaged group against a member of a targeted group… [f]or

> example, individual people of color might feel or express prejudices against White people, ... but as a group...people of color [don't] hold many positions of power...that would enable them to turn their prejudices into widely held institutional and social policy. Claims of "reverse racism" ... fail to take this power dynamic into account (61).

Claims of reverse racism also fail to account for the legacy and continued significance of White privilege and racism. In many cases, such claims minimize racism directed toward people of color by suggesting that oppression against people of color no longer exists or is not as bad as it once was and that it is the White majority who are now being oppressed.

> I'm actually frustrated that I miss out [on] scholarship opportunities and internship opportunities because [of] the color of my skin; it is frustrating (White man, 22, at a predominantly White school).

> Preferential treatment of ethnic groups. Scholarships, groups, advisors, etc. easier access based on color/ethnicity ... [People claim that you] "can't be racist against Whites," but [the] majority gets forgotten (White man, 19, at a predominantly White school).

> [Racism is] non-existent, everyone is tolerated, if anything, non-Caucasian people receive unfair benefits (White man, 20, at a predominantly White school).

> Sometimes I feel that the university...doesn't care [about me] because I'm White (White man, 20, at a racially diverse school).

> Blacks being racist against White people (White woman, 18, at a racially diverse school).

> Our campus is very diverse. The biggest issue is that there are clubs for all races/cultures that do not include me as a Caucasian (White woman, 21, at a racially diverse school).

As seen above, some individuals made claims of reverse racism because they believe that racial minorities receive unfair benefits, scholarships, and opportunities. However, these quotes do not prove discrimination against the White majority. Instead, they capture the complaints of White people who want to *continue receiving unearned privileges*, opportunities, and benefits that are typically afforded to them because of their dominant racial status.

Racist Jokes

Racist "jokes" were most common at the predominantly White school (and were briefly addressed in the anti-Asian Liquid Racism section above). Racist comments and "jokes" are often covert and incorporated into our daily interactions and are infused into the media. This requires us to do our part by being selective with the language and comments we accept from others and the types of media we consume. It also requires that we acknowledge that racist jokes are a common way for racism to thrive and to be disseminated on American college campuses, as seen below:

> My roommates often make racist jokes…It pains me and I have asked them to stop numerous times (White man, 20, at a predominantly White school).
>
> There is definitely discrimination, and jokes about how [the majority] of Black students are usually athletes, and how [the] Chinese are taking over the campus (White man, 19, at a predominantly White school).
>
> Racist jokes/comments…although I don't condone it (White man, 20, at a predominantly White school).
>
> In my opinion, racism is more of a verbal problem rather than a physical one (i.e. jokes, comments are most prevalent) (White man, 19, at a predominantly White school).
>
> Have heard people make jokes about other races (White man, 21, at a predominantly White school).
>
> Black/racist jokes (White man, 20, at a predominantly White school).
>
> I do not see very much racism on campus; however, if I do, it is usually towards international students being the center of racist jokes (White man, 20, at a predominantly White school).
>
> Many racist jokes (White woman, 20, at a predominantly White school).
>
> I have one friend who makes racist comments but plays them off as jokes, which deeply upsets and confuses me as many of my/our friends [are] of different races (White woman, 21, at a racially diverse school).

As explained earlier, liquid racism is powerful because it provides the aggressor a way to hide their racism by labeling their racist comments a "joke." However, racist comments, bullying, teasing, and "jokes" have consequences (see Chap. 2 for more on the psychological and emotional consequences of racism). Furthermore, it is irresponsible and dangerous to ignore racist jokes, teasing, and bullying since they can cause the target emotional pain and may even prompt the target to commit self-harm and, in some cases, suicide.

Research Findings on Racism in School: Quantitative Data

As previously explained, the quantitative data comes from 2500 participants at a predominantly White institution and a racially diverse institution who filled out a survey that included scales and items related to racist microaggressive experiences, racist macroaggressive experiences, racist beliefs, post-racist beliefs, perceptions of campus climate, and cultural competence. Major findings are as follows: students of color experienced more race-based microaggressions than White students; Black and Asian students experienced the highest levels of race-based microaggressions, and students of color experienced victimization by members outside of their racial group at higher rates than White students—which underscores the violence and oppression that students of color experience both vertically (by Whites) and horizontally (by other people of color).

Table 4.1 shows that there are few differences between macroaggressions experienced at the predominantly White institution and the diverse institution. Nearly 90% of Black students experienced a macroaggression at both institution types. While a smaller percentage of Latinos/as and Asians experienced a racist macroaggression, each group experienced macroaggressions at a higher rate than Whites. Table 4.2 shows the percentage

Table 4.1 Percentage of individuals experiencing a racist macroaggression by institution type and race

	%
Predominately White institution	
Black	87
White	47
Latino/a	87
Asian	81
Diverse institution	
Black	86
White	61
Latino/a	78
Asian	86

Table 4.2 Percentage of individuals experiencing a racist microaggression by institution type and race

	%
Predominately White institution	
Black	95
White	40
Latino/a	72
Asian	82
Diverse institution	
Black	83
White	57
Latino/a	73
Asian	83

of individuals who experienced a microaggression. The results show that a very high percentage of Black students experienced a racist microaggression at both institutions. At the predominantly White institution, nearly all Black students (95%) experienced a racist microaggression. Fewer Latino/a and Asian students experienced a microaggression—although the percentages are still very high. Not surprisingly, a much smaller percentage of White students experienced a racist microaggression.

The above results show that racism is still prominent on college campuses. These results are also in line with recent literature that found, compared to White students, Black and Asian students reported experiencing more racial discrimination (Gomez et al. 2011). My findings are also in line with literature revealing that White male students are less likely to be victims of racialized violence (Perry 2010). Furthermore, we cannot wish or ignore racism and racial injustice away. Direct action is required to combat racism. In summary, these results add to the bourgeoning area of microaggressions and macroaggressions, but more importantly, the knowledge presented here has the potential to inform policy, programming, and practice that can positively impact the lives, well-being, and success of all students.

References

Anti-Defamation League. (2017, March 6). *White supremacists on campus: Unprecedented recruitment efforts underway.* Retrieved from https://www.adl.org/blog/white-supremacists-on-campus-unprecedented-recruitment-efforts-underway?_ga= 1.259652554.1593255127.1485308910

Black, S., Giuliano, L., & Narayan, A. (2016, December 9). *Civil rights data show more work is needed to reduce inequities in K-12 schools.* Retrieved from https://obamawhitehouse.archives.gov/blog/2016/12/08/civil-rights-data-show-more-work-needed-reduce-inequities-k-12-schools

Gomez, J., Miranda, R., & Polanco, L. (2011). Acculturative stress, perceived discrimination, and vulnerability to suicide attempts among emerging adults. *Journal of Youth and Adolescence, 40*, 1465–1476.

Greer, T. M., & Chwalisz, K. (2007). Minority-related stressors and coping processes among African American college students. *Journal of College Student Development, 48*, 388–404.

Hardiman, M., & Jackson, B. (2007). Conceptual foundations for social justice courses. In M. Adams, L. A. Bell, & P. Griffin (Eds.), *Teaching for Diversity and Social Justice*. New York: Routledge.

Healey, J. F. (2011). *Race, ethnicity, gender, and class: The sociology of group conflict and change*. Thousand Oaks: Pine Forge Press.

Holmes, S. L., Ebbers, L. H., Robinson, D. C., & Mugenda, A. G. (2000). Validating African American students at predominantly White institutions. *Journal of College Student Retention: Research, Theory & Practice, 2*, 41–58.

Hsieh, S. (2014, March 24). 14 Disturbing stats about racial inequality in American public schools. *Billmoyers.com.* Retrieved from http://billmoyers.com/2014/03/24/14-disturbing-stats-about-racial-inequality-in-american-public-schools/

Levchak, C. C. (2013). *An examination of racist and sexist microaggressions on college campuses.* Unpublished doctoral dissertation, University of Iowa, Iowa City.

Levin, J., & McDevitt, J. (1993). *Hate crimes: The rising tide of bigotry and bloodshed.* New York: Plenum.

Lhamon, C. E. (2016). *Securing equal education opportunity: Report to the President and Secretary of Education.* Washington, DC: United States Department of Education.

Nelson, L., & Lind, D. (2015, February 24). The school to prison pipeline explained. *Justice Policy Institute.* Retrieved from http://www.justicepolicy.org/news/8775

Office for Civil Rights. (2014). *Civil rights data collection: Data snapshot: School discipline* (Issue Brief No. 1). Washington, DC: United States Department of Education.

Perry, B. (2010). 'No biggie': The denial of oppression on campus. *Education, Citizenship and social justice, 5*, 265–279.

Price, D. B., Hyle, A. E., & Jordan, K. V. (2009). Ties that blind: Perpetuation of racial comfort and discomfort at a community college. *Community College Review, 37*, 3–33.

Smith, M. D. (2014, March 31). The school-to-prison pipeline starts in preschool. *Billmoyers.com*. Retrieved from http://billmoyers.com/2014/03/31/the-school-to-prison-pipeline-starts-in-preschool/
Stotzer, R. L., & Hossellman, E. (2012). Hate crimes on campus: Racial/ethnic diversity and campus safety. *Journal of Interpersonal Violence, 27*, 644–661.
Torres, L., Driscoll, M. W., & Burrow, A. L. (2010). Racial microaggressions and psychological functioning among highly achieving African Americans: A mixed-methods approach. *Journal of Social & Clinical Psychology, 29*, 1074–1099.
Zhang, A., Musu-Gillette, L., & Oudekerk, B. A. (2016). *Indicators of School Crime and Safety: 2015* (NCES 2016-079/NCJ 249758). Washington, DC: National Center for Education Statistics.

CHAPTER 5

Microaggressions, Macroaggressions, and Modern Racism in the Workplace

I write for those women who do not speak, for those who do not have a voice because they were so terrified, because we are taught to respect fear more than ourselves. We've been taught that silence would save us, but it won't.
—Audre Lorde

Racism and Bullying in the Workplace

Many of us are afraid. We're afraid to do or say anything that will jeopardize our employment. Many of us won't confront subordinates, coworkers, and (definitely not) superiors—even when they speak or behave in racially microaggressive and macroaggressive ways. When we aren't afraid and want to speak up, as targets or bystanders, we often lack support from others in our organization and oftentimes we become the sole person who puts their "neck on the line" to address an issue. In many cases, there is a lack of policy and procedure to adequately manage instances of overt and covert racist aggression. So, many of us suffer in silence or face retaliation for speaking up, and our workplaces become toxic, hostile places that we dread going to and are eager to leave. Eventually, our emotional and mental health decline, and our employers also suffer because our creativity and productivity decline, which impacts the success of the organization. In some cases, employers will also face penalties and lawsuits because they fail to admonish aggressors, address racist incidents, and strive for a fair and

C. C. Levchak, *Microaggressions and Modern Racism*,
https://doi.org/10.1007/978-3-319-70332-9_5

equitable work environment for all employees. Needless to say, it is in the interest of both employees *and* employers to name and address racist microaggressions and macroaggressions and to hold aggressors accountable in the workplace.

But as it stands, in many workplaces, fear remains because most people need their jobs to survive. Many have a high cost of living, as well as a variety of debts, and recurring bills like crippling student loan payments, high rent, and medical expenses to contend with. Countless Americans, regardless of one's perceived class or actual class, are having a difficult time making ends meet (Gabler 2016). So, playing nice, in the face of disrespect, bullying, discrimination, and racism has become a survival strategy in American workplaces.

Employers and employees should work together to ensure that our workplaces are free from racist microaggressions, macroaggressions, and bullying. As we work toward this ideal, employers should foster work environments where people are not afraid to speak against racism, and where they are free from retaliation once they do speak out against racist attitudes, words, and actions. When incidents do occur, there should be protocols in place so that targets and bystanders can easily report racism that happened in the workplace or that involved a target or aggressor who is associated with the organization. A mediator who is trained in the area of workplace bullying, workplace violence, and cultural competence, as well as overt and covert racist aggression, should be available on-site or easily reachable off-site to provide assistance when issues arise.

Bullying and Racial/Ethnic Bullying: From the Playground to the Workplace

While I do believe that there is good in the world, I also believe that our world and society are plagued by oppressive forces; where civility is increasingly uncommon; where targets are blamed for their victimization; and where aggressors' uncivil, antagonistic, and hostile behaviors go unchecked and unchallenged in some instances and are applauded and rewarded in others. Many of us learn early on not to challenge others (even when they are wrong). We are taught messages that on the surface sound great but that have the potential to silence us and rob us of our humanity and dignity. In my view, the Audre Lorde quote at the beginning of this chapter sheds light on how toxic messages are used to teach us to "respect fear more than ourselves" (Hall 2004: 90). Such messages include "don't be a tattletale" (if someone does something that is wrong, you must not tell an authority figure; otherwise, the act of you reporting them will be worse than *their* offense); or "snitches get stitches" (if you report someone's concerning behavior, you may suffer physical harm). So, throughout life, some internalize such toxic messages and many more like them, and learn to ignore other people's offenses and to suffer in silence. Furthermore, some people actually become angry when others stand up and challenge individual, institutional, cultural, and structural racism, as well as other forms of oppression. Additionally, some have become so passive in the face of bullies and bigots that they even let children, the most vulnerable among us, suffer as targets of racism and bullying.

In recent years, there have been increased efforts to problematize bullying as a social problem and as an epidemic, and while that is commendable, I would be remiss not to mention the many targets who have already lost their peace of mind, well-being, and in some cases, their lives (Dubreuil and McNiff 2010). As a society, it doesn't seem as though the tragedies of losing young lives to the bullying epidemic has been enough to change the collective way we think about, talk about, and challenge bullying and aggressive behavior. Since we frequently let bullying and racial aggression go unchecked and unopposed, many children who are bullies carry forward their problematic behavior into adolescence and adulthood. While more research, interventions, policies, and legislation must be in place to protect children and teens from bullying and racial aggression, we also need to learn more about and address the racial aggression and bullying that adults face, particularly in the workplace.

The Workplace Bullying Institute (WBI) is one of the only formalized entities in the United States to research, disseminate results, and propose legislation (The Healthy Workplace Bill) to address workplace bullying. Their work is incredibly important because it is helping to break the silence, shame, and fear related to workplace bullying. Furthermore, if the Healthy Workplace Bill is enacted into law, we will be a step closer to eliminating racism and bullying from our workplaces. The Workplace Bullying Institute defines workplace bullying as "repeated, health-harming mistreatment of one or more persons (the targets) by one or more perpetrators" and is abusive conduct that interferes with work and is verbally abusive, "threatening, humiliating, or intimidating" (Workplace Bullying Institute 2017).

According to the Institute (2017), “27% of Americans have suffered abusive conduct at work; 21% have witnessed it; and 72% are aware that workplace bullying happens.” With respect to gender, women are targets in 60% of the cases, with 39% of women bullied by men, 21% of women bullied by women, 30% of men bullied by men, and 10% of men bullied by women (Workplace Bullying Institute 2017). In another study on racism and bullying in the workplace, Fox and Stallworth (2005: 439) introduce the term “racial/ethnic bullying,” to describe intimidation and mistreatment that individuals experience on the basis of their race or ethnicity. They found that Asians, African Americans, and Latino employees report being targets of racial/ethnic bullying at rates higher than White employees (2005: 448), with only African Americans experiencing significant levels of emotional strain as a result of racial/ethnic bullying (2005: 450). In a recent survey, half of Black respondents and one-third of Latino respondents reported being the victim of racial discrimination in the workplace (DiJulio et al. 2015). In the same survey, 26% of Blacks and 15% of Latinos reported that they had been treated unfairly because of their race or ethnicity at their place of work in the past 30 days (DiJulio et al. 2015).

Aside from the work outlined above, there are only a few articles and studies that expose and capture the horrors of workplace racism. That is why the narratives shared below are so important because they help us better understand this issue, and they bring to light the experiences of people who have endured workplace racism, who have survived, and who believe that sharing their stories will help others.

Research Findings on Racism in the Workplace

Interview Details

The interview and survey questions asked participants about their experiences with racist microaggressions and macroaggressions in the workplace. The purpose of the interview was to gain a deep understanding of (1) whether or not microaggressions and macroaggressions are present in American workplaces, and if so, how they manifest; (2) how employees and employers address microaggressions; (3) how employees cope; and (4) what employees believe would make their workplace environment more inclusive and welcoming. I found that employees throughout the United States regularly experience microaggressions in the workplace, and to a lesser extent macroaggressions.

Table 5.1 Workplace microaggressions and macroaggressions—participant information

Name	*Race and Ethnicity*	*Gender*	*Region discussed*	*Years in workforce*	*Age*
Holly	African American	Woman	Midwest and Deep South	17	36
Leo	African American	Man	Southwest and Northeast	16	29
Corrine	African American	Woman	Northeast	30	55
Fred	African American	Man	Northeast	13	29
Ralph	White	Man	Deep South	12	33
Fawn	US-born North African	Woman	Northeast	15	33
Judith	African American	Woman	Midwest	19	42
Reena	White	Woman	Midwest	30	46
Audrey	African American	Woman	Northwest and Northeast	23	36
Tatiana	US-born East Asian	Woman	Northeast	21	34
Oliver	African American	Man	Northeast, Southeast, and Midwest	19	36
Stella	African American	Woman	Southeast	20	34
Brandon	African American and Filipino	Man	Northwest and Northeast	25	42
Ruth	African American	Woman	Northeast	40	55
Joe	Latino	Man	Northeast	15	34
Pamela	Latina	Woman	Northeast	15	33
Maya	African American	Woman	Northeast	19	41
Peter	Asian American, Chinese	Man	Northeast	9	32
Roger	Asian, Indian	Man	Midwest	18	43
Tara	African American	Woman	West	14	35

In this section, I present confidential interview and survey data from a sample of 20 employees who have worked throughout the United States (see Table 5.1 for demographic information). Below, I present the interview prompt, followed by the responses of participants who provided detailed answers. Those who answered briefly were omitted for the sake of space but were included in the affirmative and negative response tallies (presented below each prompt). Some responses were not included because the interviewee did not respond. Participants' real names have been masked, and I have used randomly selected names for each interviewee. Additionally, other information that could identify individuals or institutions mentioned by the participants has also been masked. When necessary, the responses were slightly edited to remove filler words and sounds in order to increase readability.

I also masked specific states, and instead used a slightly modified version of the United States Census Bureau-designated regions when referring to geographic locations: *Northeast* (Maine, New Hampshire, Vermont, New York, Massachusetts, Connecticut, Rhode Island, Pennsylvania, New Jersey); *Southeast* (Delaware, Maryland, Virginia, West Virginia, Washington, DC, North Carolina, Kentucky); *Deep South* (Georgia, South Carolina, Florida, Alabama, Tennessee, Mississippi, Arkansas, Louisiana, Oklahoma, Texas); *Midwest* (Ohio, Indiana, Illinois, Michigan, Wisconsin, Minnesota, Iowa, Missouri, North Dakota, South Dakota, Nebraska, Kansas); *Northwest* (Montana, Idaho, Wyoming, Utah, Colorado, Alaska, Oregon, Washington); *Southwest* (Arizona, New Mexico); and *West* (California, Hawaii, and Nevada).

I conducted the interviews using the Workplace Racism, Microaggressions, and Macroaggressions Survey that I developed for the purpose of this study. The survey consists of demographic questions, open-ended questions, and closed-ended questions that are directly related to employee's experiences with microaggressions and macroaggressions in the workplace. The main interview questions were adapted from the Daily Life Experience Subscale, originally created by Harrell (1994); however, they were published and found to be a reliable measure of racial microaggressions (or microaggressions and macroaggressions as I conceptualize) in work conducted by Torres et al. (2010). Instead of asking about general racist experiences, I used the subscale questions to specifically ask about past and present racist experiences in the workplace. I also used questions from the University of Massachusetts Amherst Workplace Bullying Survey (Williams and Ruiz 2012: 10 & 15) that I modified to specifically ask about aggressors and the consequences of race-based aggression. Additionally, I used relevant literature to create interview questions that asked about employees' coping mechanisms; how microaggressions are addressed by employers; what respondents believed would make their workplaces more inclusive and welcoming for people of color; workplace climate; and the consequences of race-based aggression.

Understanding the Data

1. As noted in Chap. 2, the seriousness of a given act of aggression is largely based on socially agreed upon standards (e.g. being treated as though you are stupid is "less severe" than being punched or stabbed). Therefore, for clarity, as the questions about racist experiences progress, the severity of experiences intensifies. For example, the first question in the *macroaggression* subscale asks about experiences with racist jokes,

and the last question in the subscale asks about being physically assaulted based on race.

2. I view graduate students as employees because of the paid teaching, research, or administrative work they perform. Consequently, their experiences are included below, along with the experiences of more "traditional employees."
3. The majority of interviewees either work in predominately White workplaces or in environments where they are not a part of the racial majority, with the exception of Stella who is an African American woman and who works in an environment where her supervisor and the majority of her coworkers are African American women. Additionally, the population that Stella serves is largely African American.
4. Due to the intersection of their identities, some women struggled at times with identifying whether an experience was based on race, gender, or a combination. This also highlights the utility of my concept "oppression manifestation" (see Chap. 2) as well as intersectionality theory.

You Were Treated Rudely or Disrespectfully Regardless of the prestige associated with their particular profession or career path, interviewees experienced race-based aggression in the form of rude treatment and disrespect in the workplace. There were 14 affirmative responses, five negative responses, and one interviewee who was unsure as it relates to this prompt:

Treated Rudely or Disrespectfully

Roger (Asian Indian Man, Midwest):	Yes, most definitely to the point where you're blatantly called to your face, racial epithets. For example, I was called a "goddamned fucking sand nigger" by someone who's still a current US Senator...because I [wouldn't] deviate from instructions given [to me] by my boss at the time. The other aggression was people saying, "You're Brown, you're working for Republicans, you're a traitor to your race." These [were] White Americans [who were saying this]. It's life, you have to accept it, in the sense that you've got to move forward [although] it's hard to move forward.

Tara (African American Woman, West): Yes. Being in the military, people already think they can talk down to you because you're a woman, or you're lower ranking. Being African American [makes it] even worse. It becomes a bad stigma. And people come from places where they've never met an African American person, and so they only get their views from television or what they hear on social media or on the news. So, they use those negative views against you instantly.

Peter (Asian American Chinese Man): Yes, and I would say not necessarily from the administration but more so from the students I work with. Especially students that I may be meeting with on less-than-positive circumstances, like in conduct reviews. Some of them do hold a bit of a grudge, not understanding [what] the university's policies are, and [what my role is] as a Conduct Review officer. Sometimes stereotypes and microaggressions do come into play, in terms of them feeling like I don't necessarily understand what they're saying or [that I haven't had] the same experiences as them [because I'm Asian]; especially since most universities I've worked at are PWI's [predominately White institutions], so that comes into play a little bit.

Corrine (African American Woman, Northeast): Yes. I've worked in the executive search field at one point. I was basically hired because they needed to have diversity in their workforce. They were trying to get diverse business, but they lacked [diversity on staff]. But with me being there, there were some people [who] resented me being there. So, [I was] excluded or not told about things in the office, or things that are happening in the business. The communication was lacking, and it was intentional.

Judith (African American Woman, Midwest): Yes. Some of the things that I've experienced at my most recent workplace are related to race, and possibly gender as well. But the one that would *definitely* be race-related [happened] when the president of the college addressed [a verbal offense that was] gender-based [and] said, "I'm sure if the word nigger had been used, then it would have been a different story." I was in complete shock. [I was] the only [person of color] sitting in the meeting [and], he used the n-word. He *actually* used the word, and not one of them said a thing. I didn't feel safe bringing it up, at all. This is the president of the flipping college saying this crap. And not one person in the room, including the Dean, thought anything was wrong with it. I brought it up to the Chair of the department, and basically, what I got was the impression that [I was] being too sensitive. But [that incident] just let me know what my place was.

Brandon (African American and Filipino Man, Northwest and Northeast): In my 15 years in my field, I've had about seven different directors. At least half of [the new directors] assumed I had a lower role than my actual title. [Also, there was one new manager who] heard something about an employee that was bad, or [heard] that someone needed to be managed out or pushed out, [and he] actually assumed that *I* was that person. It was actually a young, White guy they wanted to push out. So, within three hours of him coming into the office, and talking to his higher-ups [the new director said], "We mean him?" Then I heard the other person say, "No, he's the good one, it's the other one over there." So, I'm like "Really, for real? The issue *must* be with me, since I'm the Brown guy in the office?"

Tatiana (US-born East Asian Woman, Northeast): Yes. I think it has something to do with me being Asian. Asians are known [for keeping] quiet. They don't speak up. So, then they just try to step all over you, and take advantage of you. It's been going on [in my workplace]. You get a lot of like rude comments. It's disrespectful and degrading comments. They treat you differently. I'm so surprised it still happens in this day and age in [a diverse Northeastern City].

Leo (African American Man, Southwest and Northeast): Yes. From [supervisors, coworkers], and customers. [There was] a situation [after the 2016] election. Going to work that day, here in [the Southwest, there] was a sense of false pride. A lot of people were just, really hopeful, excited for change. But it was almost [in] an ignorant sense. [They were] more brainwashed. So, it was a situation where I [went] to work and there [was] a guy, and I said a very small comment. I said, "Hey listen, let's make [our workplace] great again." Almost like a joke. [Then] he said, "*Watch your mouth*, that's our president that you're talking about now, and *show some respect*!" It was weird because we were on a very cool level [prior to that statement]. There was never a sense of disrespect [before], but I felt like that was a borderline step like, "Did you just say that to me?"

[Also], I work at a call center, so I'm taking calls from many clients from inside the country and around the world. [Sometimes] there would be a lot of people that would ask for my input [on politics] over the phone, [but] I can't share that, because I represent a company. And there would be people who didn't even care about my input; they would just talk politics. They would ask for their [account information], and then go off on Obama, and just talk about Trump. I just had someone yesterday, talk about Trump over the phone. There is just [the constant] biting [of] my own tongue. Just being the bigger person, [and] not discussing politics. Even though it's something that I am very passionate about, it's something very private to me. I don't share my views with everyone, almost like religion [it's] private to me.

Oliver (African American Man, Northeast, Southeast, and Midwest): I was fortunate to be in some environments where I was treated right. [Jack, a White faculty member I worked with in graduate school] was a really nice guy. He always held the same standards for me [that he held for] everybody else, and that's what I respected about him. I was at [an R1 research university in the Southeast] briefly, and the advisor I had there treated me as if I didn't know a lot of the material, and [like] I needed to be babied through it. If I'm always being pampered as if I don't know anything, it's harder to [learn and work] in that environment.

Not Treated Rudely or Disrespectfully

Ralph (White Man, Deep South): Me, not particularly. I'd say more so, other people. I did have students in [a Southern State] ask me if I spoke Spanish, and when I said no, proceeded to start speaking Spanish in front of me, which was a little weird (laughs). I've heard students complain about other faculty, generally foreign ones, from different countries. Primarily based on the accent, and saying that they can't understand them, and what not. But outside of that, not really. I also work at a school that's pretty much all White, which has some impact I'm sure, as well.

Unsure

Fawn (US-born North African Woman, Northeast): I feel like, it's a little bit of both [rudeness and disrespect]. It could be [related to my race and ethnicity], but I think the current principal that I [work with is] a misogynist. He makes it very well known in his statements and how he talks to women. [There have been] situations where females have reported stalking or domestic violence, and he sort of brushes it off like the girl is the issue, not so much the guy [and he has a],

> "You need to 'suck it up or deal with it' type of attitude." [Also], we have some teachers who are Caucasian; some of them are respectful, and some of them quietly look down on me. I'm not sure if it's a race thing or because I work for a nonprofit.

Treated Rudely or Disrespectfully: Microaggressive Experiences Tara explains that people hold "negative views against" African Americans which judging from her response typically manifest as racist microinsults. Peter's mistreatment can be classified as a microinsult—when students behaved rudely and treated him as though he could not understand English or their experiences. I believe that such behavior stems from the perpetual foreigner sentiment (where regardless of how long an Asian individual or their family have been in the United States, they are still perceived as a foreigner and separate from the larger American society and culture).

Corrine experienced the microinsult of coworkers not wanting her to be a part of the staff. She explains: "There were some [who] resented me being there." Black women have meaningfully contributed to this nation, and its institutions, both historically and currently. However, as noted by Corrine, sometimes we are not wanted as employees or viewed by coworkers as valuable assets to the team. While this particular example of disrespect occurred in corporate America, such behavior is not uncommon in other sectors and positions. Brandon experienced microinsults when his new directors assumed he was a lower-ranking employee compared to his actual ranking and when a director assumed that Brandon was the employee who other supervisors said they wanted pushed out of the company. Such microinsults are predicated on the belief that Black and Brown people are inferior and not suited to work in higher-ranking positions. While mistakes do happen (that are likely fueled by stereotypes and biases), aggressors are not excused from making amends and adopting anti-racism thinking and behaviors.

Tatiana and Leo endured microinsults in the form of disrespectful comments. Their experiences are not uncommon. People of color have endured and continue to endure disrespectful comments and speech that is tainted with aggressiveness, harshness, and disrespect within the workplace. Oliver experienced a microinsult from a supervisor who questioned his intelligence, knowledge base, and judgment, while Fawn didn't know if her mistreatment was due to race, gender, or the status associated with her position. However, an intersectional approach would explain that her aggressors may have been motivated by several of her identities and statuses (e.g. race, ethnicity, gender, position status).

Treated Rudely or Disrespectfully: Macroaggressive Experiences Although theoretically I categorize rude and disrespectful treatment as microaggressive, in Roger's and Judith's cases, the rude and disrespectful treatment they endured was particularly macroaggressive. Roger was called "a goddamned fucking sand nigger," which is sickening and unprofessional and shouldn't be said in any workplace—and certainly not in politics, where our leaders should model civility, respect, and cooperation. Judith was shaken when the president of her school used a racial epithet and her colleagues and direct supervisors did nothing—"He used the n-word. He *actually* used the word, and not one of them said a thing. I didn't feel safe bringing it up, at all. This is the president of the flipping college saying this crap." The behavior of the college president was unprofessional and greatly isolated and offended Judith, the only faculty member of color in the room. Furthermore, the fact that he wasn't challenged by anyone made Judith feel as though the environment was unwelcoming to people of color, which impacted her perception of the campus and her willingness to mention future incidents of racism at her job.

Bystander and Vicarious Experiences Ralph, a White educator, shares: "I've heard students complain about other faculty, generally foreign ones from different countries. Primarily based on the accent, and saying that they can't understand them, and what not." In this example, we see two of the main ways that modern racism and microaggressions thrive: (1) covertly, and (2) behind the target's back. Even the most kind, aware person who is committed to anti-racism efforts may be unintentionally impacted by racist or negative race-based comments, unless they take good care to interrupt such microaggressions when they occur. In this instance, negative race-based comments may fuel an unfavorable view of foreign faculty members, which may adversely impact how *Ralph* treats or perceives such faculty members.

Unfortunately, attacking foreign faculty and faculty of color is not uncommon. In Ralph's example, and in similar situations, some students know that making disparaging comments about foreign faculty and faculty of color (to other faculty members as well as on evaluations) can result in negative, career-impacting consequences for the targeted faculty member. Due to this unfortunate reality, foreign faculty and faculty of color need protection and support when they experience microaggressive and macroaggressive attacks to their face and behind their backs. Research shows that faculty of color receive lower evaluations compared to their White counterparts, and those evaluations will undoubtedly impact the faculty member's career and well-being (Havergal 2016; Huston 2006). On a related note, as noted in Huston's (2006) review:

> Studies show that when female faculty of color teach classes that are politically charged, such as courses on race or gender, these female faculty of color are seen as having an agenda and the class is seen as more controversial than when White faculty or even male faculty of color teach these classes. This sense of controversy could lead to lower course evaluations (604).

Even in the face of unfair scrutiny and unwarranted attacks, faculty of color who are women know that such "controversial courses" *need* to be taught, so they take up the mantle and make the sacrifice to educate students and the world, even though there may be unpleasant consequences. Therefore, schools should not only acknowledge the sacrifices made by such faculty members, they should do their best to support and protect them from microaggressions and macroaggressions.

You Were Treated as If You Were Stupid Holding undergraduate degrees, graduate degrees, completing job-specific training, and having years of related work experience was not enough to protect employees from being treated as though they were stupid. There were 12 affirmative responses, four interviewees who were not treated as though they were stupid but had similar experiences, and four negative responses as it relates to this prompt:

Treated as If They Were Stupid

Judith (African American Woman, Midwest): Yeah, that was frequent. When I would voice any sort of opinion [to a certain White male colleague], he would basically take an opposite stance just for the sake of doing so, especially in front of students. The students picked up on whatever he was putting out there. [My colleague] encouraged the students to basically disregard whatever I said, so I had students in my class that would go to him, and second guess what I had on the test, [and] second guess my grading behind my back. The guy wouldn't even give me a heads up about it. I would just have to hear [about] it from the students, "Oh yeah, I was talking to [the other professor] about this, and he agreed with me." Then when I went to him about it, in a professional capacity, looking for some professional courtesy, the gist of what he actually had come out of his mouth was that he doesn't have time to do his job *and* mine. Implying that I wasn't doing my job in the first place if the students were going to him. So yeah, the students and professors there were intentionally treating me like I [was] a complete idiot. Like I didn't know what I was doing, [and] didn't know how to teach. I had people doing all sorts of disrespectful stuff, that I don't think they would have done to another professor. And like I said, I don't know if it was race *and* gender, or race *or* gender. But whistling to get my attention like I'm a dog, [and] putting their feet up on the desk in the front of the room. I mean this is stuff that you don't expect from somebody who's an adult, technically or otherwise. Or I don't anyway. When I [went] to the Chair about it, of course, it was my fault. It was rough; it was really rough.

Brandon (African American and Filipino Man, Northwest and Northeast): [The new managers did not] realize how much experience I have. So, when I answer a question, or question their direction, they'll have to double or triple check to see if what I'm saying is correct. And then the people that they're going to [say], "Oh, actually he's right, he's actually the authority on it." Then they'll start [saying] things like well, "Yes, he's been here 15 years, but he doesn't have a master's [degree] like I do!"

Ruth (African American Woman, Northeast): I feel like things have been done, to make me *look* stupid, or to undermine my authority on something, or the way that I handled something. That's what I would say, that things have been done to undermine who I am there. That continues to happen.

Pamela (Latina, Northeast): Yes, it was in a class setting [in my graduate program]. I do obtain a fellowship [or] financial compensation. So, a part of it means [that I have] to be in class as well, so some of [what I'll be sharing] will be in relation to being in a class setting. Someone was presenting in class about doing some nonprofit work [in Central America] and the [presenter] says, "Well, does anyone know where Nicaragua is?" and then someone looks [at me and says], "It's Central America, not South America. Don't be confused."

Roger (Asian Indian Man, Midwest): Yeah. Being called stupid by a fellow colleague. [Also] when my boss had to step down as Chair. [The new Chair] did not like the fact that, here I am, a Brown guy, telling him what's going on.

[He also didn't like] people referring to me saying, "He knows what he's talking about. We don't know what he knows." [But] he didn't want to hear from me. So, they had to actually restate [what I said]. Work that I had done [was] attributed to somebody else. So, these are the types of things [I'd have to] deal with on the Republican and Democratic side. If I'd been a woman, I think it would have been even worse.

Leo (African American Man, Southwest and Northeast):	Very frequently, but I handle it very well. I'm really good at de-escalating situations. I'm very confident in my abilities. I know that I'm not stupid when it comes to what I'm good at, and what I'm passionate about. [However, my manager] doesn't respect my intelligence, [and] he sometimes comes off like I'm being stupid, but then weeks later, he'll tell me that I should apply to be a manager.
Tara (African American Woman, West):	Yes, I always had to show that I was [more] knowledgeable than the average person no matter what their race was. They always thought I was stupid. I felt that all the time.
Fawn (US-born North African Woman, Northeast):	Yeah, I would say not necessarily the people within my agency, but again with the [school I provide services to], that's a definite yes.

Not Treated as If They Were Stupid

Corrine (African American Woman, Northeast):	No. Disregarded I would say, more so than stupid. They would not [ask me for] information. So, in that respect, maybe yes. [I would be] the person working on something, and [they would] go to the person next to me, who may be a White woman; but [they knew that she didn't] work on that, and [that I did].
Tatiana (US-born East Asian Woman, Northeast):	No. With my job, I know what's needed, what to look for. [Because I have more knowledge about my job] than my supervisor, she'll look at me like she doesn't like it and like I'm a threat to her. So, it becomes hard because I know more. I've done the job, and [I've] been in this field for longer [than her, but] she feels like she can take her title and step all over me and [degrade me].

Reena (White Woman, Midwest):	Not because of my race. Gender, yeah, there's a lot of that kind of stuff, yeah.
Peter (Asian American Chinese Man, Northeast):	I wouldn't say stupid, but I think that some people have definitely characterized or believed that I wasn't as smart as *they* thought I was. Possibly because I wasn't the one to speak up quickly or [because] I take time to process things. Sometimes, I'm just indifferent about things, and I really don't give a damn. So, I wouldn't necessarily say stupid but not as smart as others.

Bystander Experience

Ralph (White Man, Deep South):	No, not me. [However], I've seen students treated like that. [In the South], a White [female] student thought a Black [female] student had plagiarized. When asked why, the response was because, "the writing was so good." So again, not me, but I've seen it.

Treated as If They Were Stupid: Microaggressive Experiences While there were no macroaggressive experiences shared in this section, there were a variety of ways that microaggressions manifested. Judith endured microinsults from students and her colleague when they treated her as if she were stupid and they gossiped behind her back—"The students and professors there were intentionally treating me like I [was] a complete idiot. Like I didn't know what I was doing, [and] didn't know how to teach." Again, we see covert racism starting behind the target's back and then eventually bourgeoning into an offensive encounter that harms the target. We also see the faculty member affirming the students' microaggressive behavior and engaging in the behavior as well. The behavior of the faculty member was deplorable and helped to foster a chilly climate that negatively impacted Judith's perception of her workplace climate.

The following individuals also experienced microinsults related to being treated as though they were stupid. Roger was blatantly called stupid by a colleague, and his supervisor refused to acknowledge his work and credited other employees for his work. Brandon, Leo, Tara, Pamela, and Ruth all shared that their intelligence and authority had been questioned in the workplace.

While the following did not report being treated as though they were stupid, they experienced similar microinsults. Corrine felt disregarded and overlooked, when her coworkers refused to approach her about information she was the authority on. Tatiana was not treated as though she was stupid, but she felt resentment from her supervisor because she was more skilled and knowledgeable than her supervisor. When Peter did not live up to his colleagues preconceived notions about how Asian males should perform in the workplace, he was treated like he was "not as smart as others." Lastly, while Reena didn't experience race-based microaggressions or microinsults, she did experience gender-based microaggressions when she was treated as though she was stupid on the basis of being a woman.

Bystander Experience Ralph experienced an incident where a White female student believed that a Black female student committed plagiarism because the latter's work was very good. Similar to how students complained to Ralph about foreign-born professors (as seen in the analysis for the first set of responses), the White student not only assumed the Black student wasn't capable of doing good work, they also *defamed* the Black student's character. Furthermore, this accusation could have seriously damaged Ralph's view of the Black student by sowing seeds of distrust and suspicion that could have impacted Ralph's future interactions with the student, as well as how he scored the subjective parts of the student's grade. As seen in this situation, we should all be careful to guard ourselves from covert venomous messages that are intended to negatively impact our view of other racial and ethnic groups.

Others Have Avoided Being Around You In most workplaces, it is expected that there will be professionalism and collegiality among employees. When employees ignore, ostracize, and avoid other workers on the basis of their race, such conduct is not only unprofessional and rude, it is also racist. Such racist behavior not only ebbs away at the target's professional and personal well-being, it negatively impacts group cohesion and collegiality. There were 10 affirmative responses, two interviewees who did not think that people avoided being around them but had similar microaggressive experiences, and eight negative responses as it relates to this prompt:

Others Have Avoided Being Around Them

Peter (Asian American Chinese Man, Northeast): I think more so my students because I supervise a bunch of them, [and] they get a little irritated with me. But also, part of my responsibilities [include] conducting diversity trainings [and] addressing things that people don't want to say or address, so there is some avoiding.

Pamela (Latina, Northeast): Yeah. I'm actively working through it. There are eight women of color in our cohort. Seven of which, identify as Black, I identify as Latina, and the seven usually engage in many [micro-aggressions]. So, there's [essentially] a women of color group, and a "sub women of color" group.

Brandon (African American and Filipino Man, Northwest and Northeast): Yeah. Some have not wanted to be around me because I don't smile too much at work. [Black people smile] to disarm White people and [to] make them think that we're less threatening. So, smiling a lot for Black people at work, whether they intend to or not, is like a disarming mechanism to let White people know, "I'm safe" or "I'm not going to hurt you," or "I'm not an aggressive Black person." [It is] my habit not to smile [and] because of that, I'm looked upon as the "mean one." I don't put up those defense mechanisms. I don't know why Black folks do that at work. [I think] we [Black people as a group] do it a lot because maybe it's a defense mechanism of how we *want* to be perceived. We do it less with each other, but we do it more with White people, whether they're on the same level, or higher, but we don't do it with each other. Like, you could be cordial [and] nice, but there's extra cheesing [or smiling] that Black people do when White people are at work, and it's just a defense mechanism coming out. It's a lot of fear that produces that

	from Black people. That's not something that Black people do because they want to, or [because] they like that person. It's like this instinctive response. I think young Black people see the adults do it, they watch their parents do it, and I think it's a learned behavior. It's cultural to behave around White people that way.
Judith (African American Woman, Midwest):	Well basically (laughs) that would be just about most of them. I'd be at their table, and no one would bother to engage me in conversation. I'd try to ease into whatever conversation was going on [and] they just stop talking, [they would] clam up.
Tatiana (US-born East Asian Woman, Northeast):	[Yes]. What she [my supervisor] does is try to isolate me from everyone and have me away from the rest. I don't communicate with them.

Related Microaggressive Experiences

Corrine (African American Woman, Northeast):	I wouldn't say they have avoided being around me, but I would say that they have *excluded me from things* that they felt free to invite others [to].
Oliver (African American Man, Northeast, Southeast and Midwest):	No, others have avoided *including* me.

Has Not Been Avoided

Leo (African American Man, Southwest and Northeast):	That would have to be a strong no. Just because of my personality. Maybe one person [avoided me], and the reason that I think of him is because he was extremely racist.

Others Have Avoided Being Around Them: Microaggressive Experiences There were no macroaggressive or vicarious experiences associated with this prompt. In terms of microaggressive experiences, Peter's experience is quite noteworthy ***and*** unfortunate. We live in a world that is in desperate need of social justice education. However, Peter shares that, as a social justice educator, he is sometimes avoided because of the nature of his work. Once we collectively realize that social justice educators like Peter are here to help individuals and institutions, and not hurt them, I believe that our society will be one step closer to the liberation of all people. Pamela describes experiencing horizontal oppression in the form of avoidance by the Black women in her program because she is not Black. We don't typically talk about horizontal oppression (unless it's Black-on-Black crime), but it does occur among and between all targeted groups.

Brandon made a brilliant comment about Black people smiling as a way to disarm White people, so they don't think that Black people are aggressive or dangerous. The stereotypes about being an angry Black woman or a dangerous Black man are incredibly pervasive. Such stereotypes supersede Black employees' creativity and credentials, and it is unfortunate.

Brandon shared that because he chooses not to engage in what he calls the "defense mechanism" of smiling, he is labeled as being mean, and people avoid him.

Additionally, Judith experienced the microinsult of being left out of conversations, while Tatiana experienced the microinsult of being avoided and isolated. While Corrine and Oliver didn't agree that others avoided them, they did explain that they experienced the microinvalidation of being excluded or not invited to participate in activities or events.

Others Have Acted as If They Were Afraid of You or Intimidated by You Many have been socialized to fear Black and Brown people and to see us as unprincipled, aggressive, and unsuited for professional workplaces. Such irrational fear and views come out in the way we are spoken to, addressed, avoided, and evaluated in professional environments. There were 11 affirmative responses, five negative responses, and four responses that were not captured as it relates to this prompt:

Others Have Acted as If They Were Afraid of Them or Intimidated by Them

Corrine *(African American Woman, Northeast):* Oh, definitely. I was working in an area where it was predominantly White men. [Then] this young [White] lady came in. I [even] sat in on her interview. That clearly should have rung a bell that I was someone whose opinion they valued, but anyway, she was hired, and she was not meeting the standards of what she claimed to have known. She was falling short. In her falling short, [she] turned it into, [me not liking her] when it was merely, *me expecting her to do the job that she was being paid to do*. So, that was her defense: "I don't like her." I had no reason *not* to like her. It was just that she was making some major mistakes that she shouldn't have been [making], if she was as experienced as she had claimed to be. She went with [the claims that], "I didn't like her," and that "she was afraid of me." These were the things that I was hearing in and around the office from other Caucasians [who told me what she was saying]. So, I knew that I could not go to her and have a conversation with her, which I should have been able to do to shut that down. So, I had to go to our boss; [but] I had to tread carefully because she was a [White] woman, and my boss was [White]. I knew how that was going to look. [However], I went to him, and I told him what I was hearing. [I told him that] I had no intention of being the "angry Black woman" in her story because I'm not going to be the antagonist. I've seen that too many times, how you get set up for that, [and] I refuse to step into that because I've been around long enough to know, see, and side-step what she was setting up. [But] he didn't settle the problem, he just quieted it, and then I knew that it was time for me to move on. I moved on within the organization but out of that group because clearly he was going to protect her at all costs, and I knew that for everything that didn't go right, she could cry, she could do whatever, and he was going to make sure that she was not held accountable. I'm never comfortable. I've been in my firm [for] 20 years, [and] I will never get comfortable because you just never know in corporate America. They could just tap you on the shoulder, [and] you're done. I don't have that comfort level that I think people who are not African Americans are afforded.

Ruth (African American Woman, Northeast): Oh, yes. Most definitely. [Ann, a supervisor who is a White woman] does it because she wants to hide the fact that she doesn't want to deal with me on any level. So, she presents it [as], "Oh, I'm intimidated by [Ruth]." So here [Ann] goes, with the White woman's cry of, "Oh, I'm afraid, I feel threatened," and then [Richard, a supervisor, who is a White man] has to play the White male savior. But he's not addressing the issue. [He should say], "[Ann] be a grown up, go to [Ruth] like an adult. You're an adult; this is a work environment." I will argue a point, yes. But I've never threatened. I've stated my point, and I will confront them on an issue, but they have no reason to feel threatened. If I intimidate you, it's because you know I'm right, and you don't want to be shown up for being wrong. It doesn't have to be spread around the office, and we can both [hear each other's] points, and clear the air, and that'll be that. But Ann has never tried to include me as a part of the staff. She'd rather have Richard do the dirty work, and she just ignores dealing with me on any level. So, it boils down to the rudeness of her coming into the office and not even saying hello. Even if

	there's an issue that she has to bring before me directly, she just doesn't do it. So, that thing, with them feeling intimidated, I really just feel like that's another ploy to be disrespectful and to exclude me.
Roger (Asian Indian Man, Midwest):	Yes. I had some people stepping away from me until they found out I worked for [an established politician]. I have been told that I look like a terrorist sometimes.
Fawn (US-born North African Woman, Northeast):	Oh, yeah. I think most of my problems really came from the principal. Since, I've been there, I've always had issues with him, and I'm not sure why. And the sad thing is, he's a man of color. I've heard him say inappropriate things, and it's not [about one] particular race, or [gender], everybody gets it. I heard him bring up something about Jews. I don't know why or how he felt so comfortable during work hours to say something about Jews. I felt it was completely inappropriate. You're a professional, you're at work, and you say something like that?
Tatiana (US-born East Asian Woman, Northeast):	Whenever there are problems with certain things, everyone comes to [me] because [I'll] figure it out. But it's only when it's problems that they'll come to me. [Other than that] they're like, "keep away from her."
Stella (African American Woman, Southeast):	Yeah, but I don't know if it was [because of] race [or due to a] lack of knowledge. [When a few of my coworkers] were new to the school, I know [they were] looking at me like, "Wow, she's so tough, and I wouldn't wanna work on a team with her." So, I don't know if it was necessarily racially based, or more so, "I don't really know her, and she seems aggressive."
Leo (African American Man, Southwest and Northeast):	This is very, very unique. [My Black male coworker Chris and I] were the only two Black men inside the branch, [and] didn't get along well, which was pretty sad. We butt heads a lot.

	He was very intimidated by my work ethic, and my personality because I was so sociable and outgoing, and he was very socially awkward. And the only reason I would say it would probably be my race, [was] because we were the only Black people inside the branch and didn't get along. He got along with everyone else. They were all Latino or White. And I got along with everyone else. For some strange reason, we just couldn't click.
Tara (African American Woman, West):	I wouldn't say afraid, but intimidated, yes. I've heard people actually say that once they've gotten to know me, I'm nothing like they thought. So, I would say. "Why? Because of the angry Black woman stigma?" and they would laugh it off, but that was [the reason]. And I've used it to my advantage because often, because of that, people wouldn't really bother me as much. If it causes you not to bother me, I'm ok with that.

Others Have Acted as If They Were Afraid of Them or Intimidated by Them: Microaggressive Experiences There were no macroaggressive or vicarious experiences associated with this prompt. As for microaggressive experiences, the narratives of Corrine and Ruth speak to the unique and unfair challenges that Black women face in the workplace. In both cases, we see Black women being targeted by White women with false accusations and character assassinations, and we see White men overlook the problematic behaviors of White women while failing to help Black women. Corrine explains that her coworker spread rumors that Corrine did not like her and that "she was afraid" of Corrine. It is my estimation that Corrine's coworker used the stereotype of the "angry Black woman" to negatively impact Corrine's reputation within their workplace. The coworker also used this stereotype to distract from her own shortcomings and lackluster work performance. Additionally, the entrenched stereotype of the "innocent damsel in distress" that needs to be rescued from some threat, such as an angry Black woman or a dangerous Black man, is ludicrous and is *very* harmful to Black people in work environments and beyond. As women, we shouldn't reduce ourselves individually and collectively to such small and offensive stereotypes, and *we shouldn't use our privilege (racially or otherwise) to harm other women or anyone else*. When people falsely accuse Black women and men of antagonizing them in the workplace, they are contributing to the oppression and racism that Black people already endure in society and within workplaces. Those committing such offenses must be held accountable for their racist dog-whistles and poor behavior. Furthermore, employers, managers, and mediators must commit to identifying such behavior, not giving it a pass, and striving to end the racist and sexist aggression directed toward Black women and other people of color in the workplace.

Stella, like other women of color (namely Fawn and Judith in previous responses), did not know whether the microaggressive treatment she experienced was based on race, gender, personality, or a combination of those factors. However, I believe the challenges women of color face in the workplace have much to do with the intersection of stereotypes related to race and gender, as well as supposed culture specific personality traits. Furthermore, this underscores the importance of using intersectionality, multiple jeopardy, and oppression manifestation theories to gain a better understanding of the unique challenges women of color face in the workplace and beyond.

Other microaggressions included Roger enduring the microinsult of people saying he looked like a terrorist, Tatiana being avoided by her colleagues unless they needed something from her, and Fawn's supervisor being antagonistic and rude to Fawn and her colleagues.

You Have Been Stared at as If You Were Abnormal or Did Not Belong The male gaze. A concept that's used in feminist discourse to highlight the sexual objectification of women and the subsequent discomfort women experience from being gawked at by men. Staring at, pointing at, unabashedly speaking about, and in some instances, touching women is unnerving, unprofessional, and objectifying behavior that reeks of male privilege and entitlement. Most civil, respectful, and professional adults know that such behavior is wrong and in recent times have made great strides to call out and challenge such behavior (even though there is still much work to be done).

This concept can also be used to explain the objectification of people of color, which I refer to as a "racist gaze" or "racialized gaze." For example, Black people are stared at and watched as though we don't belong in public and professional spaces. We are pointed at, as though we are threats that must be identified and singled out. People speak about us sometimes in stage whispers or as if we don't exist, which hearkens back to Black enslavement and subordination, where inhumane vile individuals enslaved Black children, women, and men and spoke freely in their presence as though they didn't matter or exist. We are also touched. Our bodies are violated. Our personal spaces are intruded upon. People touch our hair, pat us on the back, or make other unwelcomed contact because they believe they have the right to. In total, such objectification boils down to us being treated as though we are objects that must be ignored, despised, eliminated, or exoticized. When this "racialized gaze" or "racist gaze" occurs, the humanity of Black people is ignored and racism flourishes. There were 11 affirmative responses, six negative responses, and three responses that were not captured as it relates to this prompt:

Have Been Stared at as If They Were Abnormal or Did Not Belong

Ruth (African American Woman, Northeast):	I just experienced that at [a work event]. I was talking to [a coworker's partner], and I noticed three people, just standing there staring at me. I mean, if you want to know who I am, if you think I'm a part of the staff, then come and say something. Why would you just stand there, and stare at me? Which was different from [another parent] who was staring at me, yes, but he also came up and introduced himself and started talking to me. It was a difference, so I stood there, and stared them back down like, "What are you looking at?"
Audrey (African American Woman, Northwest and Northeast):	Yes. Now that I am in [the Northwest where] it's predominately White. When I go into [work] people stare at me like, "She's a token Black girl. What does she do? She [must be] a secretary." So, it's shocking when they [learn] that I actually have a higher role.

Tatiana (US-born East Asian Woman, Northeast):	Yeah because, there's not a lot of Asians in the area where I work, so they kind of look at you differently; they treat you differently. There's always that degradation.
Corrine (African American Woman, Northeast):	I worked for a very high-level individual, and I think for years, I noticed how people didn't recognize that I was an African American woman [over the phone]. [And when they met me] I could just see [their surprise at me being] Black.
Brandon (African American and Filipino Man, Northwest and Northeast):	Yeah, absolutely. In a lot of the cases, I would be in meetings and [was] the only Black person in those meetings, and they automatically assume, "You're the assistant," or "You must be a temp," or something other than what you actually are. And usually in first introductions, it's like, "I'm surprised you're here." You see it in the facial expressions, like wow, "It's this big progressive thing that you're here." Or for [those] who are racist it's, "I can't believe you're here." It's a reaction either way. Never mind the fact that we've always been intelligent, we've always been smart, and we should be there *anyway*. Regardless of some liberal Whites letting us in, or some people keeping us out, we end up being there, we should *always* be there. But there's always a reaction. I did work hard, but it's not like I had to overcome as much as they picture. Where they see us in squalor, [as though] we must come from squalor. So, we must have come through a lot to be on the same floor as them, and that's a different type of racism.
Peter (Asian American Chinese Man, Northeast):	Yeah, that happens a lot especially in my field of Student Affairs. The [Northeast] is a little bit more diverse, but [the Midwest] was not. Being looked at as an enigma would be the best way to explain it.

Roger (Asian Indian Man, Midwest):	Yeah. Even in hearings. I'd be sitting behind [the politician I was working for], and I was the only Indian Asian. It was very interesting, people were staring and I was told later on [that] people were wondering, "What is that Brown guy doing behind the Chairman of the Committee, and giving him information?" And it turned out it wasn't from Republicans necessarily; it was from Democrats. It was an ongoing thing where the Republicans were the ones that were giving me respect because I could do a good job, Democrats were the ones expecting me [because] I'm Brown, [to] be with Democrats, just because of my skin tone, and color.
Tara (African American Woman, West):	Yeah. [Pilots] in the air force [were] generally male, and they were White. It mostly happened with people who have been in the military for years. They look at [me] like, "Wow, that was odd to see. [It's] not just a Black person, but a *Black woman* in this uniform," so I did get stares.
Judith (African American Woman, Midwest):	That [happened at] every function that I went to in the capacity of a professor. Like I said… [I was] the only [person of color].

Has Not Been Stared at as If Abnormal or Not Belonging

Ralph (White Man, Deep South):	I don't know. I mean. I'm married to a [woman of color], so we certainly get stared at [when she visits my job]. It's probably at both of us as opposed to just me. So I wouldn't say, I get stared at because of my race. I think the relationship and the fact that it's not that common is what gets looked at. But no, in terms of, "have I been looked at funny because of my race," I would say no. Like I said, my place of work is a very White place, so no.

Have Been Stared at as If They Were Abnormal or Did Not Belong: Microaggressive Experiences Ruth's response perfectly captured the microinsult of the "racist gaze" that I mentioned in the introduction of this section, "I noticed three people, just standing there staring at me. I mean, if you want to know who I am... then come and say something. Why would you just stand there, and stare at me?" It is unacceptable to objectify Black people, or anyone, in this manner.

Audrey and Brandon experienced the microinsult of people assuming that they were filling positions that were ranked lower than their actual positions. It is wrong to assume that Black and Brown folks have subordinate positions or to display shock at their presence, as seen in Tara's response.

Corrine's response was very profound. She first explains the astonishment that some had upon learning that she was Black. It is possible that this shock was the result of (1) her voice not fitting the stereotypical voice that they imagined a Black woman to have, and (2) they were shocked that a Black woman was working in a high-level position with influential individuals.

Tatiana shares that she experienced degradation because she is one of the only Asians at her job. She explains that she is not only looked at differently, experiencing the racist gaze, but she is also *treated* differently. Similarly, Peter shares that being an Asian in a predominantly White workplace meant "being looked at as an enigma." Roger shares his experiences of being seen as abnormal for working for a Republican since the Republican Party is mostly White (Newport 2013) and since he is an Indian Asian. Judith explains that she was treated as though she did not belong at her predominantly White job soon after starting.

Has Not Been Stared at as If Abnormal or Not Belonging: Vicarious Experiences and Border Identities In Ralph's statement, he speaks to the phenomena of vicarious racism and racism experienced by individuals with border identities, such as a White partner in an interracial relationship. Being the White partner in an interracial relationship results in the creation of a border identity, because the White partner experiences the privilege of being associated with whiteness *as well as* racist stares, microaggressions, and macroaggressions that occur because they are with a non-White partner.

You Have Been Watched or Followed in Public Places as If You Were a Threat or Dangerous While this prompt likely evokes unpleasant memories of being followed around stores (particularly for Black and Brown folk), it is even more wounding when employees of color are followed around their job or watched as though they are a threat or dangerous. While this section is intended to focus solely on the workforce I'd be remiss not to include how this form of racism manifests in other spaces in society. There were five affirmative responses, eight negative responses, five responses about being followed in other places outside of work (a portion of Brandon's response fit into this category), and two responses that were not captured as it relates to this prompt:

Have Been Watched or Followed at Work as If They Were a Threat or Dangerous

Audrey (African American Woman, Northwest and Northeast):	Yes. Sometimes by security, but even while I'm at work. A lot of times my coworkers will sit there and just watch me, and I'm like, "Ok. You're clearly on the Internet surfing the Net. I'm actually doing work. Why are you watching me?" It's also not just [about being] a threat but about seeing if I'm working. They feel like they need to watch me to see if I'm doing what I need to be doing. But they're not watching my White coworkers who are clearly surfing the web. So, I rarely ever go on the Internet or anything, if I do, it's on my lunch break on my phone. For that reason, I feel like I'm always being watched.
Brandon (African American and Filipino Man, Northwest and Northeast):	In the workplace, oh yes. There's been some cases where security will ask me where I'm going, [because I] don't look like I belong there.

Have Not *Been Watched or Followed at Work as If They Were a Threat or Dangerous*

Corrine (African American Woman, Northeast): Well, we have cameras everywhere, because of the high-level individuals that we have in and around the building. So, we're constantly watched. So, I can't say that I've noticed anyone watching or following me, but then again, we have cameras everywhere. Big Brother, Big Sister are watching all the time.

Ralph (White Man, Deep South): Me, no. I know a lot of my students have. I mean, one of the things they have to do for [one of my classes] is write about what's wrong with the criminal justice system, and what needs to be fixed with it. I get a number of students who talk about how police will follow them; how they'll be followed in stores, [how] they'll be stopped and questioned and of course, they believe it's because of their race, and I'm sure it is. So, students are saying it, but I haven't experienced it.

Have Been Watched or Followed in Other *Public Places as If They Were a Threat or Dangerous*

Peter (Asian American Chinese Man, Northeast): Everywhere. Yeah it's happened a lot. Not necessarily [because] of the [possibility of me] stealing or do anything negative; I think people just have that type of mentality [that] most Asians are foreigners, and they don't really know what's happening around here. So, some of it has been negative obviously, like stealing and things like that, but some of it has been them trying to assist. Whether it's the first time I'm in that store, or the twelfth time, [they make the] assumption that it is my first time there.

Ruth (African American Woman, Northeast): Oh, yeah, that happens in the clothing stores. I can't remember the last time, since I do a lot of online shopping, but most certainly. I've been in stores and they are looking. Even if I go into a local store they're looking. They hurry up [and] rush to Black people [and ask], "Oh, may I help you?" and even though they're doing it with a smile, and trying to act all friendly, it really feels as if [they're] just rushing to watch what I'm doing here. It doesn't feel really helpful. It feels as if they're just overly extending themselves so they can watch me or let me know: "you're being watched the moment you walk in the store."

Brandon (African American and Filipino Man, Northwest and Northeast): It can happen outside the workplace but, what generally happens in those types of settings is they'll either stop pretending to help you [and will imply] "You don't belong here. What are you doing here?" Or they'll say it [more nicely like], "Can I help you? Where are you going?" So, in my view, I look like I know where I'm going, [and I'm thinking] I didn't ask you, I wasn't stopping looking at signs, and even if I was, I don't see you doing that to other people.

Roger (Asian Indian Man, Midwest): I've been followed before, [but] not very often. But [I'm] watched in airports, [I'm] gonna be watched because [I'm] Brown. I've actually been questioned like "Somebody's left their bag there…is it yours?" and I've said, "No, it's somebody else's, they just got up and left." And they question you. The following [happened when] I was a graduate student [at a Mid-Atlantic university] one month after 9–11. So, [in] October 2001, a Washington, DC, police officer follows me, flashes his sidearm, and I drive to [the university], and I'm ready to press the emergency call button that they have on these poles [around campus], and then he [drives] away. I didn't get the license plate. But you'll have that type of thing.

Joe (Latino Man, Northeast):	I would say yes. I've experienced that before. I think any person of color can relate to that, being followed around the store, based on your race or perceived class.
Tara (African American Woman, West):	Everywhere! I wouldn't say a danger or threat. Me being a woman, I feel like it's a little bit easier [for me] than for my brother. But yes, in stores, people follow you. It becomes a way of life. We expect that now, and we brush it off. I guarantee you [if] we go into any store, somebody's gonna look, especially in a high-priced area.

Have Been Watched or Followed at Work or in Public Places as If They Were a Threat or Dangerous: Microaggressive and Macroaggressive Experiences Aside from experiencing the racist gaze, where she was viewed as a threat, Audrey was also watched to ensure that she was actually doing her work. She notes that this same scrutiny was not given to her White colleagues which created a chilly climate and an unwelcoming environment for Audrey.

Brandon was watched, stopped, and questioned by security at his job. However, this is not an uncommon experience for Black people. We are followed, scrutinized, and policed as though we are a menacing threat, whether we are walking in a neighborhood or walking into an office building. It is my hope that one day this will no longer be the case. But for now, intelligent, creative, and hardworking Black men and women, like Brandon and Audrey, continue to experience the racist microinsult of being watched, followed, and questioned in American workplaces.

Peter's response is very intriguing and offers a nuanced perspective to this prompt. He explains that while people may watch him at times because they think he may do something inappropriate, it is far more common for someone to follow him because they believe he is a foreigner in need of assistance. Similar to Peter's sentiment about not receiving sincere help in stores, Ruth shares, "It feels as if they're just overly extending themselves so they can watch me or let me know: 'You're being watched the moment you walk in the store.'" Additionally, Brandon, Joe, and Tara share similar sentiments about the microinsult of being followed and watched in stores and public places. As an Asian Indian man, Roger has experienced the microinsult of racial profiling and mistreatment in airports as well as a macroaggression in Washington, DC, shortly after the September 11 attacks. During that incident, Roger was followed in his car by an officer who flashed a gun at him in an attempt to intimidate or potentially harm him.

Vicarious Experience As a White educator who has never been watched or followed as though he were a threat, Ralph explains that it has happened to his students. Ralph's statement, in conjunction with the microaggressive and macroaggressive experiences above, shows us that Black and Brown bodies are viewed as a threat regardless of age, education, location, rank, or status.

Your Ideas, Beliefs or Opinions Were Ignored or Devalued Both historically and presently, people of color, and particularly Black people have had their lived experiences and views discredited, disregarded, or diminished. Early White Americans fought for their freedom from Great Britain while denying freedom to Black children, women, and men. Furthermore, the disregard for Black ideas, views, *and* lives continues to this day. Although some policies have made it easier for us to gain entry into workplaces, that does not necessarily mean that our voices, opinions, and work will be valued or even acknowledged. There were 12 affirmative responses, four negative responses, and one unsure response. Additionally, there was one response from an ally whose anti-racism advocacy efforts were ignored, and three responses that were not captured as it relates to this prompt:

Ideas, Beliefs, or Opinions Were Ignored or Devalued

Judith (African American Woman, Midwest):	Yeah, that was pretty frequent. My ideas for how they should structure our department weren't of any interest to anyone. Anything I brought to [the Chair], it was minimized intentionally. Basically, the opposite of what I'd expect any supportive Chair to do if somebody's going through stuff.

Corrine (African American Woman, Northeast):	Oh yeah, definitely. Again, the situation with the [White] boss, and the [White] lady who was my counterpart. It always seemed like [my ideas were] received differently. If she could present something simpler or similar, it would be met with such fanfare, so that was always the case.
Brandon (African American and Filipino Man, Northwest and Northeast):	My opinions or recommendations, they'll get ignored, until maybe another, less experienced White person endorses it or says that was a good idea or poses the same idea.
Ruth (African American Woman, Northeast):	Oh, yes. Yes. [My White male supervisor Richard] has constantly tried to undermine the work that I do there until I lost total interest in the job.
Tatiana (US-born East Asian Woman, Northeast):	They don't bother to listen until they get hit in the ass with [an issue].
Pamela (Latina, Northeast):	Oh, yeah. Often, I'll raise points, such as there [being] a false binary that we continue to engage in, [that doesn't] provide an opportunity for others to engage in a conversation [about race], unless you identify as Black or White. Usually when I bring that up, it's never validated or acknowledged. It's definitely not affirmed by someone else; no one builds on the point.
Peter (Asian American Chinese Man, Northeast):	There have been times, [that] I want to go out on a limb and try something different, but there are a lot of individuals who are not able to think about new things. [They're] just trying to follow traditions and [are] not open to new ideas and new ways of thinking. So, sometimes, it's just been [an explicit] no. Other times, it's put [on] a back burner...which usually means, it's not coming back up.

Roger (Asian Indian Man, Midwest):	Oh, yeah. It's devalued as a [teaching assistant].
Oliver (African American Man, Northeast, Southeast and Midwest):	Oh yeah, definitely. [However], I tuck it away, bury it in my subconscious and focus on positive things to alter my mindset.

Ideas, Beliefs, or Opinions Were Not *Ignored or Devalued/Unsure*

Ralph (White Man, Deep South):	No. Again, I would say, for my students that is the case. Not me personally, but I would say I've witnessed it with students who are African American. Their opinions have been discounted or ignored. And I've had some complain to me how they felt like they weren't being listened to in different group projects. I wouldn't say [that my ideas] are celebrated, just accepted, not questioned.
Tara (African American Woman, West):	I've never really had an idea or belief or opinion ignored. I'm usually pretty assertive when it comes to that. In the military, I would say it was devalued, but I can't really tell you if it was because of race or if it was because of rank. They would hear me out but maybe not take account of that idea.

Ideas, Beliefs, or Opinions Were Ignored or Devalued as an Ally or Advocate

Reena (White Woman, Midwest):	I'm part of [an admissions committee], and we had a student that sent in all of her material, and in the material, it had become clear that she was Hispanic, bilingual, and a mom of [several kids]. [However, her] grade point wasn't fantastic, but she had explained it in her personal statement. She had written that she [suffered a devastating personal loss], and [that] explained her low-grade point average. I'm sure [it] was a rough experience for her to have to write about and to tell

an admissions committee. We admitted a White man with a fairly significant [mental condition] into our program, whose essay was a little challenging to read, but he explained how [he] worked through some of the issues that [we] might be concerned with [because of his disorder]. And [even though] his grade point wasn't fantastic, [my colleague] without a doubt said, "We have to admit him!" [And I thought], "But not the Hispanic woman?"

Like it really felt like, we had come down to a racial issue. Based on somebody's identity you're making a decision about whether they can come into this program or not. She didn't have anybody else interviewed; none of the Whites were interviewed. It was really disturbing, and I felt like I was participating in it by even being in the interview, but I also didn't want her to make the decision by herself, and not have that particular, potential student supported. I didn't want her to feel like, this is the way the program is, or that this is a representative of how we feel about [her] value.

So, it was icky. It was not pleasant. She had to drive in. She had an hour drive, and the interview maybe lasted 20 minutes. It was ridiculous. As soon as she opened her mouth and started talking to us, [my colleague] was like, "Yes, of course!" Which is exactly what I thought when I read the personal statement and looked at her references. [And I thought], "Why are we doing this? What did we just do to this person?" And to feel like [I] participated in it, only because [I] wanted to make sure that this [student] was in a safe environment, felt awful. I can't let it go, it's too upsetting, and something happened that needs to be addressed.

Ideas, Beliefs, or Opinions Were Ignored or Devalued: Microaggressive Experiences Corrine and Brandon had their ideas ignored, and found that the same or similar idea was endorsed if a White person presented it. Tatiana shared that her input is generally ignored unless people need her to resolve an issue. As a Latina, Pamela believed that her opinions were ignored during discussions on race. Judith, Peter, and Roger had their ideas ignored and their concerns minimized when broaching issues with their coworkers and supervisors.

Ideas, Beliefs, or Opinions Were Ignored or Devalued: Bystander and Vicarious Experiences While Reena did not have her opinions ignored or devalued because of her race, she did have her input initially ignored when she was advocating for a prospective student. Reena was a bystander who did her best to challenge her colleague's biased views and to ensure that the prospective student was treated fairly. Even though Reena's colleague was persistent in her dissent and opposition toward the Latina applicant, Reena was steadfast in her pursuit of fairness and anti-racism on the admissions committee. In this case, Reena is a great example of how a sincere and effective racial justice advocate should operate.

Additionally, Reena's colleague committed a microinvalidation toward the Latina applicant when she discounted the personal tragedy that the applicant endured, while readily and accepting the personal circumstances of a White male applicant. I believe this type of microinvalidation is rooted in the fact that White and non-White people are granted different degrees of empathy. Unfortunately, when a person of color experiences a personal tragedy, they don't receive the same degree of empathy as a White person who experiences a similar tragedy. We see this in the news coverage of missing persons where White people and "[W]hite women in particular benefit from a higher intensity of coverage than other missing persons" (Sommers 2016: 310). In terms of drug use, "While the crack cocaine epidemic, for instance, produced a response mostly through the criminal justice system, the opioid epidemic has led mostly to a public health response" (Lopez 2016), namely because the crack epidemic impacted poor people of color, and the opioid epidemic is impacting White people. The racial disparity in empathy is rooted in racism, and overcoming it is a crucial component in tackling modern-day racism.

You Have Been Left Out of Conversations or Activities Intentionally excluding an employee from an activity or conversation is rude, unprofessional, and in many cases, develops into the common bullying tactic known as social exclusion. Social exclusion is a form of bullying and should not be accepted in any environment and certainly not in the workplace, where solidarity and team work are important. Social exclusion sends the message to the target that they do not belong among a certain group of people, or within a certain environment, and when directed toward people of color, aside from being a microinvalidation, it is a form of racist bullying. There were 14 affirmative responses and six negative responses as it relates to this prompt:

Have Been Left Out of Conversations or Activities

Leo (African American Man, Southwest and Northeast): That happened a few times. People would just forget to invite me, or [if] the guys [were] going out to drink and they [knew] that they [were] gonna end up at a country bar [where there have been racist incidents], they [didn't] invite me. That's happened a few times, and then I'll see them on Snapchat or Facebook tagged, and I'm like, "Oh, well thanks for the invite guys!" It's kind of awkward. That's happened a few times.

Corrine (African American Woman, Northeast): I'll be having a conversation, and I'll be like, "I didn't know that happened," or "I didn't know that was happening," or "Should I be involved in that?" And [a colleague will say], "Oh, you were left off of that e-mail? I thought I put you on [the listserv]," or "Oh, I put you down first. I don't know. [Your name] must have come off." And you know, I'm just pleasant about it. Like I said [in a previous response], I will *never* audition for the antagonist or the angry Black woman in their story, because that's what they're looking for you to play. [They] can't make me play that, so I'm like, "Oh, ok, no problem. But now that I know, can you forward that to me?" So, once I have the evidence, it's no disputing...who all got [the e-mail].

Judith (African American Woman, Midwest):	Yeah, definitely. [People] would stop talking when [I] came into a room, and you'd just know that they'd been talking about you. That's the kind of crap that had been going on at that point. [A colleague in my department] would be talking to [other people] about me. I'd say hello, [and] they wouldn't even look me in the eye, [they] wouldn't even acknowledge my presence. That kind of thing, or they would just clam up when I came into the room.
Audrey (African American Woman, Northwest and Northeast):	I've been left out of some conversations, but I feel like they're ones that I don't want to know about (laughs). Activities, not really.
Brandon (African American and Filipino Man, Northwest and Northeast):	Yes. A group of management came in with significantly less experience, and one of the things that [a colleague who is a White woman] shared with [the staff of color, although she was a racist as well], was that the current director said, "Wow, this office has a lot of people of color!" The office is Black, Brown, [and] predominantly women of color, and it's not the type of environment where they both came from, with mostly White men. Slowly but surely, he started purging people out, [and] the Black assistants started disappearing. They started hiring some White people that were not so skilled, and not so experienced, and started bringing in their social friends, like their after-work friends, [and] they started getting hired and had no experience. Then me and this Indian woman were actually assigned to start training them. The next thing you know, they're part of [important work] discussions, and they're leaving me and the Indian woman out. [They were having]

impromptu meetings in the Director's office, [with] the door closed. [It was] a very odd experience watching that. I went to [Human Resources] for that, but unless you have a recording, or an actual e-mail, it's just your word, and that doesn't weigh anything. Most [Human Resource offices] are structured to protect institutions *from* individual workers. So, in most of these cases, if you make an accusation of racism or anything of that nature, or sexual harassment they will pay you out to not say anything as opposed to taking any type of institutional hit. To answer your question, that's the context, but I started being left out of meetings.

Ruth (African American Woman, Northeast): Oh, most definitely. [My supervisor who is a White man] put me in meetings...[that] I have nothing to do with. But the meetings I should have been on [that] have to deal [directly with my job], those are the meetings [he] excludes me from. So now I'm not in either meeting. I'm not in the meeting where I belong, and I don't go to the [inappropriate] meeting because it makes no sense to me. Why am I taking a half an hour out of my morning every [week], to sit in on a meeting, and to hear about things that have absolutely nothing to do with me. He wants me to feel excluded, and more off to the side, as if I'm not really needed there. But then on the low, [he's] always coming to me for answers. So, this is [his] way of having [his] cake and eating it too. So, that's why when he comes [and asks me questions], even when I do know [an answer to his question, I say], "Oh, I don't know, I have no idea." I'm not even interested in finding out what the answer is for [him] anymore. Which I used to do. Now, [I'm] totally uninterested because I don't feel like I get the support I need.

Peter (Asian American Chinese Man, Northeast):	Yeah, that's happened a lot as well. I think that also has to play into the fact that I have a quiet demeanor most of the time. I go about my business. I do what I have to do. [However], there are individuals who don't feel it's important to include everybody. As I've said [in an earlier response], there's sometimes when I, depending on the day, depending on my mood, depending on how I'm feeling, may throw out a really radical idea, and sometimes I have a stigma put on me [because I don't] "toe the line" so to speak.
Pamela (Latina, Northeast):	Yeah. I believe it's because of my ethnicity. I find out about things that have happened, whether it's like a gathering or a meeting, but it's been other times when they have included me.
Fawn (US-born North African Woman, Northeast):	Conversations. I would say yes for conversations. They may know that a student who [I work with] has been missing for like two weeks, and the school staff will know, but they [fail to relay] that information. So, I find out way after, but that's not always, it's here and there.
Oliver (African American Man, Northeast, Southeast and Midwest):	Study groups at [predominately] Caucasian [graduate] institutions, that was always constant.
Holly (African American Woman, Midwest and Deep South):	Oh, all the time. [However], some of those conversations, I did not want to be a part of.

Have Been Left Out of Conversations or Activities: Microaggressive Experiences Leo's response offers a nuanced insight into this microinvalidation. Even though some people claim that they are not racist and are inclusive, that doesn't mean that they are not complicit in racism. As we see with Leo's coworkers, instead of standing in solidarity with him, they patronized an establishment that wasn't welcoming to Black people. Being a friend and an ally to people of color means standing against racism and using one's privilege and buying power to boycott businesses and places that are hostile and unwelcoming to people of color. The coworkers' silence and support of such an establishment is deeply troubling and indicates a lack of awareness at best and approval of racial hostility at worst. Furthermore, I doubt that there is a lack of awareness in this case since Leo's colleagues did not invite him because they were *already aware* of a previous racist incident at the bar and that's why *they* decided not to invite Leo. Ending racism requires *all* people of all races doing their part. This includes standing in solidarity with people of color and not supporting racist individuals or businesses.

Judith was blatantly shunned and excluded by her coworkers. These microinvalidations were precipitated by a coworker who exhibited bullying behavior in the form of social exclusion and disrespect (as noted in an earlier response by Judith). While Audrey and Holly shared that, depending on the conversation topic, they do not mind being excluded, especially if the conversation can be deemed unprofessional.

Brandon's response revealed a deeply disturbing display of nepotism and racism. What makes this particular display of nepotism, racist, was the director's shock at the number of people of color initially working in the office upon his arrival, followed by the systematic removal of people of color from positions, *and then* the subsequent filling of those positions by the supervisor's White, low-skilled friends. This situation could have been avoided with clear policies against nepotism and a human resources representative who was committed to anti-racism efforts and fostering a diverse and inclusive workplace.

There is much to unpack in the work relationship of Ruth and her supervisor. It is clear that communication has broken down and that the relationship is strained. Ruth has become despondent and disengaged because of her supervisor's attempts to exclude her from meetings where her input would be valuable and where she would gain important information related to her job. Aside from excluding Ruth from relevant meetings, the supervisor devalued Ruth and her contributions by only seeking her input in secret (in order for others not to learn how much he actually relies on her expertise). Peter believes that he is excluded because of his quiet demeanor and punished by exclusion because he doesn't always "toe the line" and maintain the status quo while Pamela felt that she was specifically excluded because of her ethnicity (as she explained in a previous comment).

Others Have Expected Your Work to Be Inferior Even though this prompt is associated with microinvalidations on the subscale I used, it can easily be associated with microinsults since such treatment belittles targets. Therefore, conceptually, I consider this particular prompt to be on the border of microinsults and microinvalidations. This prompt is connected to the racist stereotype that some people of color lack the work ethic and intellect to produce excellent work. There were 12 individuals who experienced this microinvalidation while seven did not. One individual did not provide a response.

Others Have Expected Their Work to Be Inferior

Holly (African American Woman, Midwest and Deep South): Yes, at times, they have. When I worked at [a predominately White Midwestern hospital] I had a [White male] coworker tell me, "Let me tell you something, when you walked into that pharmacy, and they saw a Black face, you were already judged!" I felt so inferior. I would get nervous around all my colleagues. I couldn't speak. It was almost as if the articulation that I did have went out the window. I knew there was something going on emotionally.

One of the major challenges or turning points, [was that] I was not a certified pharmacy technician. [My manager] advised me [that] due to new state laws, I had to get certified. So, I had to take a test, [and] I failed [although I went on to pass it later]. When I went back to work, I told my managers, but then that same guy [who made the Black face comment], I told him [and] he told all the pharmacists, [and] all the technicians. From that time, I saw a change in their behavior. A change in the way that they treated me. A change in their confidence. Even my manager [was impacted], she told me, "None of the pharmacists want to work with you."

They already had some issues with me because of my race or my skin color, but that just made things a little more challenging for

	me. That was one of the hardest things that I had to walk through. The embarrassment of not passing; [but] not just the embarrassment, [it was] how everyone treated me, because it actually caused them to [be angry]. One pharmacist was *angry* that she had to work with me, [another] pharmacist actually lied and said that I didn't finish my rounds in a certain amount of time. I was going to confront her, but I just didn't want to deal with the drama. She already had a wall built up when she saw that she had to work with me. There was a lot of judgment. [So] I changed. I went through a major change and went through specialized training. [Then] I started thinking of new ideas to become more efficient in the workplace [and] was able to multitask. I was doing so well that [my most troubling coworker] went to my manager and said that I was doing a "wonderful job."
Brandon (African American and Filipino Man, Northwest and Northeast):	Yes. Me and the Indian woman [introduced above] experienced this. In terms of trying to push us out, the director had the people that *we trained*, start to *oversee some of our work*. In terms of "double-checking" some of our work, under the guise that everybody's work needs to be second looked. But we noticed that it was me and her, and one other person that he wanted pushed out, that was overlooked by the White kids that we trained.
Corrine (African American Woman, Northeast):	I go out of my way to be superior. I always feel the need to make sure that I cover myself. I've always felt the need to go that step further, just to cover all bases.
Oliver (African American Man, Northeast, Southeast and Midwest):	Yeah. I tend to use that as motivation, in order to survive in the environments that I've survived in. In academics, your stuff has to be really polished, so they can believe you. [You must be] more polished than the guy next to you, so I would say, in my work, my stuff was more polished.

Fred (African American Man, Northeast): Yes. I feel like I've often received a follow-up question of whether I think I'm capable of doing [a task], how much help I need, do I need further explanation on what I'm doing, and just more people wanting to put their hands into the process to make sure I'm doing the job correctly.

Judith (African American Woman, Midwest): Well I'm assuming that they did, especially when it came to students. They definitely lacked any confidence in me even when I had [confidence] in myself. Eventually, my confidence started [decreasing] because I wasn't getting support from anybody there. And every time students would go to [the other professor] behind my back, they basically [got approval from him].

Audrey (African American Woman, Northwest and Northeast): Yes. I think when I first started, they knew my [professional] background. So, when my boss hired me, she saw my resume, and she knew I had great experience. But one of my colleagues, every time I turn something in, she's always looking to find how she can critique it. She finds personal pleasure in it.

Ruth (African American Woman, Northeast): Yeah, of course. This is the thing that [Madeline, a White female lawyer who I used to work with did]! [I was] taking college courses. [And] she had the nerve to say, "Oh, I didn't realize that you had graduated high school." And I just looked at [her] and blinked. There is an assumption [that Black people are inferior].

Tara (African American Woman, West): Yes. Oh, my gosh! They would expect me to do things on a [higher] level, [but] they would not [expect] that [of] other people. My work would have to be perfect. [When I needed an evaluation done] on how well I was doing, my supervisor [should have written] that report, [but] I've often written my own report because my supervisor didn't want to or made me do it. But that doesn't normally happen and I was like, "Why is that happening to me?" I found myself asking that a lot. I have no problem being stellar in everything I do, and I think that they thought that could break me

	in the military or make me flustered. But I performed at a stellar level in everything I [did] and [since I had] to write my own reports for myself, it made me write better reports for my peers and my troops. So, I take everything that's a challenge and turn it into a positive because people waste energy trying to be negative, and it becomes such a strong positive for us if we face it correctly.
Roger (Asian Indian Man, Midwest):	Yeah in some cases, yes. Professionally, I know people have expected [my work to be inferior].

Others Have Not *Expected Their Work to Be Inferior*

Tatiana (US-born East Asian Woman, Northeast):	What happens is...I get all the effed-up files, and so from there, I have to figure out how to fix it. Then anyone who has an effed-up file [will] say, "Go to Tatiana, she'll be able to help you with these effed-up files."
Peter (Asian American Chinese Man, Northeast):	I would say no because I really haven't experienced it that much. I also set a really high standard for myself. And I think people are able to get that. Part of that I think is the [stereotype] of Asians being hardworking and being on top of their game, so while not inferior, it might just be a different [expectation].

Others Have Expected Their Work to Be Inferior: Microaggressive Experiences Brandon's supervisor not only systematically fired and replaced employees of color (as outlined in the previous section), but, according to Brandon, the director is still forging a crusade to push all workers of color out of the organization, including Brandon. Requiring that Brandon's work be "checked" by junior staff members, who Brandon trained, is not only degrading, but it helps create a narrative that Brandon's work is substandard. This can then be used as justification to push Brandon out of the workplace.

In Holly's response, we learn that she endured microinsults *and* microinvalidations. First, we learn that Holly experienced a microinsult in the form of a racially charged comment from a coworker. Holly shares that the comment was enough to shake her confidence: "I felt so inferior. I would get nervous around all my colleagues. I couldn't speak. It was almost as if the articulation that I did have went out the window." Furthermore, when she failed a job-related exam (that she passed on a second attempt), Holly experienced microinvalidations when her coworkers and supervisors were convinced that failing the exam meant that her work would be inferior (even though her workload consisted of completing the *same* tasks that she had been exceptionally executing prior to taking the exam). She explains, "They already had some issues with me because of my race or my skin color, but that just made things a little more challenging for me." While Holly was understandably deeply impacted by her coworkers' microinsults and microinvalidations, Corrine and Oliver used people's assumption of their inferiority as motivation to prove that they are knowledgeable and exceptional employees.

Fred, Judith, and Audrey all experienced the microinvalidation of colleagues and supervisors lacking confidence in their work and questioning their judgment. Ruth experienced microinsults and microinvalidations when a White supervisor questioned her intelligence. Tara also experienced a microinsult when her supervisor was unwilling to write her an evaluation, a practice that was common for supervisors in Tara's workplace.

Related Microaggressive Experiences While they did not experience this particular microinvalidation, the experiences of Tatiana and Peter are still noteworthy. Tatiana experienced a microinsult as a result of her colleague's disrespectful treatment. While they recognized her expertise, and good work ethic, they also took advantage of her by giving her the less prestigious and more difficult cases to manage. Their behavior was quite exploitative, in that they did not give her the respect that she deserves, all the while expecting her to carry a heavy and difficult workload. In Peter's case, he believed that his coworkers didn't expect his work to be inferior, in large part, because of stereotypes about Asians being hard workers and intellectually superior.

You Have Been Mistaken for Someone Else Because You Are a Member of the Same Racial Group While this microinvalidation may seem trivial, misidentifying someone because of their race or skin color is quite problematic. This particular microaggression is concerning for two main reasons: (1) it shows a lack of awareness and respect when one assumes that all people in a given racial group are the same and when little attention or respect is given to the *different cultural and ethnic subgroups* within a given racial group; and (2) this typically means that people in a given racial group are painted with broad generalizations, leading to the erasure of their individual qualities.

Reach outside of your comfort zone, and aim to *genuinely* get to know people from *your own* racial, cultural, and ethnic groups, as well as *people from other racial, cultural, and ethnic groups.* I think you'll find that there are beautiful and inspiring things about all groups and about yourself. I also think that such a journey will increase your knowledge and decrease any implicit or explicit biases you may have. While leaving our comfort zones might be challenging, it's worth it, as we individually and collectively work toward dismantling racism. In the words of one of my favorite authors, Mark Twain: "Travel is fatal to prejudice, bigotry, and narrow-mindedness, and many of our people need it sorely on these accounts. Broad, wholesome, charitable views of men and things cannot be acquired by vegetating in one little corner of the earth all one's lifetime." There were 12 affirmative responses and eight negative responses as it relates to this prompt:

Have Been Mistaken for Someone Else Because They Are a Member of the Same Racial Group

Holly (African American Woman, Midwest and Deep South): Yes. If they call me someone else, I always say, "I'm the other Black lady." This brings a little light to what they did, that's how I answer.

Pamela (Latina, Northeast): This White woman, said to me, "You must be so-and-so's sister, right?" and I said, "Why, do you think that?" And she said, "Well, you guys look alike." I said "Do we? Because we're not the same actually, and we don't look alike at all." So yes.

Leo (African American Man, Southwest and Northeast): (Laughs) Oh, my goodness. This one guy just got hired [and] everyone is like, "That's your twin brother," and I'm like, "He looks *nothing* like me." So many people say it. I just spoke to him for the first time yesterday. [He's a] really cool cat. [I] can't even hate on him. [But] it's just weird how everybody makes everything awkward [by saying], "That's your doppelganger. That's your competition." [But] I'm like, "No, I'm my *own* competition."

Audrey (African American Woman, Northwest and Northeast):	Yeah, all the time. People are like, you look like so and so. I mean that's in work and outside of work too (chuckles). You know, the "all Black people look alike" kind of thing.
Tara (African American Woman, West):	Oh yes. You know we all look alike (said sarcastically followed by laughter). We had one other African American girl in our squadron. She was younger than me, I have dreadlocks, I look different from her, I was a whole shade [different than her], and they would constantly call her my name, and me her name. And it's weird because we use only last names, and you cannot mix the two up. I couldn't even say that her name sounded similar. It is what it is, and all you can do is correct them.
Peter (Asian American Chinese Man, Northeast):	Yeah, that happens a lot. Most people have a stereotype of what an Asian looks like and [they think], we all look alike, even though we really don't. [Furthermore], I've only been to two or three national conferences [for work], but I want to say that that's happened at every conference.
Fred (African American Man, Northeast):	That actually happens to me fairly often. I don't know if it's more of a "*big* Black man" thing, [or] just a "Black man" thing. Whenever there's another large Black man, particularly with facial hair, I get confused for that person quite often. [This happens] regardless of how different our dress styles are, how different our voices are, [or] how different our personalities are. In 2014, when I was an assistant director of a [youth program] one of the staff members was a guy named [Horatio]. The entire summer, people would call me Horatio, and call him by my name. I don't understand how over the course of three months, [they couldn't] keep up with the fact that we [are] different people. It made me feel like it was on purpose.

Brandon (African American and Filipino Man, Northwest and Northeast):	Yeah. I was going somewhere and was misidentified as a supervisor of custodians. I was going into another building [on my job site] and passed by where the custodians were. [There were] only Black men or Hispanic men and the assumption was that, I was either working with them, or they are working for me, and that I wasn't in higher administration.

Have Not *Been Mistaken for Someone Else Because They Are a Member of the Same Racial Group*

Maya (African American Woman, Northeast):	No, that hasn't happened to me personally. But it has happened to a colleague here, it was pretty bad. She was mistaken for hotel staff. It was bad, it was just a really bad experience, but that hasn't happened to me personally.
Corrine (African American Woman, Northeast):	In my current office, there [are] literally four African American women and we all work in different departments, it's not a big firm. Prior to that, at one point, there were only two [African American women]. But I was the only one on the executive floor. We were in different areas, and different departments, and even in my previous positions, I was the only African American, so no I can't say yes to that.
Judith (African American Woman, Midwest):	No, I was the only one (laughs). I couldn't have hidden even if I wanted to. The only way I could hide was by not attending. That's the only way I could do it.

Have Been Mistaken for Someone Else Because They Are a Member of the Same Racial Group: Microaggressive Experiences This is one of the only microaggressions that occurs where the target typically *has* to respond. Holly, Ruth, and Pamela responded to this microinvalidation by being direct and by immediately calling the aggressor out on their offensive behavior. While Leo was direct, he also redirected the conversation to focus on his merits instead of his race. Instead of calling the aggressors out on their racist behavior, he wanted them to recognize his own distinctions and work.

Audrey and Tara suggest that this particular microinvalidation is connected to the stereotype that all Black women look alike; similarly, Peter explains that this microinvalidation is connected to the stereotype that all Asian men look alike. While Brandon being mistaken for a member of the same racial group was a brief occurrence, Fred was mistaken for another Black coworker for an entire summer. We don't know for sure whether it was on purpose or whether it was simply negligence and ignorance at hand, but we do know that Fred experienced a series of microinvalidations that reflected a disregard for his lived experiences and individuality.

Bystander and Vicarious Experiences Maya shares that her coworker experienced the microinvalidation of being mistaken for someone else because of race. Even though her coworker was working in a white-collar professional capacity, she was nonetheless mistaken for hotel staff because of the stereotype that hotel hospitality, housekeeping, or other domestic laborers are typically women of color.

You Have Been Mistaken for Someone Who Serves Others This prompt is connected to racist stereotypes about service work and *who performs* such work. While the original question uses maids and janitors as examples of "someone who serves others," in some cases, employees were mistaken for someone who was expected to manage undesirable situations or who did not have as much authority as the employee actually did. There were eight affirmative responses, 10 negative responses, and two responses that were not captured as it relates to this prompt:

Have Been Mistaken for Someone Who Serves Others in Their Workplace

Holly (African American Woman, Midwest and Deep South):	[Two pharmacists] were talking about another pharmacist that left his wife for a pharmacy technician. [One of the pharmacists] referred to that technician as "the help." I stopped and I turned toward him, and I said, "The help? That's how you look at me? I'm 'the help' to you? Let me explain to you, when a Black person hears 'the help' it just sounds so degrading." He

said, "That's not what I meant." And I said, "I understand that, but don't use that tone." I don't know his heart, because I'm not God, so I don't know. So, I believe it when he says that he out of ignorance didn't realize how that could offend someone, but I just wanted him to know.

Peter (Asian American Chinese Man, Northeast): Yes. While at [a Midwestern school that I worked at], we had a night-shift janitor that was also Asian who actually didn't look anything like me. There was a time [when] I was on call, [and] I had to respond to a situation. [At this job] I didn't have specific attire, we could be in whatever attire we wanted to. By the time I got [to the site of the incident], the parent was there as well. And the student [said], "Why is the janitor here?" And I was like, "I'm not the janitor, I'm not him. I'm the on-call administrator, and I'm here to assist the situation." I think by the student saying that, it disregarded who I was to the parent. That took [away] my authority in terms of trying to solve the situation.

Fred (African American Man, Northeast): Yeah. I have also been mistaken, as one of the ground-level employees, instead of a supervisor. Despite the fact that I dress differently than the ground-level employees did.

Judith (African American Woman, Midwest): Oh, I definitely have been mistaken [for not being] a professor. They didn't know who I was when I first got there and was at one of their functions. And people would start talking, and they'd be surprised to find out that I was a professor. Surprised I have a PhD.

Have Not *Been Mistaken for Someone Who Serves Others in Their Workplace*

Maya (African American Woman, Northeast): It hasn't happened with people here at work, but as a part of my position I plan meetings; so, it's happened when we're at other places by hotel staff. They never [think] that I'm the meeting organizer. They always want to go to somebody

	else, but I'm actually the person running the meeting. So, that's happened outside, but I don't ever think it's happened [at] work.
Ruth (African American Woman, Northeast):	No, because they know that I'm sitting in an office so they know what I do there. [In fact], after [my supervisors] can't fix [an issue], and they [can't] handle it, they come and dump it on my desk for me to fix it. And that was part of the problem that I had with Richard, I would say, "Don't come and bring me this, after you have broken it. You created this mess. Don't come and bring it to me like I'm the cleanup woman." So maybe that's right, maybe they *do* see me, on some level as "the maid who will fix it for us." I don't know, I don't know what the mentality was there.
Oliver (African American Man, Northeast, Southeast and Midwest):	No, I don't think so. I bury this stuff. My experiences made me super strong. Mentally strong, and you know, if an African American male can't keep their temper in this society, you're going to jail, prison, or nobody's gonna hire you.
Tara (African American Woman, West):	(laughs) Never. I will say, I've been to [stores], and somebody thought I worked there, and I was like, "I do not even have the shirt on that matches the store! What is wrong with you?" Generally, it is a blatantly racist older White man or woman. It is always them.

Have Been Mistaken for Someone Who Serves Others: Microaggressive Experiences Referring to employees as "the help" is disrespectful and objectifying. Not referring to an employee by their name and calling them "the help" trivializes their humanity and individuality beyond the work that they perform. It is clear why Holly would be offended by her supervisor using that term to refer to an ex-employee who held the same position as she did. I would also note that in this situation, the pharmacist's intent or lack of knowledge does not give him a free pass. Such speech is unprofessional, offensive, and microaggressive, and the pharmacist should have been held accountable for it. As for other experiences, Peter was mistaken for a janitor because he shared the same racial background as the janitor at the school, while Fred, Judith, and Maya were mistaken for lower-level employees.

Although Ruth did not experience the microinvalidation of being mistaken for a maid or janitor, she did experience a microinsult that was similar to what Tatiana experienced (as shared in an earlier response). The behavior of Ruth's supervisors was also quite exploitative, in that they did not give her the respect that she deserves, and they expected her to resolve difficult issues that arose. Ruth shared, "Maybe they do see me, on some level as, 'The maid who will fix it for us.'"

You Have Been Told that You Were "Too Sensitive About Race" Racism is insidious and complex. It harms race relations, making it difficult for us to coexist and to live peacefully together. Therefore, we *all* should be thoughtful about and concerned with improving race relations and ending racism in the United States. Claims about being "too sensitive about race" are antithetical to anti-racism goals and are used to shut down conversations about racism and its impact on people of color and their allies. There were 10 affirmative responses and 10 negative responses as it relates to this prompt:

Have Been Told that They Were "Too Sensitive About Race"

Reena (White Woman, Midwest): Well, yeah. Mainly from other White people, when I'm trying to be an advocate, or voice an experience that maybe isn't the voice of the general, dominant group.

Judith (African American Woman, Midwest): Yeah, yeah, definitely. I got the message after the first couple of times that I [went] to the [department] Chair [a White male]. When I came to him with any issues [he would say], "Oh, you're being too sensitive. Just try to laugh it off and make a joke out of it the next time it happens," like he expected it to happen again. [He suggested that] I should just deal with it.

Brandon (African American and Filipino Man, Northwest and Northeast): One of my White coworkers started going through my Facebook [page]. My page was public at the time. It's not public anymore, but at the time it was public.

Although I've never had a conversation with [my coworkers] about race or racism, or anything about social oppression, or anything political, I *do* have those discussions on my Facebook page with my friends and family.

I'm sensitive about police brutality [and things] along those lines. I think most of my posts at the time, were about police brutality. Outside of work, I have a history of dealing with community [organizing], so I would volunteer for community organizations and coalitions that dealt with police brutality cases. In one case, I did media for [a high-profile police brutality case in the Northeast], so I do have particularly sharp views when dealing with police brutality. So, they would approach me on that. [They were] more upset with *my opinions on police brutality than police brutality itself* (laughs). That's insane. They care more about a Black person's feelings *about* police brutality than the actual act itself.

Ruth (African American Woman, Northeast): [My supervisor Richard] tried to tell me [I was too sensitive] ... [when someone] made a remark about slavery. He said, "Well you know, if I take it to her, she's going to say it wasn't meant that way." I [told him], "I know the game, I know exactly what she's going to say."

[Then another coworker] drew a [racist image]. I had to question myself, "Ok, if I bring this to him, is he going to start seeing me like I'm trying to pull the race card?" But in my spirit, [I was like], "I can't let this ride" because it was blatant. And I told him, "It's not just what I think. You're getting ready to have [people] walking through the door. What if one of them assumes the same thing?" So, he said, "Take it down" and I took it down.

I also thought that Richard wasn't [racist], but the more that I've perceived his behavior over

	the years, he does have a level of it. If I confronted Richard directly and said, "I really think some of your behaviors are racist," he would be so insulted by that, but he doesn't seem to understand that [he] in his own way has tried to ostracize one of the few Black employees that [he] has on this job. [He] has systematically turned [our organization] into a place that will only cater to White [people], and [has held] meetings on how to go about diminishing bringing in [people] of color. [On another note], when I interviewed at [another job], the first thing [a White female supervisor] said was, "We're not racist here." And that always struck me, if you have to open your mouth to say it, there's an issue. Either there is an issue *or* there has been an issue, or you wouldn't automatically feel as if you had to defend it. Don't approach me because I'm a Black woman and think I'm automatically gonna think you're a racist. No, no, I don't dig it, I don't dig that. If that's one of the first things that you're saying to me, meeting me, there's an issue, and most likely it's coming from you because you're the one who approached it.
Peter (Asian American Chinese Man, Northeast):	When I do my diversity trainings I always try to push people into thinking more abstractly about who they are, [and] what they are. I do get called sensitive about [diversity related issues] because I'm just trying to get [people] to have a deeper understanding and a deeper mindset about race.

Roger (Asian Indian Man, Midwest): Yep, by faculty and grad students, most recently. I've even been told that when I was working on Capitol Hill. Some people [would] say, "It isn't about race." And I'm like, "Dude, race impacts everything."

Have Not *Been Told that They Were "Too Sensitive About Race"*

Leo (African American Man, Southwest and Northeast): The only time that ever happened was last year. I don't like to vent a lot on social media, but there was a time when I shared a lot of videos of police brutality. That's the thing that really hurts because of my experiences [with police brutality]. I've had people comment and say insensitive things [when] they've never experienced [it] or [have] been in that position, and it's frustrating. It's insensitive things. [Like with] the whole, "All Lives Matter," belittling "Black Lives Matter."

Fred (African American Man, Northeast): No, and that's probably more of a me thing because I tend to avoid even getting into those conversations with some people, [especially] with Americans. European people, we talk race a lot because I feel like people from other countries seem to be more sensitive about race. I feel like, White [Americans] are starting to feel victimized. They feel like they're victims because we feel like victims, and they're tired of getting the blame for it. So, you get that kind of a reaction at times from American White people, opposed to European White people, who have pretty much decided that, they are wrong, and are actively trying not to be, and trying not to offend [too] often.

Corrine (African American Woman, Northeast): No. I tend not to talk about certain subjects, like religion. I think they know my feelings just by the things *I don't say.* Sometimes, your position is *known* by [giving off the attitude of], "I'm not even having that conversation with you, because that's not gonna go well." They know that I have children. I have a son who I was concerned about when certain things [like police brutality, happened] in the media, and they can't begin to identify with that at all. As a Black mother, I've always [been concerned about his safety], even when he was younger. When he was younger, he got stopped by police. Sometimes I hear conversations that they have, [when police brutality happens] in the media, and it's just lost on them. For me to try to make them understand would almost be pointless, because they just can't identify. It's like, we're in two separate worlds [in terms of] how we view things, and we totally process [things] differently. But as a Black woman, I just never get into a conversation about race.

One thing that I've learned in order to survive, [is not to let anyone] force me into any conversation, [especially] not in the office. There's a certain level of respect you will always get from me, and I have no intentions of allowing you to make me act in any sort of way to try to confirm whatever your feelings are about African Americans or minorities or women, especially women of color. They immediately want to think that we got an attitude. They have their preconceived images of how we behave, and I just don't intend to play into that ever. And they're quite surprised sometimes.

In some way, it's unfortunate, but I always feel like their experience with me will shape the experiences for others. Whatever I do will be how they view Black women as a whole, or Black people or minorities. I feel that sense of burden so that [I don't] hinder anybody, [and] so maybe [I'll dispel] negative views. I'm still being me and I'm still being real, but that's always in the back of my mind.

Tara (African American Woman, West): No. I usually don't talk about it with people, because people will say stuff that will irritate me. The direct rule [in the military] is that, you will not talk about race, religion, and politics. No matter how big the topic was in the United States. They did not want that because it can cause issues, and you have to work with people in close quarters.
It completely irritates me when somebody says, "All lives matter." It does, but all lives are *not* being attacked. [Hearing it is] a slap in the face. It was a White man in my class who said, "Saying all lives matter, to a Black person who believes Black lives matter is like having a bunch of people at a table eating a meal, and the Black person doesn't get a meal, and [the other people] say 'Well, all people need to eat.' But that Black person is not getting a meal." That was really profound to me because, that's exactly how I feel. I'm not getting fed, but you're gonna say, "Well all people need to eat." It's a slap in the face.

Have Been Told that They Were "Too Sensitive About Race": Microaggressive Experiences Reena experienced horizontal oppression from other White people when she attempted to highlight targeted voices and experiences. Following some racist incidents at her job, Ruth was convinced that her supervisor was at best racially insensitive, and at worst actually racist. She was also concerned about mentioning racist incidents to her supervisor because she didn't want to be accused of "playing the race-card." Ruth's experience highlights the need for on or off-site mediators who have extensive cultural competence and anti-racism training.

As a diversity trainer, Peter has been called sensitive about race. However, it is also his job to be aware of race-based issues. We need to protect individuals like Peter who conduct such important work related to diversity and anti-racism because it is clear that some people harbor resentment toward such professionals.

After seeking out Brandon's social media page, his coworkers approached him about his posts on race and police brutality. He shares,

"They care more about a Black person's feelings *about* police brutality than the actual act itself." When she reached out to her supervisor for help and assistance after experiencing racist treatment, Judith's supervisor dismissed her concerns. Similarly, Roger's concerns about race and race-related issues were also dismissed by colleagues.

Some interviewees experienced this microinvalidation outside of the workplace or refused to discuss race out of concern that there would be unfavorable consequences. Similar to Brandon, Leo experienced this microinvalidation on social media; however, Leo's experience didn't involve coworkers. Fred, Corrine, and Tara thought it best to avoid race-related conversations in the workplace.

Someone Has Told You that They Don't See Race While it is true that race is a social construction, racism has *real* consequences. Therefore, pretending that racial diversity doesn't exist is disingenuous and discounts the past and present struggles against racism. There were 13 affirmative responses, five negative responses, and two responses that were not captured as it relates to this prompt:

Have Been Told by Someone that They Don't See Race

Leo (African American Man, Southwest and Northeast):	[Yes from] my customer. I spoke to [her] on the phone, a few days ago. We were really getting along and really clicking, joking, laughing, and getting to know each other. The conversation was steering away from banking, and she got so comfortable that she goes, "I have to ask you. Are you Black? Are you White?" I laughed and I go, "I'm not allowed to share that unfortunately." And then she tried to keep digging in, and the next question she asked me was, "Well, do you like collard greens?" I was dumbfounded for like three or five long seconds (laughs). I didn't know how to answer that, and then I eventually came up with an answer and I said, "I love all food, and collard greens are one of them." And she goes, "Well, race doesn't matter, I don't see any race…but I just wanted to know. I didn't know how your feelings would be with the election and Donald Trump."

It's crazy how much people vent to people over the phone that they don't know. They just go off. You see that person's true colors, because there's no filter, and they know once they hang up, they're never going to speak to that person ever again. That's what that lady did: she took advantage. The conversation first started out being comfortable, [and] ended up being uncomfortable to the point where I'm like, "Well ma'am, do you have any other questions about banking?" That's just the short version. There was a lot of other stuff that she said, but it was definitely weird.

Corrine (African American Woman, Northeast): Oh, they always say that (laughs). I've had conversations, and they always go back to their one Black friend or whatever. *We all see race.* And I'm more comfortable if you talk about race. I think it's more real because we both know it's there. It's White privilege, [to] get a pass on something that I don't get to do [in terms of not talking about race].

Ralph (White Man, Deep South): Yeah. Some of the students in their essays [write it]. The White students might say, "Police brutality is an issue, but personally I don't see race." So, there's probably a significant number of students who hold that view. I've certainly heard it but it's not applying directly to me.

Reena (White Woman, Midwest): I have had students that say they don't see race. That's a challenge. I do address it. I name it [and] I say, "You know, there's actually a name for what you just said, it's color-blind racism." It's what we taught people in the nineties, in the eighties when we were still in that mode of "teaching tolerance." Which taught people, "Race doesn't matter, and we're all the same," until we realized what we were really saying was [that] we're erasing race instead of acknowledging the similarities between folks. What we're really doing is not acknowledging the important part that race plays in relationships, living, and being part of the world.

Peter (Asian American Chinese Man, Northeast): Some students still say that to me. But the most vivid experience was in one of my grad school classes when I was in [a graduate program in the Midwest]. We were talking about race and diversity one day, and most of the [graduate students] in the room, they were like, "While we are trying to educate everyone it's important for us *not* to see race, because that really diminishes what [we're] trying to do in terms of educating [our] students." On some aspects, I do agree with them because you want to be equal to everybody, and you want to educate everybody in a similar fashion. [But] when you're saying you don't see race, you're also saying that you don't see a large part of what everybody else sees.

Stella (African American Woman, Southeast): Yes. This might be racial, because it's never the Black teachers that's saying it; it's always the White teachers. In the area that I work in, the students that we teach [are] low income, we have a high ESL [English as a Second Language] population, whether it's Spanish or Haitian or French or whatever the case may be, and there are [White teachers that] are like, "It doesn't matter the color of the skin. You know I really don't see that, I'm just trying to teach the child." And I'm just like, "You can't say you don't see [race] because the majority of our building is African American." So you can't just say, "'I don't see it, [and] all children are the same.' [Because] they're not." If you look at our school, and one of the schools that's in the northern part of the county, you're gonna see a clear difference. Not just in the students, but you're gonna see a clear difference in the school buildings. So you can't just say, "I don't see color." You have to take that into account, you really do.

Judith (African American Woman, Midwest): That would be quite a few people there. [Students and faculty] don't see race when they look at me; they don't see color. They believe America is a melting pot, but they don't believe in race. And then, some like [my colleague in my department], he's supposed to be a [social scientist] and understand aspects [related to race]. They had him teaching a class on race and identity. This person is supposed to understand concepts like race and ethnicity, yet [he was racist toward me] (as outlined in previous responses); it was fascinating.

Brandon (African American and Filipino Man, Northwest and Northeast): Oh, yeah, they like saying that they "don't see race." They don't see race, but they benefit from racism, [and] they'll pretend to be a good liberal friend. That's the thing about White bourgeois feminism. Its goal is to work along with the White male in getting access to the spoils. To get a piece of the pie of what the White man is enjoying. By that extension, you can also have bourgeois Black nationalism, and bourgeois Latino nationalism too, where their whole thing to is to have a place at the White man's table, at the expense of their own people. Because they're not looking to change the social structure, they're trying to get included *in it* to have the spoils.

Fred (African American Man, Northeast): I've been told that by several people. My response is usually that, "*it's impossible not to see race*." I understand the point that they're making, but if I asked you if I was Black, you would say yes; and if I asked you, if you were White, you would probably want to respond that you don't see race, but you are, and you *do* see it. There's one thing to state that you respect people of all races, but not seeing race is a completely unrealistic thing.

Have Been Told by Someone that They Don't See Race: Microaggressive Experiences Leo's response shows us that people who conduct service work are at a constant risk of harassment. He shares that while his conversation with a client was initially pleasant, her speech eventually reduced to racial harassment. After making racially insensitive remarks toward Leo, she went on to say that race did not matter and that she does not see race. However, this is nonsensical based on her behavior during the earlier portion of the conversation. People like Leo's client claim to be color-blind because they probably believe doing so relinquishes them from taking responsibility for their racist speech and behavior.

Corrine makes a good point that ignoring race and pretending not to see race is a product of White privilege and is not a freedom that is awarded to people of color, since they are often mistreated on the basis of their race. Ralph, Reena, Peter, Stella, and Judith experienced this particular microinvalidation in educational environments, which underscores the importance of cultural competence and anti-racism training for students, staff, and educators.

In Brandon's response, he gave a scathing critique of people who pretend to be color-blind. He shares, "They don't see race, but they benefit from racism." Fred shares that it is "impossible *not* to see race," and "there's one thing to just state that you respect people of all races, but not seeing race is a *completely unrealistic* thing." Fred is correct—pretending not to see race *is* unrealistic. Instead, we should aim to understand and respect other races, ethnicities, and cultures so that we can move toward achieving interracial solidarity and eradicating racism.

You Have Heard an Offensive Joke or Comment About Your Group As mentioned in Chap. 2, racist jokes are often fueled by hidden intentions. Oftentimes, macroaggressors make racially offensive jokes and comments *with the intention of being offensive*, and if confronted about their words or deeds, *they hide their true intentions by saying that they were simply joking*. There were 12 affirmative responses and eight negative responses as it relates to this prompt:

Have Heard an Offensive Joke or Comment About Their Group

Audrey (African American Woman, Northwest and Northeast):	Oh, yes. Actually, the first time that I was shocked to silence was when I was [overseas for work], and one of my colleagues there offered to take [a colleague and I to go sightseeing]. He's Indian but lives in [a predominately Black

	country]. So, he [says], "I can't find a job [here] because all the Black people are taking all the jobs because of affirmative action. My wife and my daughter they have a little bit of a shot at getting it because Affirmative Action [benefits women too], but I can't find anything," and he's like, "You people," and I was [thinking], "What?" I was so shocked. I was [thinking], "I'm in a car with this guy, and he's driving me in the middle of nowhere; and I can't even [address him] like I [normally would], because I need him to drive me back where I need to go." I looked back at my [Asian female] colleague [but] she kept her mouth shut. Two months later, he ended up getting fired.
Brandon (African American and Filipino Man, Northwest and Northeast):	Yeah, so there was a lawyer [who was] part of the [institution's] legal team, [who started] making these microaggressive comments about Black men. Because [I am] half Asian, [he thought] that I would probably go along with it. Maybe he thought, "Oh, he's half Asian. He's not too Black." Or maybe he thought, my Pakistani boss at the time, would be down with it too. But we weren't down with that. Because I'm half Black and half Asian, there's an assumption from White people that I have anti-Black tendencies. Therefore, they feel [as though] in private they can talk to me about anti-blackness under the assumption that I may not identify with Blacks.
Leo (African American Man, Southwest and Northeast):	All the time (heavy sighs). It's gotten to the point that I've become numb to it. I would show up late to a party because I didn't want to be the first person there [and] sometimes they'll make comments [like], "Leave it to Leo to be late." Sometimes, I'd have to de-escalate it, "Of course, it's the *Black* person that's gonna be late," then they'll laugh and say a racist joke, I'll say a racist joke, and then it will kind of just end like that. That's what I face a lot out here. That's just one situation, but it's an everyday thing.

Fred (African American Man, Northeast):	Well yeah, I hear lots of jokes about my racial group. I guess, I never really take them negatively. For one, I have thick skin, and two, I'm very racial when I joke also.
Corrine (African American Woman, Northeast):	Yeah, it's definitely overt. I call it out in a nice way, and ask, "What are you trying to say?" [Even though] I clearly know what they're trying to say. It changes the mood in the room, but I'm ok with that. I'm not stopping [them] from [having their] conversations, but I will never make [them] feel comfortable [about having] those conversations. It is not acceptable, and I don't think it's funny.
Fawn (US-born North African Woman, Northeast):	Oh, all the time. I wouldn't even just say with race, necessarily, it's more so a religious thing. Now, I'm not a practicing Muslim. I was born into Islam. I am more spiritual than I am religious, but I have heard people say comments about Muslims, and it makes me uncomfortable because even though I'm not a practicing Muslim, it bothers me because I have family that are practicing Muslim.

Have Not Heard an Offensive Joke or Comment About Their Group

Stella (African American Woman, Southeast):	Not at work.
Ruth (African American Woman, Northeast):	No, I've never heard that. (Laughs) I've never heard it to my face, maybe they've said it amongst each other. But no, I've never heard anyone tell a racial joke.
Pamela (Latina, Northeast):	I can't recall one. I think the other thing too, is that it happens so often, that at times, I can't retain them because it's just so much. I know that it's happened for sure, but I just don't have any examples for it.

Have Heard an Offensive Joke or Comment About Their Group: Macroaggressive Experiences Audrey and Brandon show how pervasive anti-Black sentiments and comments are. A colleague who was stationed in a predominately Black country had no qualms about making anti-Black comments in Audrey's presence. Brandon shares, "Because I'm half Black and half Asian, there's an assumption from White people that I have anti-Black tendencies." While Brandon's revelation might be shocking to some, I hope that it will inspire people to speak up when they hear bigoted or racist comments about *any* group. We have to make it the standard and not the exception to stand against racism and bigotry when it arises.

Fawn shares that the macroaggressive comments that she heard were not only race-based, but also based on religion. While religion-based microaggressions and macroaggressions are outside the scope of this project, research in this area is sorely needed to understand and eradicate the antagonism that people of different faiths experience.

Leo and Fred admit that they also make racist jokes and comments—sometimes in response to aggressors' comments, and sometimes they initiate such speech. However, I don't think we should normalize toxic speech or excuse it under the guise of joking. Such language is inappropriate regardless of the setting.

You Have Heard Stereotypes About Your Group We must work together to end racist stereotypes and beliefs because those who hold racist views about a group may eventually *act* in racist ways toward members of that group. As explained earlier, racist beliefs are rarely restricted to one's mind. They oftentimes escape through one's words and actions. However, I am hopeful because we have the power to dismantle stereotypes by replacing them with correct and positive information. There were 15 affirmative responses, three negative responses, and two that were not captured as it relates to this prompt:

Have Heard Stereotypes About Their Group

Ruth (African American Woman, Northeast):	I think they assume the stereotype about Black women. That we're gonna start pulling off earrings and greasing up our faces because we're getting ready to fight. [They've] never seen that from me. I've had [coworkers] stand over my desk yelling and being argumentative; they have never heard me raise my voice in return.

But I feel year after year, new people come in, [and] these are the [stereotypes] that get repeated. And [the new coworkers] expect a certain behavior. And I'm like, "Where is it coming from? Why would you assume [negative things about me] when I've been nothing but kind to you? Where is it coming from?" The sad thing is, I think that one of the main ones that was spreading most of those rumors was Ms. Beck, the other Black person in the office. I just think it's part of a stereotype.

Leo (African American Man, Southwest and Northeast): I had a coworker say, "Leo, is getting so skinny, you used to be fit, what's going on? You gotta get back to being buff." She's a Mexican girl, and was like, "You know the White girls out here, they like, buff Black dudes." That was a form of stereotyping. Then we had a potluck, and I go, "Hey do you want some food?" and she says, "No, no, I'm dieting, my boyfriend just said I was fat." And I go, "I don't think you're fat," and I knew exactly what she was going to say next, because I've known her for a while, and she's very comfortable and loose. And she was about to say it, and I cut her off, and then I said, "Well then again, I'm Black," and then she goes, "I was just about to say that," and then I go, "I know."

Stella (African American Woman, Southeast): Yes. I think [one particular coworker] was a racist. I'm so glad she retired. I say that because she was always talking about how her grandson's father is Black, [and] she always had something to say about his part of the family. [She would say], "He just happens to be a good father, [and] he has a job." [And I'm like], "He's *supposed* to have a job, isn't he? (laughs) He's *supposed* to take care of his kids, isn't he?" And it's the manner in which she said it like, it's not expected of him to have a job, and it's not expected of him to be such a good father, or to be so involved in her grandson's life, but she's a racist. I can't take her.

Brandon (African American and Filipino Man, Northwest and Northeast):	Yeah, the comments that I've indirectly heard was that Blacks are always angry. I heard that at the workplace. [My White coworkers] said that to a young girl who was Black. She's from the Caribbean, [and] did not grow up here. So when dealing with White racists here, she's not too sensitive to White racist microaggressions. And a [White colleague] said to her, "You're very nice, I thought you would be more mean." And she thought that was a good thing, and when she told me they said that, I'm like, "You realize what they're saying?" Then she realized, [what they were] saying. From an African American cultural experience, we can pick up certain things that other Blacks don't pick up right away because of our experience here. And so, the White people feel like they can get away with certain things with them. Or they'll say something like, "Oh, you must know how to dance. You should come with us after work. We'll have some beers and dance." Like how do you know that I'm good at dancing (laughs)?
Judith (African American Woman, Midwest):	Only from the students. The professors would be careful not to say anything.
Pamela (Latina, Northeast):	Yeah. I've definitely been around people who have had conversations [like], "We need to make sure that they stop coming into the country." The stereotype being that every Latino is an immigrant, and all we have to offer is cheap labor.

Have Heard Stereotypes About Your Group: Macroaggressive Experiences
Ruth was directly impacted by stereotypes that label Black women as "angry and aggressive." Horizontal oppression also came up in her response when she mentioned that the person who was spreading such stereotypes was the only other Black person in the office. Leo heard stereotypes that related to Black male body types and Black male sexuality; Pamela heard

disparaging comments about Latinos and immigration; and Stella heard stereotypes about Black men being substandard fathers. Brandon provides a nuanced perspective on how Black Americans react to stereotypes compared to other Black people. Lastly, Judith mentions that she has heard racial stereotypes from her students. As previously mentioned, it is important that we foster work environments that are free from racist speech and behavior so that employees can do their jobs without experiencing racism.

You Have Been Called a Name or Verbally Harassed Verbal harassment can cause emotional pain and distress for the target and can also lead to penalties for the aggressor and employer. These reasons alone should be enough motivation for employers and employees to foster workplace environments that are void of name-calling and verbal harassment. There were 10 affirmative responses, nine negative response, and one that was not captured as it relates to this prompt:

Have Been Called a Name or Verbally Harassed

Leo (African American Man, Southwest and Northeast): Yes, I have. I've been called the n-word, monkey, baboon. I can't remember all of the names, because honestly, whenever I come across racism, I get upset, but I [also] get [sad] because it's 2017.

Pamela (Latina, Northeast): Yeah, it happened on the street. I was on campus. A White man walks by, and I was with a colleague of mine who identifies as Black, and we're both walking down the street, and it's at night, [and a] man yells out, "I hate niggers," directly at us. I didn't know what to say.

Have Not Been Called a Name or Verbally Harassed

Ruth (African American Woman, Northeast): No. I've never been called a name, or verbally harassed, but I had to stop stereotypical behavior. I didn't like the fact that one day [a White coworker said], "Yeah, yeah, we can go back to the hood." I stopped her, and I said, "Excuse me, but I don't live in the hood." She started

	blinking really quickly, and she realized what she said, and then tried to clean it up. But no, if I let [her], then [she was] going to continue this behavior and feel as if I'm supporting it; as if [she was] making some, "Black connection" with me because [she was] speaking, or acting in a [stereotypical manner]. [Another coworker also behaves] in a stereotypical manner, [and] to tell the truth, I'm a bit offended by it.
Judith (African American Woman, Midwest):	Two stupid things that had happened. One, some creep had yelled nigger out the window of the truck and kept going. I was just walking, minding my own flipping business, but other than that, at a local store. I'm from the Deep South, and I hadn't experienced the kind of stuff that I had to deal with [in the Midwest].
Fawn (US-born North African Woman, Northeast):	No. I don't "look" like I'm from the Middle East, so I don't believe that I've ever had anything directed toward me. But I hear it in conversations. A lot of my Latino friends [will] say an Arab joke, or make a comment. And I look at them, like, "Do you not remember what I am?" They often forget that I am not Latina.
Tara (African American Woman, West):	Maybe once, and it was from a little kid. I was like a teenager, and he spit at me, and called me a nigger.

Have Been Called a Name or Verbally Harassed: Macroaggressive Experiences As Leo mentioned in a previous comment, he works at a bank call center and is exposed to varying levels of racial harassment from customers. In this response, he shares some of the racially macroaggressive and derogatory names that he has been called. Pamela was also called a racist slur as she was walking on her campus. While Ruth was not called a name or verbally harassed at her job, she was offended when her White colleagues spoke to her in stereotypically Black vernacular and one made a comment about the "hood"; and although it did not occur on the job, Judith was called a racial epithet in the college town that she worked in.

Fawn can pass as Latina and heard derogatory comments about Arabs from her Latina friends (who did not know or remember that she identifies as an Arab). Tara was called a racially derogatory name by a child, which shows that cultural competence, awareness, and respect must be taught early since racism is learned early.

You Received Offensive Phone Calls, Letters, or E-mail Since modern racism tends to operate covertly, most aggressors in the workplace are unlikely to leave evidence of their racist words and actions. Nevertheless, there are instances when racism in the workplace is obvious and unmistakable. There were three affirmative responses, one related experience, 14 negative responses, and two responses that were not captured as it relates to this prompt:

Received Offensive Phone Calls, Letters, or E-mail

Leo (African American Man, Southwest and Northeast):	[On] phone calls, the person doesn't visually see me, but they start to create their own picture of who they're talking to. I had this one person that was upset about a fee, and [I told them] that I'd go check to see if [I could] get a refund. [I found out that] I couldn't give back the refund. The guy was not cool about that, and went off, [and said], "Are you Black or White? Answer the damn question! You must be a fucking [n-word]." He just went off.
Corrine (African American Woman, Northeast):	I've had an assistant hang up a phone on me because she said she didn't like the tone of my voice. Actually there was no tone. I know she wouldn't have done it to anyone else.

Related Experience

Reena (White Woman, Midwest):	It bothers me that this situation happened and the way that it did. [I invited a White anti-racism activist and educator to] come and speak on campus. And she spent quite a bit of time off script, not with her general lecture that she was going to give, but [instead was] almost combative with students. One of the White male students (one of many), left after a short period

> of time, and immediately contacted the Dean of Students. (Another White man) went on this rant [about whether] this was really appropriate; [and whether] they [should] have brought this person to campus. He was so offended. Then it snowballed into many White students saying they were really offended that she was calling them racist and that she was calling them out because of their conservative beliefs.
>
> It really kind of snowballed and the person it landed on wasn't me. It [landed on a coworker who specializes in diversity], and he's African American. He ended up with the bulk of the e-mails, the discussions, the angry students. Not me, I didn't end up with it, but he did. He got a lot of flak for that. So, yeah, that was rough, but I wasn't the one who ended up with all the bullshit. I wasn't the one who ended up with it, and that's the part that was really upsetting. I brought her here. I rounded up the money. I sent the e-mail out. I was the one who contacted her. I was the one who organized all the travel. I brought her here. And when she got into the lecture part of what she was doing, I was like, "This is what I thought she was gonna do," but she stood up front for quite a while and just went off on the president, [and] we're a small, conservative campus. I felt like I hurt people [when I really wanted] to support faculty, staff, and students of color by bringing somebody in that was going to challenge White students.

Received Offensive Phone Calls, Letters, or E-mail: Macroaggressions and Related Experiences Leo and Corrine both experienced offensive phone calls at work. While Leo's aggressor used blatantly racist slurs, the behavior of Corrine's aggressor was less extreme and was microaggressive in nature. Reena invited an anti-racism activist and educator to her school whom some White students opposed. Consequently, she experienced some backlash; however, her African American colleague experienced the brunt of the macroaggressive backlash, which greatly impacted Reena.

You Had Personal Property Damaged Although people of color and their allies experience property damage at the hands of racists, based on my sample, this macroaggression was uncommon in the workplace. There were two affirmative responses: (1) Ruth believes that a coworker, who was previously horizontally racist toward her, discarded her personal property, and (2) Peter did not elaborate on the circumstances. Additionally, there were 11 negative responses and seven responses that were not captured as it relates to this prompt.

You Have Been Threatened with Physical Assault As expected, being threatened with physical assault in the workplace was uncommon in my sample. This makes sense because such threats are antithetical to what it means to be professional. There were two affirmative responses; however, Oliver and Roger did not elaborate on the circumstances. Additionally, there were 13 negative responses, and five responses that were not captured as it relates to this prompt.

You Have Been Physically Assaulted or Harmed Being physically assaulted in the workplace was uncommon in my sample. This is unsurprising because one would assume that violence in the workplace would result in adverse consequences for aggressors and employers and would generally be avoided. There was one affirmative response by Roger. However, to protect his identity, the specific circumstances will not be shared. Additionally, there were 13 negative responses and six responses that were not captured as it relates to this prompt.

I included the following questions to capture racist microaggressions and macroaggressions that were outside the scope of the modified Daily Life Experience-Frequency Subscale. The questions below deal with topics such as employee coping mechanisms, how microaggressions are addressed by employers, and what respondents believed would make their workplaces more inclusive and welcoming for people of color.

Are There Other Ways that Racist Microaggressions Manifest in Your Workplace? Audrey, Ruth, and Peter were all impacted by stereotypes in the workplace. While colleagues attempted to use "the angry Black woman" stereotype against Audrey and Ruth, Peter's subordinate bombarded him with racist behavior, while refusing to learn what microaggressions are. Ruth also experienced horizontal oppression from her Black colleague who spread rumors about her that were rooted in negative stereotypes about Black women. Ruth also felt targeted by her Latina colleagues who she believed wanted to exclude her. Holly experienced microaggressions and macroaggressions from an aggressive White male coworker. Judith had her authority questioned by students and was ostracized by coworkers and supervisors.

Audrey (African American Woman, Northwest and Northeast): I think the general stereotypes that people have about African Americans, especially Black women being loud and angry. When you need to say your point, [you have to be careful] that it doesn't get mistaken that you're being [an] angry Black woman. I'm from [the Northeast], so a lot of times, I'm used to being more direct, but I realize in [the Northwest] that's not really the way people do things, they talk in circles.

Ruth (African American Woman, Northeast): [I confronted the Black coworker who spread rumors about me, and said], "I thought we were trying to be friends, but you keep [saying negative things about me] around this building that I know are coming from you, and I can't deal with it anymore," and she was like, "I don't say anything more about you than anyone else around here." I didn't tell her that it hurts more coming from [her] because the other ones are not up in my face trying to be my friend and asking me for [things]. [I've also experienced exclusion from my] Spanish coworkers.

Peter (Asian American Chinese Man, Northeast): Yeah, we have an administrative assistant here. We have conversations a lot. So we have a pretty good relationship [and] we joke around a lot. But pretty much once or twice a week, she'll think it's fun to come up behind me, and do these "karate moves" and every time, I say, "Microaggressions." And every time she's like, "I don't know what they are," and I'm like, "Go look it up."

Holly (African American Woman, Midwest and Deep South): I worked at [a multinational shipping company], and I had bad run-ins with my supervisor. He was very immature. [He was a] Caucasian male. Initially, it began as yelling; he would yell at me in the workplace.

[One day] we finished our work for the night [and] he yelled at me, and I just stared at him, and then he walked off. I was so upset because that was not the first time he had a major issue. He always had a major, major problem with me, and I never knew what it was. Now at [this particular company], they have a rule that if a package is too heavy, you must have help with it for safety reasons. [Then] I overheard him ask a coworker, "Did you do that thing I asked you to do?" and she said, "Yes. I started on Friday." And that particular day was a Monday, and the "thing" that she started on Friday was, she [began refusing to help] me with the 100-pound packages. They were my height, about five feet tall, [and] she refused to help me.

[Then] one night...[my] manager came up to me, and he was upset. I didn't want any trouble. I didn't want any drama. And he yelled at me so bad, [that] I just left, I went home. I couldn't take it anymore. I've never felt so insulted in my life, and so I left and went home. So, that was a Friday night, [and] on Monday, in front of everyone, [the manager] came to me and said, "What happened Friday?" And I said, "I really did not feel well Friday (referring to the way he treated me and talked to me)." [Then] he said, "Oh, so you're gonna go with that? That's gonna be your excuse? What's your problem?" So, at this point, I'm flabbergasted, [and] I said, "Ok. I'm gonna answer your question. My problem is that I feel that you have a prejudice against me." He said, "I really want to hear this!" and he became aggressive, very aggressive and he jumped toward me, as if he was gonna hit me. I couldn't believe it. He said, "Oh, you're gonna tell me, I wanna know how do you feel that I have a prejudice against you?" And I said, "This is not the time, the place, or the environment for that type of conversation," and so he said, "No, we're gonna talk about this right now!"

I was flabbergasted at his lack of maturity and so, I contacted HR. I typed up six different occurrences that I had with him because when he called me out in front of everybody, that was the straw that broke the camel's back. I did contact HR, [and] he was already under investigation because he called a young lady the n-word. When I turned in my report, [because] he already had one [pending] investigation; he went ahead and resigned in order to avoid being terminated so he could be eligible for rehire, should he apply in the future.

Judith (African American Woman, Midwest): I had students who would essentially question my authority. There was one who basically was pouting after I refused to let him take an exam that [he] had known about [but he missed]. So, he called in his advisor to a meeting with me. I was offended by that because nobody else had ever had that crap happen to them. I feel like it's my own fault, after years of that kind of stuff, you start to internalize. I'm trying to get over it, but you internalize the emotions, that's part of why I quit, [and] for my health. That was not good, not good at all.

How Do You Cope with Racist Microaggressions in Your Workplace? Corrine coped by covering her tracks and by documenting problematic behavior in the workplace. Judith admits that she didn't have the best coping mechanisms in the past but now utilizes methods that work better for her. She also shares, "There's something to be said for human touch, you know, there just is. If you're all alone, and you don't have any contact with another human being who's sympathetic to your situation, then it just weighs on you, [and] I started not coping too well." Her description shows the value of having allies, advocates, and close confidantes who can stand in solidarity with us as we struggle to survive and recover from racial microaggressions and macroaggressions. Judith's point about having close confidantes is also reflected in the statements from Holly, Maya, and Audrey where they shared how they relied on emotional support from family members and friends.

Reena's coping methods included speaking to an ally and educating herself so that she increased her awareness while unlearning any harmful messages that she may have absorbed during socialization. Her statement speaks to my belief that prejudices, stereotypes, and racism are learned. Therefore, we can also unlearn them. Oliver, Leo, and Stella explain that they cope by letting racist incidents go. Oliver and Leo specifically cope by laughing. Oliver laughs and reminds himself that racists are foolish, "It's ignorance because the true nature of the human being is his *character*, not his friggin skin...if you're caught up in race then something's really wrong with you (laughs)." Leo explains that he laughs to keep himself calm. He shares, "It's a situation where I don't want to rile myself up. Black people have to police themselves. Black people can't be angry."

Brandon notes the importance of leaving toxic work environments, and while I agree with him, I will note that, if a target decides to leave, they should be strategic in *how* and *when* they leave. They should be sure to take care of themselves and make sure that they are not leaving without having a plan for how they will cover their personal needs and obligations. Ruth explains the importance of letting incidents go for her emotional and physical health. In fact, she believes that holding on to racist incidents made her feel worse than the original incidents did. In his response, Roger talks about the power of participating in activities that allow him to safely disengage from toxic situations.

Corrine (African American Woman, Northeast): I had a boss, she didn't care for me. A White woman. She used to look me up and down, from head to toe every day to see what I had on. Literally, head to toe, every day. And she would nitpick everything that I did. So, I knew that I had to document, whatever I did, and whatever conversations we had. I would print out our conversations, because I tried not to talk to her face-to-face. Anything that she asked me to do, I made sure that it was printed out, double-checked with her, and [then I] had her sign off on it. Because there were times that she told me to do things, and I did what she asked and [then she said], "No, that's not what I asked you." People [like her] can try to set you up for failure. Thank goodness, I [documented our interactions] because she blamed me [for something], but I had the documentation of what she told me to do. I had the smoking gun. All I did was cover myself. I made sure I kept my notes and made sure I got her approvals printed out. I had my own little book of stuff for her, and thank goodness I did.

Judith (African American Woman, Midwest): The way I used to cope with it isn't good. I wasn't really coping with it too well. When I first started there, just talking to family about it [helped]. But it occurred so often, that they got fatigued, or [they weren't there with me and] if somebody's not physically present for it, it's just draining. You know, there's something to be said for human touch, you know, there just is. If you're all alone, and you don't have any contact with another human being who's sympathetic to your situation, then it just weighs on you, [and] I started not coping too well. But the first year, I could cope by talking to others and basically when I had time, I continued doing some of the research I was trying to do. Looking up things, trying to work on finding articles for a project I had a while back. [Now] I draw or read. That's how I sometimes cope with stress now.

Holly (African American Woman, Midwest and Deep South): I normally talk to a friend about it.

Maya (African American Woman, Northeast): I heavily rely on my family, my sister. She gives me a legal perspective on things, in terms of what's ok, what's not ok.

Audrey (African American Woman, Northwest and Northeast): Luckily I have my husband, so a lot of times, I'll come home and be like, "Can you believe what happened?" and I tell him. So, he's kind of like my release, but it's not as satisfying like [the East Coast] where you can just deal with it head on. The first person of color I met [in the Northwest] said, "Find your support network now." She offered for me to come to her mentoring program, just because she realizes it's important to have a circle. She knew it was going to be things that I was going to go through that I was going to need support with.

Reena (White Woman, Midwest): The first thing that I am drawn to do, is to find an ally to go and talk to, and to say, "This just happened. Please tell me that I'm not misinterpreting this, or validate the fact that I am really pissed about this, and this is something that I *should* be pissed about." [I do this] with people that I know are safe people, and I know are going to be honest with me and say, "Yeah, that was a big deal. You're not overreacting. That was horrible, [and] that shouldn't have happened that way. How can we respond to it? What can we do." That's the first thing that I do.

And then, I'm constantly called to remind myself to do things that put me in the position where I feel like, I'm doing what I need to do. I'm educating myself, I'm reading what I need to be reading, I'm paying attention to what is happening in other cultures. [I also ask myself constantly if I] am paying attention to the right perspective; [and] am I speaking in a way that is acceptable and inclusive? It makes me feel better, to feel like I'm trying to do the best that I can. I'm constantly trying to undo what's been done.

Oliver (African American Man, Northeast, Southeast and Midwest):	I just laugh, sometimes I don't blatantly laugh, but I think you gotta learn to laugh about it, and move on. [Racism] is more ignorance than anything. It's ignorance because the true nature of the human being is his *character*, not his friggin skin. How you treat people, how you respect people, how you listen to other people, how you communicate, those things are the most important things, and if you're caught up in race then something's really wrong with you (laughs). What happened to you, that you're dwelling on something so petty, something so negative, and you aren't judging people by their character, the real nature of an individual human being.
Leo (African American Man, Southwest and Northeast):	Whenever I'm nervous, afraid, or scared I use laughter and jokes. Primarily for myself, not because I think it's funny but to laugh it off. To calm myself down, because it's a situation where I don't want to rile myself up. Black people have to police themselves. Black people can't be angry. You can't go out accusing and pointing, and you don't want to feel like the victim. You don't want to play the victim because that can also be turned around on you. I have those thoughts constantly going in my head, that I have to police myself. I have to watch the way that I talk. I have to watch the way that I act. Even the way I walk. We have to police ourselves.
Stella (African American Woman, Southeast):	(chuckles) Because I value my job, and my freedom (laughs), a lot of stuff I have to let roll off my shoulders…simply because it's ignorant, pure ignorance.
Ruth (African American Woman, Northeast):	At first I think I internalized it, and I think it was making me angry. I think it was making me feel worse because when I think back on it now, those were the years when my pressure got worse than it ever had. Inflammation with my

knees and ankles, and [issues with my hip]. I really think all of that could have been a byproduct of internalizing anger, and I just had to start letting that stuff go. That means I can't respond to their negativity, I can't feed off that. I can't take every instance personally. So, I just developed a thicker skin, and I just start letting it go. [Also], the more that I started [removing responsibilities that were not mine from] my desk, the calmer I became. Unless it affects me directly, I'm gonna let it go, and I've been feeling a whole lot better.

Roger (Asian Indian Man, Midwest): Sometimes cussing, reading books, playing video games, [or] talking about it. One of the ways I also like [to cope] is by watching a movie.

How Does Your Employer Address Racist Microaggressions in Your Workplace? Reena and Audrey had supportive supervisors who helped them manage and recover from microaggressive incidents, and Stella's direct supervisor did her best to address any issues that arose and to offer mediation to her employees. Ralph notes that the president of his school is seemingly aware of microaggressions and offered assistance to the university community, but Ralph is not sure what such "assistance" would look like. Similarly, Pamela notes that her school has an Office of Diversity and Inclusion, but she thinks that the office does not effectively help members of the university community learn how to address microaggressions or about one's own implicit biases. Leo says that his employers offered some diversity and awareness training; however, some of the employees didn't take the trainings seriously; and Peter believes that his employer could have been more proactive about addressing microaggressions.

Fred, Holly, Roger, and Ruth feel as though their supervisors were dismissive and tried to cover up incidents while Brandon and Tara believe that their employers deflected any accusations of racism and revictimized targets. Lastly, Judith's supervisors were not helpful at all since she suffered macroaggressions from the president of her school as well as microaggressions and dismissive behavior from her direct supervisor.

Reena (White Woman, Midwest): My director encourages me to address the issue that I'm having. [Whether] it's happened with another employee, [or] if it's happened with students, we'll talk about ways to handle it. But the larger university, they're a little behind on how to address microaggressions, [and how to] create macro-level policy that's going to impact micro-level issues. I think they're kind of lost, so I don't think they're really doing much.

Audrey (African American Woman, Northwest and Northeast): [On the East Coast] my boss was really supportive and would deal with it head on. Usually I would handle it myself, and then I would tell her.

Stella (African American Woman, Southeast): The principal doesn't like a whole lot of "he said, she said." So she brings both parties together. It's kind of like a mediation about their differences. I've [had] some White [supervisors and] depending on their values, they would do the same thing that my principal [a Black woman] does [in terms of mediation]. [But] I have met some that would go to the side that's closest to them and not try to defuse the situation.

Ralph (White Man, Deep South): I haven't heard of any incidents. I know they have different policies in place. The president [of the school] sent out an e-mail to everybody after Trump got elected about [how the school will address any issues that arise]. What exactly that means, what they would do, I have no idea. But supposedly, they say they would do something.

Pamela (Latina, Northeast): I don't think that they're doing a great job. I know there is an Office of Diversity and Inclusion, but I haven't seen anything explicit [about how targets should] handle themselves in the moment, and how to identify your own implicit bias. There isn't anything explicit around that.

Leo (African American Man, Southwest and Northeast): They have presentations, and they have little training simulations [about] what to do, and what not to do. A lot of people make light of the situation, which is funny, because the one's that make light of the situation are the ones that [behave in racist ways].

Peter (Asian American Chinese Man, Northeast): I think they try to, but it's more of a reactionary aspect as opposed to a proactive aspect.

Fred (African American Man, Northeast): They're very dismissive.

Holly (African American Woman, Midwest and Deep South): I feel that some of my managers have tried to cover it up or pretend that it doesn't exist.

Roger (Asian Indian Man, Midwest): They don't (laughs). It is swept under the rug, or you're told that you're responsible for the violence that happened to you.

Ruth (African American Woman, Northeast): I think it's swept under the rug. I don't think that [my supervisor] gives any real thought to it, and he tries to quickly sweep it away as fast as possible because he doesn't want to deal with it.

Brandon (African American and Filipino Man, Northwest and Northeast): From what I've seen, they address racism by calling the person that called them a racist, *a racist*. They try to deflect [any accusations].

Tara (African American Woman, West): It was ineffective, because the "good ol' boy club" of older White people would protect each other, and [then] you have to defend yourself against them. [They won't take a] chief or a captain out because of racism. What they [would] do is move them to another base. Even if it was something in writing, and they could prove it, they wouldn't ever get rid of them.

Judith (African American Woman, Midwest): Technically, the employer was the one doing it.

What Do You Believe Would Make Your Workplace Environment More Inclusive and Welcoming for People of Color? In terms of what participants believe would make the workplace more inclusive and welcoming for people of color, Holly suggests that we have more empathy for one another and engage in meaningful dialogue with each other. Similarly, Reena highlights the importance of having a dialogue about inclusion that centers the voices and experiences of people of color. Ruth suggests that all employees and supervisors should partake in a seminar that focuses on diversity and microaggressions.

Leo, Oliver, Tara, and Ralph argue that a diverse staff would help. Ralph also mentions that in academic environments, "trying to make students aware of what they say, and what they do, and the impact it has on other people" would be beneficial. Corrine imagines that a diverse senior staff and a mentoring program would be helpful in changing the climate in her workplace. Judith also mentions the utility of having a mentoring program and holding aggressors accountable.

Fred notes that ending cliquey behavior among employees and supervisors would be helpful in creating an inclusive environment. Similarly, Brandon argues that having managers who are fair would go a long way in improving the workplace climate. Audrey argues that ending nepotism and hiring a diverse staff would be a positive step forward. Pamela reasons that horizontal oppression must be addressed to change the climate in her program.

Holly (African American Woman, Midwest and Deep South):	Dialogue and more empathy.
Reena (White Woman, Midwest):	That's a great question. I think it would help, if as a faculty, we spent more time talking about [inclusion and campus climate]. I think, getting more ideas and listening to our students of color that have either graduated from our program or are currently in it [would] help us navigate [those discussions]. I'd have to call in folks who have experienced our program to help us really get to the point where we could understand what the barriers are and what the issues are that folks are experiencing in the classroom. It would be a really vulnerable space because there are so few of those students who have

	either graduated or are participating in our program. It would have to be dealt with in a really sensitive way.
Ruth (African American Woman, Northeast):	I think that they need to [hold] a seminar on diversity with the entire staff. Certain behaviors that they have need to be brought to their attention, [such as] the [behaviors and words that] people of color find offensive. That's the number one thing. And the number two thing is having real interaction with people, not trying to undermine or go behind their back.
Leo (African American Man, Southwest and Northeast):	It would have to be a little bit more diverse, and that's hard to say because I'm not in a diverse state.
Oliver (African American Man, Northeast, Southeast and Midwest):	I think having a more diverse workplace forces people to always have to think. If [your staff is] 95% Caucasian, and from the same place, they're all gonna influence each other to think the same way. But if [an employee] doesn't have anybody to grab a hold of and hang onto preconceived notions, [they're] forced to progress their thinking. So, diversity in the workplace is extremely helpful for progressive thinking and eradicating racial stuff.
Tara (African American Woman, West):	Add more people of color. The more people of color, the more you have to understand us. [The small amount of] people of color leads them to believe that people of color cannot handle this job, they cannot do it, and so they mess with us and say, "We don't want this person in here. This is our little clique." Add more people of color. They may not like it, but it would definitely make sense if there were more people of color there.
Ralph (White Man, Deep South):	More non-White faculty would be a good start. I think a diverse faculty would be useful. I'm not too familiar with students' experiences on campus. Certainly, trying to make students aware of what they say, and what they do, and the impact it has on other people, is probably something that needs to be done.

Corrine (African American Woman, Northeast):	I think just more African Americans, or more minorities in senior-level positions. There are very, very, very few. It's very few of us still in the whole company. I guess [it's] an oxymoron, [but] you can have people of color in higher positions and *still* not feel welcome. Because some of them get there and forget how they got there, and they're not helping the next person up. But a friend of mine, a Spanish woman, she left my company, and went [to another company]. She said they had mentors. She mentioned [that having a mentor] helped her so much, to fit in. Not even as a minority, just to fit in. Period. I think that's a great idea to have mentors. To have people who volunteer. Who you can go to, to help you learn the lay of the land. If you have a nice, diverse group of [mentors], I think that's helpful.
Judith (African American Woman, Midwest):	A faculty mentor that actually has authority to do something if there is some sort of racial incident at the school or [who can address the] microaggressions that are occurring. [And] instead of minimizing [racism], they go ahead and acknowledge it, and try to work with someone to try to deal with it. [And] not just deal with it on the side of the person [who's] the target of it but deal with it on the side of the people who are doing it. I'm tired of it always coming back to the person that's the [target], [where the target] has to make adjustments and cope, instead of tackling [racism] where the problem starts: from the person who is the aggressor.
Fred (African American Man, Northeast):	A more inclusive environment on both ends. [Management and employees] should actively try to avoid "cliquey" behavior. I know working at camp, that's something that's focused on heavily before the children even arrive. Like, you're not going to sit with the same people that you've been sitting with all the time. Try to get more of an openness [toward] understanding other people.

Brandon (African American and Filipino Man, Northwest and Northeast):	I originally thought, if you had more people of color in charge, it would help [inclusion and fostering a welcoming environment]. [But] if anybody's in charge, they should just be fair. People should feel like they should be rewarded based on good work and feel like their job security is based on that, not because they are a part of a particular club or clique.
Audrey (African American Woman, Northwest and Northeast):	Welcoming diversity instead of hiring people that [the managers] know and are comfortable with [but who are] not necessarily qualified to do [the job].
Pamela (Latina, Northeast):	I think that it would be [beneficial] to include research, different scholarship, different evidence-based [work] that talks about the harm that exists in pitting groups against each other that have the same common denominator. Also, talking about experiences of different groups, just to be aware.

In Your Own Words, Please Describe How Your Experience with Racist Microaggressions in the Workplace Has Affected You Many of the interviewees were negatively impacted by microaggressions. For some, experiencing microaggressions was damaging not only to their professional lives but also to their personal lives and emotional well-being. Judith discloses that microaggressions and macroaggressions have profoundly distressed her: "I would say that it's made me question everything that I've worked so hard for... [Whether I should have gotten my PhD]. Who I am, whether or not I'm even a competent person, or whether I even deserve to be there. Even though it wasn't me who was the problem, it just made me blame myself." Roger explains, "It impacts you in your personal interactions with other people, most particularly, those you most love. The detriment to your personal well-being, and how you're interacting with somebody else is unimaginable." Holly shares, "It placed a burden on me. I felt emotionally drained at times, I felt inferior at times, and my stress levels had increased." Similarly, Corrine shares, "It affected me. It affected my sleep. I was stressed." Fawn shares, "I've lost focus and the love of what I was doing."

Other interviewees reasoned that microaggressions not only ruined their work environments but also harmed their sense of self and their interactions with others. Pamela fears that she has internalized negative messages about her race and she knows that she must work hard to dismantle those beliefs. Tara argues that depending on the target's mental health, microaggressions in the workplace can linger and impact the target's future jobs and interactions. Maya feels stuck in her current position. Unable to leave, and not wanting to stay, she explains, "I feel like I can't truly express my opinions. I feel like I can't be myself in order for me to even move on. And it's debilitating. It forces me to be someone that I'm not, which is really difficult. I do think that takes a toll on me emotionally." Audrey explains, "It eventually wears on you as you get older… always having to struggle and think [about] what people are thinking about you. And it's not only from White people. It's from other people of color too… They all have their stereotypes about Black people."

Some interviewees believed that microaggressions in the workplace are problematic because they adversely impact productivity and group solidarity. Reena argues that microaggressions were a waste of time and a drain on productivity. She explains, "I think about the amount of time I spent being irritated, frustrated, angry. If I could have all that time back, other things may have manifested over the last two years." Similarly, Oliver argues that microaggressions not only, "[take] away from the big picture" but are also "divisive."

For one interviewee, the persistent presence of microaggressions at the workplace was a deal breaker, while it served as inspiration for another interviewee. Brandon understandably has a low tolerance for racist microaggressions and argues, "In 2017, if your job is racist, quit. Just leave." Conversely, the microaggressive experiences that Peter encountered inspired his career aspirations of obtaining a position with more power and influence where he can address microaggressions more broadly and in a "proactive and consistent manner."

In her statement, Ruth advocates for more awareness and argues that people need to learn what microaggressions are so that they can avoid them and stop offending others. She also expresses concern about racist microaggressive behaviors being taught to younger generations. Similarly, some interviewees were concerned about the impact of microaggressions on children and in learning environments. Stella hasn't experienced many microaggressions in the workplace because she works in a predominately Black neighborhood, works with a predominately Black staff, and has a supervisor who is a Black woman. However, she is concerned about the way that some of her White colleagues interact with Black children. Stella shares, "Who is to say that in your teaching, your feelings about our race [aren't] coming out toward these kids, when you get upset, when you're yelling in a classroom, when you're handing out consequences in a classroom?" Fred also hasn't been impacted too much by microaggressions, but he is concerned that they are manifesting among children. Similarly, Ralph wasn't affected by microaggressions but believes microaggressions and their consequences should be demystified in teaching environments.

Judith (African American Woman, Midwest): I would say that it's made me question everything that I've worked for. Everything that I've worked so hard for. [Whether I should have gotten my PhD]. It made me question everything. Who I am, whether or not I'm even a competent person, or whether I even deserve to be there. Even though it wasn't me who was the problem, it just made me blame myself. So, I think dealing with racist microaggressions makes you break down essentially because you keep internalizing the messages that you're getting from these types of aggression. Not just somebody who's questioning your credentials. It's somebody who's questioning your intelligence. Questioning your competence.

I know there are some people who can deal with it for years on end and not have negative consequences, but at some point, I think for a lot of people, it makes you question your identity, makes you question who you are. Part of that raises your stress level. [It] also raises the negative consequences that stress and racism bring. And makes you feel like you're not even a full person, a real fully human person anymore when you're dealing with that kind of thing. Makes you feel less than, and like you can't do your job right, and of course you get it internalized and you start having problems doing your job which of course feeds into the whole self-fulfilling prophecy problem. So, if it were younger me, I would say that the degree was definitely not going to solve any problems with regard to race and microaggressions that I've experienced. It definitely is not a shield; it makes it [even] more difficult in some aspects.

Roger (Asian Indian Man, Midwest): It impacts you in ways that you may not even know. It impacts you in your personal interactions with other people, most particularly, those you most love. You don't realize it at times.

The detriment to your personal well-being, and how you're interacting with somebody else is unimaginable. [It] impacts me in a manner that is so subtle. It's like a poison pill that's there, and it's eating at you. It's like a cancer. It's a malignant cancer because it's not ever gonna go away.

Holly (African American Woman, Midwest and Deep South): It placed a burden on me. I felt emotionally drained at times; I felt inferior at times; and my stress levels had increased. It also caused a little paranoia because you question that person's character after any type of microaggression. You always wonder, and it affects your trust. When you cannot trust your coworker or management, that affects your work performance.

Corrine (African American Woman, Northeast): When I was going through the last situation that was really, really toxic, I knew I needed to get out of it but did not have someone who I could go to for help. I had to figure it out by myself. So, I stayed prayed up. Every morning, I used to go in there, I'd be prayed up. My [sibling] would call me five o'clock in the morning [and] pray over me just to go to work. I kept saying, "Either I'm here to teach something, or I'm here to learn something." Maybe more patience, maybe something to pass along. It affected me. It affected my sleep. I was stressed; and when you're stressed out, plus you have to perform, it affects your health, it affects you in many different ways. I had to find a way out. So, I just thank God that another position opened up that I could go to. [But again] it can affect your health; it can affect your family, [it can affect everything]. Even [after] 20 years, I still dot my i's and cross my t's. I'm never that comfortable, and maybe that's what I need. I never have felt like I can relax, or I'm one of them, or I get a pass for the things that I see many others get a pass for. So as long as I'm always mindful of that, it keeps me sharp, and it keeps me employed.

Fawn (US-born North African Woman, Northeast): The purpose I came in with, has definitely changed. In terms of how I work with my students, and how I work with professionals. It's definitely impacted the way I think and the way I move, when I'm at work. I've lost focus and the love of what I was doing because of these things happening.

Pamela (Latina, Northeast): A part of growing up, had a lot to do with suppressing my own ethnic and cultural identity. [Being in] my current environment brought back a lot of feelings, and a lot of ideas I used to have growing up that negatively impacted my own confidence and image, and how I perceive myself in relation to others. Not just others who are like me but others who [are in the] dominant culture. In my previous work environment, I had been around people that were like me, whereas now, I'm in [a] predominantly White space. I think the other thing [about] experiencing racial microaggressions is [that we're] conditioned to not even know when they occur because they're so common place. It's almost as if [I've] accepted [them], so I have some internal work that I have to do.

Tara (African American Woman, West): I would say microaggressions, depending on your personal mental health, can be something you carry with you for a while. [On] every job, [you may] constantly be worried about [racism]. But on the other side of the scale, it can be something to push you to show them you are an overachiever, no matter what comes your way, [and that] you can do it, [and] nothing is gonna stop you. It all depends on the person's mental health and well-being, and how much can they take.

Maya (African American Woman, Northeast): This interview is very revealing. Obviously, I've been dealing with it. I do think it's biggest impact for me has a lot to do with thinking about leaving [and] how I move on. Because so much of it is happening at a senior level, I am now concerned about [trusting] these people to serve as references for me. I feel like I'm beholden to them in some way. I feel like I can't truly express my opinions. I feel like I can't be myself in order for me to even move on. And it's debilitating. It forces me to be someone that I'm not, which is really difficult. I do think that takes a toll on me emotionally. In some ways, it forces me to try to find ways to move on without references, so it's a very difficult situation to be in. I think working someplace small makes it extremely difficult. There's no way that you can talk to human resources without it getting to a senior level, so I really feel like I don't have any support here to even address the issues. [However], this place, for as much as I've had problems in the last few years, has afforded me so many opportunities. I was able to go back to school, get my degree. But it was under different leadership. So, the change in leadership, definitely led to where I'm at now. In many ways, I am so grateful for the opportunities that I've been given, that I don't want to seem ungrateful, but at the same time, I do recognize that I'm not happy with where I'm at, at the moment. To me, I realize that I can't change the organization, so I really do need to find someplace else. But it's difficult when you don't trust the people who are going to speak up for you when you're looking for a [new] position.

Audrey (African American Woman, Northwest and Northeast): I think microaggressions are a huge problem right now. Not only in the workforce but with people on the streets. It definitely impacts me because I'm the one experiencing it, and it also makes me think like, "These people are smiling in my face, but what are they really thinking about me?" And in general, I think it's not good for society because we keep manifesting these stereotypes amongst ourselves about people of color. How do we break these stereotypes that have been going on for centuries?

Stereotypes aren't people, but for whatever reason we can't seem to get away from the stereotypes, because it's embedded in everything that we do, and some people are even taught that at a young age. I mean, I look at my [child] and [my child's] friends, her best friends are White, Asian, Spanish, and they don't see color, but at some point, it switches, and it becomes that they do see it because they're taught that by their parents, or their family, or just interactions that they experience. It eventually wears on you as you get older, dealing with it and always having to struggle and think [about] what people are thinking about you. And it's not only from White people. It's from other people of color too. I've experienced it from Indians, Asians, Hispanics. They all have their stereotypes about Black people, so it's coming from all angles, so you never really know who[m] to trust because they can be thinking the worst of you too.

Reena (White Woman, Midwest):	I wonder if productivity would be improved exponentially if racial microaggressions weren't happening. I think about the amount of time I spent being irritated, frustrated, angry. Expressing those things, addressing them, and then doing what I need to remediate those things, I think if I could have all that time back other things may have manifested over the last two years.
Oliver (African American Man, Northeast, Southeast and Midwest):	It takes away from the big picture. Whatever the big picture of the organization is, it subtracts from the big picture and slows it down. It's divisive. The person that you have these preconceived notions [about] may have the answer. But because you're in that [bigoted] state of mind, you're not ready to work with them. You may have the ability to help nourish [their] idea, but by putting up a wall you don't come close to bringing that idea to life.
Brandon (African American and Filipino Man, Northwest and Northeast):	If [your work is] not going to be rewarded, then you have to find a space where it will be. [In] 2017, if your job is racist, quit. Just leave.
Peter (Asian American Chinese Man, Northeast):	When I first got to [my current position in the Northeast], one of our directors at the time preached [the motto that]: "Education is a business, and our business is education." And that's always really stuck with me because if our business is education, then as the administrators of this business, [we need to be knowledgeable]. [If we can't] recognize issues, such as [microaggressions], which I feel are very important, how are we able to help the "next generation" [of] student's progress. [Additionally], if our faculty and our staff are not willing or comfortable to learn about [microaggressions] or address things more proactively, instead of reactively, how are we really ever able to affect our students in a more

positive way, in a more enlightening way so that they're more worldwide and abstract thinkers?

I try to be as up-to-date with the issues that are happening around us and issues that are happening in the field, [and] in the world. Hopefully, if I can go into the mid-level and executive level I can potentially change [things] in a broad way. I do what I can do in terms of doing my training sessions and working with the faculty and staff as well as my students, but I think that [microaggressions] definitely need to be addressed in a more proactive and consistent manner.

Ruth (African American Woman, Northeast): People need to understand, what they assume to be common behavior could really be microaggressive behavior that's offending people around them. It's not always the blatant remarks [of] calling someone a racist name, or making a racist statement. It's the subtle behavior, that's the hardest thing for any of us to change. [And] how do you stop that behavior [from moving] to the next generation? Because [at first], I see it from the adults, but I also start seeing the same behavior from the children. You can see it begin when they walk in, and they think they have the authority to walk in that office and talk to me as though I'm on their level, with authority. Or they can walk in my office, and go and pick up something, or touch something, or do something without asking permission to do it because they feel they have the entitlement to do that. It's a measure of learned behavior, disrespect, [and] a sense of entitlement that [they] don't have to answer to a person because they're Black. It's interesting, but that's what I would say, it's the subtle behaviors that people have to work on changing.

Stella (African American Woman, Southeast):	It doesn't affect me on a personal level, [but] it affects me on a work level. [If] you have these racist ideals about African Americans [and] you're teaching these kids every day, who is to say that in your teaching, your feelings about our race isn't coming out towards these kids-when you get upset, when you're yelling in a classroom, when you're handing out consequences in a classroom? How much of this is actually based on whatever behaviors were displayed, or was it based on how you feel towards them as a race?
Fred (African American Man, Northeast):	Because I have a fairly strong sense of self, experiencing [microaggressions] hasn't affected me greatly. It's more of an indication of how other people are raised, then it is an indication about me. I teach when it's called for, and when I can. Otherwise I just move on as if it didn't happen; it's just another part of the day. If anything, I would just say, working in education, a lot of microaggressions are way more prevalent with the children and the families, than they are within the staff. So, a lot of what we deal with has to deal with the kids' reactions to each other, like the whole, "Black girls don't have pretty hair," and stuff like that, and, "Black boys being more athletic than non-Black boys," and things of that nature.
Ralph (White Man, Deep South):	Like I said, I haven't really had any experiences. I would just say that, myself and anybody else in [education], should make sure that [we] are actually aware of what [microaggressions] are and [how they] can have a seriously negative impact on students. Maybe it might seem like it's nothing significant to a White faculty member or a White student, but it can be very detrimental to non-White individuals, and I think that needs to be recognized and addressed.

In the Past Two Years, Which of These Categories Describes the Person or People Who Were Behaving in Racist Ways Toward You in Your Workplace? Table 5.2 shows who was behaving in a racist way toward the study participants. For this sample, most aggressors were coworkers and individuals who fall into the "Other" category like customers and students. It is unsurprising that coworkers would be the most common type of aggressor because we spend more time with and around our coworkers than someone of a lower rank than us, who we might not see in our immediate work environment, and who might be wary of being disrespectful because of the power dynamics. People in the "Other" category also make sense, because these are people who typically encounter targets for a limited amount of time. Customers and patrons may be more likely to direct microaggressive and macroaggressive behavior toward a customer service representative

Table 5.2 Categories of individuals behaving in racist ways toward participants

Participant name	*A coworker*	*Someone of lower rank than you*	*Your supervisor*	*Someone of higher rank (but not your supervisor)*	*Other*
Holly			✓		
Leo	✓				✓ Customer
Fred					✓ Parents of students
Judith	✓		✓		✓ Students
Reena	✓			✓	
Audrey	✓	✓	✓	✓	✓
Tatiana	✓	✓	✓	✓	✓
Stella	✓				
Brandon	✓	✓	✓	✓	✓
Ruth	✓	✓	✓		
Joe					✓ Clients and patrons
Pamela	✓				
Maya			✓	✓	
Peter	✓	✓	✓	✓	✓
Roger	✓	✓	✓	✓	✓
Tara				✓	✓
TOTAL (N = 16)	11	6	9	8	10

N = 16, Corrine, Oliver, Ralph, and Fawn were omitted from the chart because they didn't list any aggressors who they can easily hang up on and never interact with again. An angry, microaggressive or macroaggressive client can decide to never visit the target's establishment again while students, particularly college students, can drop a class, never take a course with the instructor again, or leave a microaggressive or macroaggressive review online or on course evaluations without consequence.

Consequences of Microaggressions

As outlined above, microaggressions and macroaggressions can negatively impact targets and allies in a variety of ways, leading to physical, emotional, and professional problems. Detailed results for each prompt are presented in Table 5.3 but will be presented here in terms of the percentage of respondents who agree and the percentage of respondents who disagree with the prompt.

"Experiencing racist microaggressions at work has negatively affected my work performance." About 50% of the sample agreed and 50% disagreed. While microaggressions may impact morale and work performance, most employees need their jobs or recommendations from their

Table 5.3 Consequences of microaggressions

Consequences of microaggressions	*Strongly agree*	*Somewhat agree*	*Somewhat disagree*	*Strongly disagree*
Negatively affected work performance	28% (n = 5)	22% (n = 4)	17% (n = 3)	33% (n = 6)
Lowered my self-confidence	28% (n = 5)	22% (n = 4)	0% (n = 0)	50% (n = 9)
Less satisfied with my job	47% (n = 8)	12% (n = 2)	18% (n = 3)	24% (n = 4)
I've stayed home from work	22% (n = 4)	11% (n = 2)	0% (n = 0)	67% (n = 12)
Negatively affected my emotional health	28% (n = 5)	50% (n = 9)	0% (n = 0)	22% (n = 4)
Negatively affected my physical health	33% (n = 6)	6% (n = 1)	17% (n = 3)	44% (n = 8)
I have considered changing my job	39% (n = 7)	28% (n = 5)	0% (n = 0)	33% (n = 6)
Increased my stress level	53% (n = 9)	35% (n = 6)	0% (n = 0)	12% (n = 2)

$N = 18$, Corrine and Oliver were omitted from the results because they did not answer these questions current employer to get a new position—which may motivate them to produce great work. However, Brandon shares, “I strongly agree. Because at some point, you wonder why you’re still here. You start to wonder why you’re there, and then the next thing you know, you spent the last 15 minutes staring at your computer screen. Over that question.”

“Experiencing racist microaggressions at work has lowered my self-confidence.” About 50% of the sample agreed and 50% disagreed. Brandon disagreed with the statement, sharing, “No. Maybe at one point, but not now, because I understand what the conflict is, it’s not me. It’s them, it’s the system at play in those folks. I know I’m dope as hell and when I moved up, I moved up because of my merit. So, I know I belong. And they know that too.”

“I am less satisfied with my job because I have experienced racist micro-aggressions.” Out of the sample, 59% agreed and 42% disagreed. Ruth shares, “Oh, yes, yes. I strongly agree with that. That’s why I stopped trying as hard, I’m not putting forth anymore effort.” Regarding her job in the military, Tara shares, “I agree strongly. The job is a fun job, but I didn’t get to enjoy it because of microaggressions.”

“I have stayed home from work because I have experienced racist microaggressions.” Out of the sample, 33% agreed and 67% disagreed. Judith shares, “I admit it. Strongly agree. It was several times that I had stayed home from work. I took a sick day, several sick days.” Ruth shares similar sentiments: “I would somewhat agree to that because there’s been days when I just couldn’t.”

“Experiencing racist microaggressions at work has negatively affected my emotional health.” About 78% of the sample agreed and 22% disagreed. Leo explains, “It has temporarily affected my emotional health. I would have to say, somewhat agree.” Relatedly, Tatiana also believes that microaggressions at work impacted her emotional health: “It drains you with all that negativity, and trying to black things out.”

“Experiencing racist microaggressions at work has negatively affected my physical health.” About 39% of the sample agreed and 61% disagreed. Brandon and Judith are two participants in the sample who strongly agreed with this prompt. Brandon explains, “Yes. Strongly agree. Working late in the last 15 years, I probably gained 100 pounds, of which I lost 60 pounds of it in the last year.” Judith shares, “I’m recovering now. But that was definitely a factor.”

“I have considered changing my job because of the racist microaggressions I have experienced at work.” About 67% of the sample agreed and

33% disagreed. While Ralph strongly disagreed, he shares, "Strongly disagree. But I probably would, if I did experience them." Also, Tatiana explains that she wants to change her job, but her main concern is finding another job first.

"Experiencing racist microaggressions at work has increased my stress level." About 88% of the sample agreed and 12% disagreed. Holly strongly agreed and shares, "When I left [the Deep South], I shared with a friend that I need[ed] to recover. Because I was emotionally upset... emotionally I needed to recover from the opposition." While Joe shares, "I try not to let it overpower me," which truly sums up the experiences of many targets of workplace bullying, microaggressions, and macroaggressions.

Major Themes

Microaggressions were more common than macroaggressions in this particular sample. Some of the interviewees felt trapped in their jobs. They wanted to leave but felt as though they didn't have the means to change jobs yet, which added to their emotional distress and their discontentment with their workplace. For example, Maya and Tatiana both wanted to leave their jobs but felt trapped, and Maya shared, "I feel like I'm beholden to them in some way...I feel like I can't be myself in order for me to even move on. And it's debilitating."

Through the narratives of Pamela and Ruth, we see how painful and disruptive social exclusion and horizontal oppression can be in the workplace. In Pamela's workplace, she was excluded by Black women and felt as though there was a distinction between "women of color" (meaning Black women), and "subwomen of color" (meaning non-Black women of color). Ruth felt deliberately excluded by Latinas in her workplace. In these examples, we see a lack of solidarity between women of color in the workplace. However, if this chasm can be overcome, it would ideally provide a network of allies and support given that both groups of women face obstacles related to racism and sexism in the workplace.

Tatiana and Ruth experienced similar microaggressions and exploitation. They were both mistreated by coworkers and supervisors. However, when issues arose, their coworkers and supervisors expected them to fix the issues. Specifically, in the case of Ruth, her supervisor engaged in unquestionably exploitative behavior by expecting her to conduct work that he was unwilling to pay her for (these details were masked in order to protect her identity).

Oliver and Reena make the point that microaggressions waste so much time and they ruin employee's morale. As seen in their examples, workers of all races and backgrounds are impacted by covert racism. Corrine, Tara, Audrey, and Ruth all mention that they encountered the "angry Black woman" stereotype in their workplaces. Trying to paint Black women as unfriendly, angry, and mean is another way to classify them as lacking objectivity and professionalism. Furthermore, spreading such a stereotype is not only unprofessional on behalf of the aggressor, it is a form of character assassination that harms the target, group cohesion, and workplace climate.

What Can Be Done?

Navigating the American workplace as a person of color can truly be daunting. As we have seen above, racist microaggressions, macroaggressions, and workplace bullying are present in all types of workplaces. However, discussing racism and bullying in American workplaces is still taboo in many respects. Workers are expected to be "professional" at all costs, which is coded language that really means to "buck up, get over it, and get your work done without complaint." Even though the target may be experiencing soul-crushing, morale-reducing, and creativity-killing racism and bullying. As mentioned in the Introduction to this book, oppression thrives in silence, so we must change our current workplace culture so that targets and bystanders are encouraged to come forth, seek assistance, and speak out when racism and bullying occur. Additionally, employers and managers must have the tools needed to readily and effectively address issues as they arise.

Furthermore, employers and managers must stop siding with aggressors and bullies. As it stands, there are few repercussions for aggressors, and in many cases, it is the target who loses their job, not the perpetrator (Workplace Bullying Institute 2017). Oftentimes, when issues are raised, employers and management will focus on the "intent" of the aggressor's words or deeds. However, as I have previously mentioned, regardless of the "intent" of the word or deed, workplace management should take the target's perspective and feelings into account and should also hold aggressor's accountable by offering consequences that range from "teachable consequences" (DiMarco and Newman 2011: 17) to more severe sanctions.

Aside from the advice offered in Chap. 7 of this book, I believe that the following guidelines (modified from the United States Department of Labor Workplace Violence Program 2017) provide good direction for employers, management, and employees who are committed to fostering a safe and fair work environment that is free from racist microaggressions and macroaggressions.

(1) Employers should set standards of what is considered acceptable speech, behavior, and performance for all employees, including supervisors and management. These expectations should be listed in job announcements as well as mentioned during interviews and during any orientations and training.
(2) Employers and management should promote civil, respectful, and kind communication between all parties associated with their organization.
(3) Employers and management should provide learning opportunities designed to provide techniques on how to effectively deal with conflict resolution as well as how to respond to microaggressions and macroaggressions.
(4) Employers, managers, and employees should be responsible for their own behavior.
(5) Employers should hire a mediator who is trained in the area of workplace bullying, workplace violence, cultural competence, and identifying race-based aggression. This person should be available on-site or easily accessible off-site to provide assistance when issues arise.
(6) Employees should report instances of racist microaggressions and macroaggressions when they occur and cooperate with any related investigations.
(7) Managers and supervisors should take all reports of racism seriously and should conduct related investigations in a respectful and timely manner.
(8) Managers and supervisors should also provide support to targets as well as feedback and teachable consequences to all aggressors involved.
(9) Employers should create a knowledgeable threat assessment team to evaluate risks posed by employees and all individuals associated with the organization.
(10) Employers should provide ongoing awareness, cultural competence, and anti-racism training or programming for all employees, management, and supervisors.

References

DiJulio, B., Norton, M., Jackson, S., & Brodie, M. (2015). *Kaiser Family Foundation/CNN Survey of Americans on Race*. Kaiser Family Foundation. Retrieved from http://files.kff.org/attachment/report-survey-of-americans-on-race

DiMarco, J. E., & Newman, M. K. (2011). *When your child is being bullied: Real solutions for parents, educators & other professionals*. Poughkeepsie: Vivishpere Publishing.

Dubreuil, J., & McNiff, E. (2010, October 15). Bullied to death in America's schools. *ABC News*. Retrieved from http://abcnews.go.com/2020/TheLaw/school-bullying-epidemic-turning-deadly/story?id=11880841

Fox, S., & Stallworth, L. E. (2005). Racial/ethnic bullying: Exploring links between bullying and racism in the US workplace. *Journal of Vocational Behavior, 66*, 438–456.

Gabler, N. (2016, May). The secret shame of middle-class Americans: Nearly half of Americans would have trouble finding $400 to pay for an emergency. I'm one of them. *The Atlantic*. Retrieved from https://www.theatlantic.com/magazine/archive/2016/05/my-secret-shame/476415/

Hall, J. W. (2004). *Conversations with Audre Lorde*. Jackson: University of Mississippi Press.

Harrell, S. P. (1994). *The racism and life experiences scales*. Unpublished manuscript.

Havergal, C. (2016, January 21). 'Biased' students give BME academics lower NSS scores, says study. *Times Higher Education*. Retrieved from https://www.timeshighereducation.com/news/biased-students-give-bme-academics-lower-nss-scores-says-study#survey-answer

Huston, T. A. (2006). Race and gender bias in higher education: Could faculty course evaluations impede further progress toward parity. *Seattle Journal for Social Justice, 4*, 591–611.

Lopez, G. (2016, January 25). Why are black Americans less affected by the opioid epidemic? Racism, probably. *Vox*. Retrieved from https://www.vox.com/2016/1/25/10826560/ opioid-epidemic-race-black

Newport, F. (2013, February 8). Democrats racially diverse; Republicans mostly white. *Gallup*. Retrieved from http://www.gallup.com/poll/160373/democrats-racially-diverse-republicans-mostly-white.aspx.

Sommers, Z. (2016). Missing white woman syndrome: An empirical analysis of race and gender disparities in online news coverage of missing persons. *The Journal of Criminal Law and Criminology, 106*, 275–314.

Torres, L., Driscoll, M. W., & Burrow, A. L. (2010). Racial microaggressions and psychological functioning among highly achieving African Americans: A mixed-methods approach. *Journal of Social & Clinical Psychology, 29*, 1074–1099.

United States Department of Labor. (2017). *DOL workplace violence program*. Retrieved from https://www.dol.gov/oasam/hrc/policies/dol-workplace-violence-program.htm

Williams, E., & Ruiz, Y. (2012). *Against workplace bullying*. Amherst: University of Massachusetts, Amherst.

Workplace Bullying Institute. (2017). *The WBI definition of workplace bullying*. Workplace Bullying Institute. Retrieved from http://www.workplacebullying.org/individuals/ problem/definition/

CHAPTER 6

Microaggressions, Macroaggressions, and Modern Racism in the Media and Popular Culture

This is the press, an irresponsible press. It will make the criminal look like he's the victim and make the victim look like he's the criminal. If you aren't careful, the newspapers will have you hating the people who are being oppressed and loving the people who are doing the oppressing.
—Malcom X

As a proud Xennial, whose formative years happened during the 1980s and 1990's, I understand that the media has had a great impact on American society and in my personal life, for better or for worse. Much to my parents' chagrin, my first words were not "mama" or "dada"; they were the lyrics, "Beat It" from the Michael Jackson megahit of the same name. I remember the joy I felt when my grandmother presented me with my Nintendo Entertainment System (NES), how I loved playing it throughout my childhood, and how I still cherish it as a prized possession decades later. I also recall the pride of watching Spike Lee's "Do the Right Thing," because he filmed it in my neighborhood and captured the beauty of Bed-Stuy. Also, I was so moved by Radiohead's album "In Rainbows" that I used one of the songs as my "wedding march" song. The list could go on because there are songs, television shows, video games, and films that mean so much to me and that have inspired me and helped me. When you really reflect on it, it's amazing how an artist can change the world through their art and how their work can touch individual lives in profound ways.

C. C. Levchak, *Microaggressions and Modern Racism*,
https://doi.org/10.1007/978-3-319-70332-9_6

While no piece of media is without fault, there are some that get it right. Prot et al. (2015) explain that media with positive and counterstereotypical messages can reduce stereotypical views and attitudes. As it relates to race and race relations, there are amazing artists who make the world a brighter and more pleasurable place through their work and who also intend for their work to elevate all communities and for it to improve race relations. Additionally, some pieces are diverse and display a wide variety of races, ethnicities, and cultures; some provide an honest, nuanced view of what it means to be a person of color, specifically, a Black person in modern-day America; and some are affirming and show people of color in a positive light. Therefore, in this chapter, aside from presenting examples of microaggressions, macroaggressions, and modern racism in music, television, films, sports, news, politics, and social media, I will focus on what is edifying, constructive, and affirmative in terms of race in the media.

The Impact of the Media on Us

As captured in the Malcom X quote at the beginning of this chapter, the press has historically harmed race relations and oppressed groups through its irresponsible, inaccurate, unfair, and stereotypical portrayals of oppressed groups (X 1994: 93). Furthermore, one could argue that the press and the media at large *still* perpetuate harmful messages and stereotypes that negatively impact how targeted groups are viewed and treated. Prot et al. (2015) share a number of disturbing facts about the media and race-based stereotypes, including the following, "Media-based ethnic stereotypes are especially influential for individuals who do not have direct contact with depicted minority members (283)." So, if a non-Black person has never had direct contact with a Black man and all they are familiar with are media portrayals of Black men as violent and criminal, those stereotypes will influence their beliefs and behavior when they encounter a Black man. This can potentially explain the common microaggression that some non-Black people engage in when they cross the street when a Black man approaches them out of an unfounded fear that he will harm them or steal from them.

"[E]ven a single exposure to stereotypes in the media can influence real world evaluations of minorities" (Prot et al. 2015: 284); therefore, we should all be mindful of what we are exposing ourselves to and we should pay special attention to what children are exposed to. We should also be doing our best to ensure that White *and* non-White children aren't learning about people of color through stereotypical racist depictions and images. One way to address this concern is by including stereotypical messages or representations as a part of TV Parental Guidelines. That way, parents and guardians would be able to make an informed decision about whether they want their child to view a particular piece of media. If we believe that it is useful to warn people about media that contains violence, profanity, and sexual content, then it is also appropriate to warn people about media that contains racist images and depictions.

"[P]ortrayal of ethnic minorities in American television news is more negative than fictional programming...overrepresentations of African American criminals on local and network news can lead to a strong mental association between this group and criminality, creating the perception of African Americans as violent and deviant" (Prot et al. 2015: 284). It's important to acknowledge and address the biases that local news producers and management have against African Americans. Instead of engaging in sensationalism and presenting news stories that portray African Americans as deviant and criminal, news producers and management could instead highlight African American small businesses, African American involvement in philanthropy, and African American involvement in innovations that will benefit local communities and the larger society. It is the responsibility of news producers and management to decide whether they want to present "news" that is biased and disheartening, or if they want to present news that highlights the best of humanity.

"[M]any video games undermine perceptions of minority groups by first, excluding them from taking on main character roles, and second, portraying them through stereotypic images" (Prot et al. 2015: 284). The lack of diversity in video games could very well be linked to the lack of diversity in the gaming industry. The International Game Developers Association reported that 67% of game developers are White, 3% are Black, 9% are East Asian, and 7% are Latino (Weststar and Legault 2015). Furthermore, even though Blacks (53%) and Latinos (51%) are just as likely to play video games as Whites (48%) (see Duggan 2015: 21), Blacks make up only 11% of video game characters and Latinos represent around 3%, while Whites represent about 80% of video game characters (Williams et al. 2009).

In the following sections, I treat mainstream songs, television shows, movies, video games, news stories, social media, and behavior within politics as social artifacts that provide insight to modern race relations and racism. Using a convenience sample of material from the United States that was created approximately within the last two decades, I examine manifestations of racist microaggressions, macroaggressions, and modern racism within pop culture, media, and politics. The examples below are *not* an exhaustive list and mainly focus on Black- or African-American-centered examples. A summary of microaggressions and macroaggressions in the media is presented in Table 6.1.

Table 6.1 Microaggressions and macroaggressions in the media

Media type	*Microaggressive examples*	*Macroaggressive examples*
Television, Film and Video games	Racist stereotypes and tropes Portraying people of color as though they are dangerous or stupid because of their race	Gratuitous violence, cruelty, and aggression toward Black and Brown bodies Racialized sexual violence Racial slurs
Music	Songs that praise or excuse racist behavior or racist artifacts like confederate flags	Songs with racial slurs or songs that glorify or glamorize violence toward Black and Brown bodies
Social media	Comments or memes that refer to people of color as dangerous or inferior, and those that are dismissive about the concerns, safety, and lives of people of color and their allies	Threats of physical and sexual assault on Black and Brown bodies, as well as comments that include racial slurs Images and videos that show violence toward Black and Brown bodies
Sports	Admonishing players for having anti-racism beliefs Using racist stereotypes to unfairly scrutinize Black women Devaluing Black women's work	Racist remarks Racist online bullying of athletes
News	Villainizing individuals and communities of color Downplaying and ignoring the contributions of people of color	Showing violence inflicted on people of color for ratings (oftentimes without a content warning) such as the brutal beating of Rodney King or the murder of Philando Castile
Politics	Not genuinely embracing egalitarian, pluralistic, and anti-racism values Not being genuinely interested in helping communities of color Obstructive racism in politics	Blatantly racist comments Policies that result in the physical, mental, emotional, and/or economic harm of individuals and communities of color

Television, Film, and Video Games

Microaggressive and Macroaggressive Messages

Television shows, films, and video games can be entertaining, uplifting, and informative, particularly when they contain positive or prosocial messaging (Prot et al. 2015). However, I would be remiss not to mention common racist microaggressions and macroaggressions found in these forms of media. Microaggressive messages within television shows, films, and video games often rely on racist stereotypes and tropes, and they portray people of color as though they are dangerous or stupid because of their race. An example would be scripted shows and reality television shows that portray African Americans as criminals or shows that chronicle the crimes and deviance of poor Black and Brown folk while glossing over the crimes and issues in predominately White and affluent neighborhoods.

Television shows, films, and video games with macroaggressive messages use racist slurs and show gratuitous violence, cruelty, and aggression toward Black and Brown bodies. Examples include films and television programs that show brutality toward Black and Brown bodies in the form of sexual violence or the horrific enslavement of Black people. While we should never forget the horrors of slavery, we should also show the success, beauty, and intelligence of Black people.

Diversity and Representation

We live in a diverse society, and our films and television shows should reflect this. A demonstration of American diversity can be seen in the casting of *13 Reasons Why*. While the show has been criticized for the way it handled some topics, it is exceptional in terms of racial representation. *The Walking Dead* also has a diverse cast with important characters who are in interracial relationships. *Horizon Zero Dawn* is a visually stunning video game that has a red-headed White female lead along with diverse support characters. As the player travels the world in Horizon Zero Dawn, they encounter racially, ethnically, and culturally diverse characters, which makes the game even more realistic and immersive.

Nuanced and Intricate Views

Excellent documentaries often provide a rare view of their subjects, as was the case in the documentary, *What Happened, Miss Simone?* The Netflix documentary about Nina Simone did not exploit or disparage her. Instead, it showed the personal, professional, and political accomplishments of an extraordinary cultural icon who worked to overcome the issues she faced. *Black-ish* is an amazing family comedy that captures the complexities of being Black in modern-day America. It manages to entertain with solid performances and sound comedy while also navigating issues such as racism and politics. The comedy *Atlanta* captures the intricacies of being a Black Xennial and Millennial in the United States and chronicles struggles related to managing relationships and attaining financial security. *Get Out* exposed the ugliness of modern racism and the genuine concern that many Black people have as it relates to safely navigating modern-day America. Since modern racism thrives in silence, it is a good thing when the media captures the concerns and struggles of being Black in a society that can sometimes be anti-Black.

Positive, Empowering, and Affirming Messages

The character Akosua Miller in *American Koko* is an intelligent, outstanding Black woman, who is also a champion for social justice. The show is exceptional and is inspirational for all people, particularly Black women who work in the area of social justice. Having an agency dedicated to managing microaggressions, macroaggressions, and modern racism is not only a good idea for Akosua's fictional world, it is a good idea for our world too.

I would be remiss not to mention the amazing and affirming work of Issa Rae. I've seen myself, my friends, associates, and family in the characters she has created and in the work she has produced. Her work is realistic, and it is a tribute to blackness, Black love, and Black lives. From the storylines to the carefully selected music, many of the projects she produces and are otherwise involved in are outstanding and realistic representations of blackness.

Music

Microaggressive and Macroaggressive Messages

Music that perpetuates microaggressive messages includes songs that devalue the feelings, concerns, and experiences of people of color. An example would be songs that praise or excuse racist behavior and racist artifacts like confederate flags. Such messages are toxic and harmful because they teach impressionable minds that racist behavior and artifacts are acceptable and justifiable. Music with macroaggressive messages includes songs with racial slurs or songs that glorify or romanticize violence toward Black and Brown bodies. In these cases, such harmful messages can be horizontally racist in nature when they are performed by artists of color.

Positive, Empowering, and Affirming Messages

Esperanza Spalding's "Black Gold" is an amazing work of art that is inspiring and affirming for Black people. While the song seems specifically dedicated to inspiring Black boys, as a Black woman, I too find it incredibly uplifting. In a world where Black people have negative messages and cruelty directed at them constantly, "Black Gold" is a reminder that we are still precious and worthy of tenderness.

Brown Skin by India Arie is also an amazing song about Black beauty and Black love. It celebrates the beauty of Black and Brown skin, the type of skin that is often disregarded and disrespected. India Arie's lyrics are like a nurturing and soothing balm to skin that has been pummeled by microaggressions. It is a gift, and it is truly affirming.

Social Media

Microaggressive and Macroaggressive Messages

Social media can be incredibly inspiring and useful. It brings people together from all over the world and unites local communities, but it can also be toxic. Many of us have experienced direct or vicarious victimization online when anonymous and seemingly invincible aggressors have made comments about groups that we identify with or groups that we stand in solidarity with. It can be downright brutal sometimes, creating bruises and scars that we can't see but that we can surely feel.

Microaggressive messages on social media include comments or memes that refer to people of color as dangerous or inferior and those that are dismissive about the concerns, safety, and lives of people of color and their allies. An example would be a widely circulated meme that portrays Black men as threatening. Macroaggressive messages on social media include comments that include threats of physical and sexual assault on Black and

Brown bodies, comments that include racist slurs, and images or videos that show violence toward Black and Brown bodies.

Positive, Empowering, and Affirming Messages

Although the Internet and social media can at times seem like a wasteland, void of positivity, there are spaces online that are inspiring, encouraging, and committed to upholding anti-racism ideals. While we all find inspiration from different sources, I encourage you to search for online spaces and communities where you will find affirmation, empowerment, and allies.

Sports

Microaggressive and Macroaggressive Messages

One could make the argument that modern-day sports are devoid of racism and prejudice because "winning is the only thing that matters in sports." This leads some to suggest that athleticism and skill are more important than an athlete's race or ethnicity. However, upon closer examination, it is clear that racism exists in sports and sports culture. Colin Kaepernick being shunned for his anti-racism beliefs and activism is certainly microaggressive in nature.

Simone Biles, Gabby Douglas, and Laurie Hernandez are possibly among the best gymnasts of all time. I cried as I watched their performances during the Rio Olympics. I cried because I was in awe of their strength, excellence, and skill; and I cried, because as I watched them, I fully understood the importance of representation and how meaningful seeing them is for all girls and women, and particularly Black and Latina girls and women. Yet, regardless of their superior athleticism and brilliance, Biles and Douglas have experienced racism during and after the Olympics, some of which was macroaggressive in nature. Biles experienced racist harassment from social media users after she appeared as the love interest of a White artist in a music video (Callahan 2016), and she was also the target of racist remarks from a White gymnast who was jealous of Biles' superior performance (Whiteside 2013).

Douglas experienced horizontal and vertical microaggressive and macroaggressive comments about her appearance, as well as comments about her allegedly having a bad attitude (an accusation that is often hurled at Black women). The bullying that Douglas endured was offensive and hurtful and reflects the unfair judgment that Black women experience in their personal *and* professional lives (Schuman 2016).

Serena Williams shared that she has also been the target of macroaggressive verbal remarks:

> Growing up, I was told I couldn't accomplish my dreams because I was a woman and, more so, because of the color of my skin. In every stage of my life, I've had to learn to stand up for myself and speak out. I have been treated unfairly, I've been disrespected by my male colleagues and—in the most painful times—I've been the subject of racist remarks on and off the tennis court. Luckily, I am blessed with an inner drive and a support system of family and friends that encourage me to move forward. But these injustices still hurt (Williams 2017).

Additionally, aside from being one of *the greatest* athletes in the world, it can be reasoned that the intersection of racism and sexism is the cause of Williams receiving fewer endorsement dollars than lesser athletes (Bain 2017). The fact that Williams was cheated out of endorsement dollars is inexcusable. Furthermore, the racism, sexism, mistreatment and disrespect that Williams endures sends the message to women of color, and particularly Black women, that even at our best, we won't be fairly compensated or treated fairly because of incorrect assumptions and offensive stereotypes about our worth.

News

Microaggressive and Macroaggressive Messages

Some of the content presented by mainstream and alternative news media outlets is racist and has far-reaching negative consequences for Black and Brown communities. Black people in particular are villainized, and our positive contributions are downplayed or downright ignored. Examples of microaggressions in the news industry include the overrepresentation of Black people as criminals across various news outlets. Macroaggressions in the media include showing violence inflicted on people of color, such as the brutal beating of Rodney King or the murder of Philando Castile. Seeing such violence causes vicarious harm to the Black community and our allies. I also believe that it desensitizes people to violence against Black and Brown bodies, which makes it easier for some people of color to develop self-hatred and to lash out at other people of color, or for some White people to devalue the lives of Black and Brown people.

Nuanced and Intricate Views

Although journalists of color aren't well represented in American newsrooms (Maksl and Liu 2016), there are journalists and commentators of color who offer meticulous analyses of race in the United States and honest commentary. At the time of this writing, some of the most notable voices and commentators include Van Jones, Angela Rye, Bakari Sellers, Charles Blow, Ana Navarro, Shaun King, April Ryan, and Amy Goodman. While all outlets have their flaws, shortcomings, and missteps, (at the time of this writing) there are news sources such as "Democracy Now!", NPR Code Switch, and Colorlines that offer nuanced views on Black and Brown individuals and communities and analyses in line with anti-racism ideals.

Politics

Microaggressive and Macroaggressive Messages

Microaggressions in politics often manifest as obstructive racism (see Chap. 2)—a term I created while considering the treatment of President Obama during his presidency. Obstructive racism halted President Obama's agenda in many ways. Additionally, macroaggressions in the political realm manifest when politicians make blatantly racist comments and when they support policies that result in physical, mental, emotional and/or economic harm to individuals and communities of color.

Positive and Empowering Messages

In my estimation, an upstanding political leader works for the good of *all* people. They have great leadership skills and are also compassionate, civil, trustworthy, and honest.

They care about the voices and needs of targeted groups, they care about social justice, and they care about the betterment of society. Additionally, they would not place their loyalty to party and re-election fears over the people they serve, and they would certainly not engage in microaggressions and macroaggressions *of any kind*. Furthermore, as citizens, we all need to be more politically aware and active to ensure that women and men who are committed to social justice, anti-racism efforts, and interracial solidarity are chosen to lead us. There is much at stake, and we must do our part to ensure that the right leadership is elected. It is up to us.

References

Bain, M. (2017, August 31). Only sexism and racism can explain why Serena Williams doesn't earn more in endorsements. *Quartz Media*. Retrieved from https://qz.com/490859/only-sexism-and-racism-can-explain-why-serena-williams-doesnt-earn-more-in-endorsements/

Callahan, Y. (2016, October 24). Simone Biles responds to racist comments about music video appearance. *The Root: The Grapevine*. Retrieved from http:// thegrapevine.theroot.com/ simone-biles-responds-to-racist-comments-about-music-vi-1790889220

Duggan, M. (2015, December 15). *Gamers and gaming*. Pew Research Center. Retrieved from http://www.pewinternet.org/2015/12/15/gaming-and-gamers/

Maksl, A., & Liu, Y. (2016). *ASNE diversity survey*. American Society of News Editors. Retrieved from http://asne.org/content.asp?contentid=447

Prot, S., Anderson, C. A., Gentile, D. A., Warburton, W., Saleem, M., Groves, C. L., & Brown, S. C. (2015). Media as agents of socialization. In J. E. Grusec & P. D. Hastings (Eds.), *Handbook of socialization* (2nd ed., pp. 276–300). New York: Guilford Press.

Schuman, R. (2016, August 17). Why isn't Gabby Douglas smiling? How a champion gymnast became the Olympics' easiest target. *Slate*. Retrieved from http://www.slate.com/articles /sports/fivering_circus/2016/08/why_gabby_douglas_has_been_the_target_of_so_much_unfair_petty_criticism.html#lf_comment=558137544

Weststar, J., & Legault, M. J. (2015, September 2). *Developer satisfaction survey 2015: Summary report*. International Gamer Developers Association. Retrieved from https://c.ymcdn.com/sites/www.igda.org/resource/collection/CB31CE86-F8EE-4AE3-B46A-148490336605/IGDA%20DSS%202015-SummaryReport_Final_Sept15.pdf

Whiteside, K. (2013, October 9). Race remark 'out of line,' parent of world champ says. *USA Today*. Retrieved from https://www.usatoday.com/story/sports/olympics/2013/10/09/ gymnast-apologizes-racist-comment-world-champion/2952905/

Williams, S. (2017, July 31). How black women can close the pay gap. *Fortune*. Retrieved from http://fortune.com/2017/07/31/serena-williams-black-women-equal-pay/

Williams, D., Martins, N., Consalvo, M., & Ivory, D. D. (2009). The virtual census: Representations of gender, race and age in video games. *New Media & Society, 11*, 815–834.

X. M. (1994). *Malcolm X speaks: Selected speeches and statements*. New York: GrovePress.

CHAPTER 7

The Future of Race and Racism in the United States

We have to change ourselves in order to change the world.
—Grace Lee Boggs

Oppression or Liberation?

As I write these words, many are disheartened and tired because of the daily onslaught of covert racism and the recent displays of overt racism as seen in the violence and domestic terrorism that occurred in Charlottesville, Virginia. The future of race and racism in the United States appears bleak, and it is hard not to wonder if we are inevitably moving closer to a dystopian society.

It's intriguing how some of the most popular books and television shows in recent times are set in dystopian societies. Many of us love the idea of a person who can survive the worst and still stand. Some of us may even play with the question of whether we could survive certain dystopian societies and post apocalyptic realities. However, I wonder how many of us have actually thought about how we would respond if *our world* worsened and dystopia and domination came knocking at our door.

Some feel as though we are a few policies and protections away from such a dystopia, so considering our responses is not an exercise in futility. Would you collude with the oppressor or resist tyranny? Would you ignore the persecution of targeted groups and their allies, or would you stand in

C. C. Levchak, *Microaggressions and Modern Racism*,
https://doi.org/10.1007/978-3-319-70332-9_7

solidarity with them? Would you let fear consume you, or would you commit to plans of action?

For some of us, it feels like we are already living in a dystopia. People of color are persistently impacted by internalized, horizontal, and vertical racism. We are supposedly free and equal, but I wonder if we are *truly* free and equal, if anti-blackness and racial oppression are rampant in American society? Are we truly free when students of color are unable to pursue their education without the constant bombardment of racist microaggressions (Chap. 4); when employees of color must contend with oppressive microaggressions in the workplace (Chap. 5); and when the media propagates oppressive stereotypes (Chap. 6)?

Even though the state of race relations seems grim, there is hope. Hope that is real and powerful. Hope that is born out of the encouragement and support of allies and advocates, as well as supportive acquaintances, associates, colleagues, friends, partners, and family; and hope that is born out of the determination of those who have resisted and who have won. This hope reminds me that we can make a difference.

As noted in the quote by Grace Lee Boggs at the beginning of this chapter, we can change the world for the better, but we must first change ourselves (Democracy Now 2015). We can generate long-lasting positive social change if we are *intentional* about increasing our *empathy*, taking *care* of ourselves and others, and if we have a willingness to *stand against* all forms of racism and oppression. We can win with hard work, dedication, education, hope, and diligence.

Liberatory Consciousness

In her work, Love (2013: 602) identifies a liberatory consciousness as a mindfulness that is "practiced … each time we are faced with a situation in which oppression or internalized oppression is evident." According to Love, a liberatory consciousness requires awareness, analysis, action, and accountability/allyship.

Awareness "involves developing the capacity to notice, to give our attention to our daily lives, our language, our behaviors, and even our thoughts" (Love 2013: 602). I believe that awareness in this sense also means taking responsibility for your own growth and avoiding behaviors and thoughts that are internally, horizontally, and vertically oppressive and that are not "consistent with [the] values of an equitable society" (Love 2013: 603). Analysis includes thinking about what needs to be done to resolve issues that arise while action involves "deciding what needs to be done, and seeing that action is taken" (Love 2013: 603). The last step in developing a liberatory consciousness includes accountability and allyship. This requires that we are responsible for our actions and our community and that we stand in solidarity and alliance with targets of racism. With intentional choices, we can develop a liberatory consciousness, but first, we must be aware.

Committing to Anti-racism Efforts and a Liberatory Consciousness

Our biases have been learned over time. They are *not* innate, which means that they can be changed. We can learn to do better and to treat others better. However, this requires some important steps as follows: (1) identifying our issues, (2) not being defensive when others point out our shortcomings, (3) recognizing our privileges, (4) admitting our flaws, (5) *actively* standing against racism and oppression when they manifest, and (6) *actively* supporting targets and anti-racism advocates and activists. Although taking some of these steps may be uncomfortable at times, it will be worth it once we begin to reap the benefits of liberation in our own lives, our communities, our country, and the world.

Although many will expect us to be passive and silent in the face of racism and evil, we should do all that we can to resist the progression of covert and overt racism within our society. Racism and oppression are diseases that must be erased. Words matter, actions matter, and we should be intentional to call out and peacefully organize against racism in all forms. Now is *not* the time for complacency, especially when racism exists in all segments of our society and when people of color and their allies are losing their lives, as well as suffering physical, emotional, mental, economic, and professional harm.

We must work hard to keep this illness from spreading in our hearts and minds and to the next generation. They deserve more, we deserve more, and our world deserves more. Again, feigning ignorance, claiming colorblindness, ignoring racism, denying racism, and making exceptions to who is worthy of love, respect, and liberation is harmful to anti-racism efforts. Please remember, you are worthy of a better world, so let us acknowledge racism and then work together to address it.

Promoting Anti-racism Efforts and a Liberatory Consciousness in Our Relationships

I know that challenging family and friends about anything is no easy task and that doing so is especially difficult when we are confronting them about their bigotry. However, *interrupting and denouncing* their microaggressive and macroaggressive comments and behaviors is a step in the right direction on our journey to end bigotry and racism.

Engaging in bystander intervention training and taking responsibility for your learning will be extremely helpful and will provide you with the skills and confidence needed to interrupt sexist *and* racist behavior alike. As explained in Chap. 1, bystander intervention training and de-escalation training offers skills that everyone should have because *everyone* should be working to eradicate racism. We don't have to wait for someone to be physically assaulted or for a macroaggression to occur before we intervene.

If an acquaintance, associate, coworker, classmate, family member, or friend shares their bigoted thoughts, or if they behave in racist ways, we have the social responsibility to intervene and set boundaries so that their behaviors do not continue or escalate. Silence will not work. In silence, racism grows, mutates, and worsens, so we must stop it early on. For some aggressors, having a prosocial encounter with *one* person is enough to end their bigotry while others will benefit from prosocial encounters with a variety of people. In other situations, the person who confronts them is what matters; while a microaggressor or macroaggressor might not value what their parent or family member says, they might be inclined to listen to a friend. But what matters is that we all do our part to challenge microaggressors and macroaggressors and to establish firm boundaries so they know that we won't tolerate bigoted speech and behavior. We can't let the fear of rejection, or even a sharp rebuke, keep us from addressing bigotry. If we desire to have a strong civilization and strong relationships, we must be civil, respectful, and gracious to one another. There will be times when we won't get it right, but if we wholeheartedly commit ourselves to doing better, we will reap the benefits of peace, interracial solidarity, and the reduction of racism.

Supporting Leaders and Policies with an Anti-racism Focus

We must require more from our leaders. We need for them to clearly condemn hatred and bigotry when they arise. Crandall and Eshelman (2003) note: "when social norms are ambiguous, and do not overtly sanction prejudice, discrimination is significantly more prevalent (420)." Therefore, we should expect a higher standard of behavior from all leaders, especially from our elected officials and institutional leaders because unless bigoted behavior is challenged by those we trust to guide us, racism will persist and potentially increase.

We must become intentional about supporting institutional and political leaders who hold anti-racism views and who will introduce or support anti-racism policies. We also need to support policies, procedures, and practices that will work together to protect individuals and groups from racism in all of its forms, hold aggressors accountable, and protect our social spaces and institutions from hate and aggressors. There must also be protections for *those engaged* in anti-racism efforts. Calling out racism is *not* racist, and calling out bigotry does not mean that you are bigoted toward those you are calling out. While individuals and institutions alike benefit from the brave efforts of social justice advocates and educators, these courageous individuals need to be supported through anti-retaliation policies, procedures, and practices.

Furthermore, as anti-racism policies and procedures are being created, we need input from the people of color who are directly impacted by the issue that the policy is intended to address. For instance, if we desire to combat racism and sexism in the workplace, we need input from women of color so that their experiences can influence workplace policy and proposed solutions.

We also need bold policies and procedures that are specifically designed to dismantle structural racism so that all people can enjoy racial, social, political, and economic justice. Additionally, we need macro-level anti-racism policy that will impact micro-level issues and behaviors. Without progressive policies, change is oftentimes slow, and aggressors' behaviors often go unchecked and unchallenged. For instance, without progressive policies, interracial marriages would not be legal, and it would still be legal to segregate schools.

Collective Action

Although many of us are resilient and strong on our own, we are more powerful when we are united and use collective action to achieve our goals. Jobin-Leeds (2017) shares, "organized action can turn fear and hopelessness into a transformative movement." He also provides "7 actions that we can take right now" to address oppression: in all of its manifestations: (1) have a bold vision and focus your attention on attaining it (e.g. stopping racism on your campus); (2) focus on self-care, resiliency, and being led by love in the work you are involved in (e.g. take care of yourself and others engaged in anti-racism efforts on your campus); (3) get involved with a social justice organization (e.g. volunteer at a local social justice organization where you can learn and practice social justice values and related skills, while giving back to the community); (4) attempt to reach a wide audience (e.g. use language, posters, and social media posts wisely); (5) cultivate valuable skills related to community and coalition building (e.g. observe campus and community leaders to learn important communication and management skills); (6) stay aware of current events and information related to the social change you want to achieve (e.g. use reliable sources for information and news updates); (7) protect vulnerable groups and courageously advocate for liberation (e.g. support targets of racist microaggressions and macroaggressions) (Jobin-Leeds 2017). Collective action has worked in the past, and it will work in the future. It's our move now.

Liberation

Embracing education is key in fighting oppression and striving toward liberation. Several studies have shown the benefits of cultural competence and awareness education in reducing racist beliefs and prejudices. Rudman et al. (2001: 865) found that students who participated in a course on prejudice and conflict showed significant reductions in their levels of prejudice. Another study found that long-term awareness training resulted in a reduction of implicit racial bias (Devine et al. 2012). Similarly, in my dissertation research (Levchak 2013), I found that students with higher levels of cultural competence held fewer racist beliefs. Following the rationale that racist beliefs precede racist behavior, it is realistic to argue that cultural competence education and awareness training are important elements in changing beliefs, reducing microaggressions and macroaggressions, and moving toward liberation.

Relatedly, Bobbie Harro's Cycle of Liberation (2013) gives us hope and shows us that, with intentional thought and action, we can move past the oppressive beliefs and behaviors we learned during the socialization process and, instead, create long-lasting positive social change through individual and collective efforts.

The Future of Race Relations and Racism in the United States

If we stay on our current course of action, and at times, inaction, then future race relations in the United States will be bleak. We'll continue to experience microaggressions and macroaggressions in our schools, workplaces, and within the media, as well as on the streets, in stores, restaurants, gyms, and doctors' offices. We'll continue to be horrified and heartbroken by racism, and we'll continue to question what year we're living in and why so little has changed when we see acts of racism occur before our eyes. However, it does not have to be this way. We do not have to live in a dystopia. There is a better way.

If we take responsibility for our own learning, growth, and awareness; if we commit to interrupting the racist behaviors of those in our lives; and if we are intentional about supporting leaders who are guided by anti-racism principles, then we will see a better America and a better world—one that I and many other people are longing for. There is much work to be done, but there is hope.

References

Crandall, C. S., & Eshelman, A. (2003). A justification–suppression model of the expression and experience of prejudice. *Psychological Bulletin, 129*, 414–446.

Devine, P. G., Forscher, P. S., Austin, A. J., & Cox, W. T. L. (2012). Long-term reduction in implicit race bias: A prejudice habit-breaking intervention. *Journal of Experimental Social Psychology, 48*, 1267–1278.

Harro, B. (2013). The cycle of liberation. In M. Adams, W. Blumenfeld, R. C. Castañeda, H. W. Hackman, M. L. Peters, & A. Zuniga (Eds.), *Readings for diversity and social justice* (3rd ed., pp. 618–625). New York: Routledge.

Jobin-Leeds, G. (2017). What can we do? 7 actions we can take right now. *When we fight, we win.* Retrieved from http://us12.campaign-archive2.com/?u= ed535f51bbb0886f9f4383b8e&id=a1267ac707

Levchak, C. C. (2013). *An examination of racist and sexist microaggressions on college campuses* (Unpublished doctoral dissertation). University of Iowa, Iowa City.

Love, B. J. (2013). Developing a liberatory consciousness. In M. Adams, W. Blumenfeld, R. C. Castañeda, H. W. Hackman, M. L. Peters, & A. Zuniga (Eds.), *Readings for diversity and social justice* (3rd ed., pp. 601–605). New York: Routledge.

Rudman, L. A., Ashmore, R. D., & Gary, M. L. (2001). "Unlearning" automatic biases: The malleability of implicit prejudice and stereotypes. *Journal of Personality and Social Psychology, 81*, 856–868.

Glossary

Acquaintance microaggressor/macroaggressor an aggressor the target knows slightly.

Active listening concentrating on what a person is saying to you, as well as their tone of voice, and their body language.

Anti-racism thoughts, speech, behavior, procedures, practices, and policies that oppose and resist racism in all of its forms.

Awareness being mindful of, and interested in, one's surroundings; in terms of race, it also means being alert and thoughtful about race, racism, and injustice.

Bigotry intolerance and/or aggression toward others (typically toward targeted groups, but can be directed toward anyone).

Collective action working with others in solidarity to achieve a goal or to bring about social change.

Covert racism racism that is underhanded and subtle but very insidious.

Cultural appropriation when a member of the dominant culture steals aspects of a targeted culture.

Cultural competence an awareness of and a respect for cultures that differ from our own; the ability to work effectively with others across cultures.

Diverse institution (academic) the majority of students are non-White (even if White students are the largest racial group, they do not outnumber minority groups when all minority groups are combined).

C. C. Levchak, *Microaggressions and Modern Racism*,
https://doi.org/10.1007/978-3-319-70332-9

Dog-whistles coded language used to stealthily convey racist rhetoric.

Empathy the ability to understand a person's pain, difficulties, or struggles from their perspective.

Horizontal oppression/racism behavior that reinforces oppression or racism and is committed by targeted members *against* other targeted members or is committed by dominant members *against* other dominant members.

Implicit biases attitudes and stereotypes that we hold toward other people unconsciously.

Intentional microaggression/macroaggression an act of aggression that is premediated or deliberate.

Internalized oppression holding views about yourself or your group that support systems of oppression; it can manifest in the form of internalized sub- ordination within targeted members or internalized domination within dominant members.

Intimate microaggressor/macroaggressor an aggressor the target has a close relationship with.

Liberatory consciousness mindfulness to help us navigate and overcome manifestations of oppression.

Long-lasting positive social change long-term change that benefits individuals, families, groups, communities, and society.

Macroaggression a blatant or obvious form of aggression; in this work, it typically refers to manifestations of racial aggression, but it can manifest as other forms of identity-based aggression, such as a gender-based macroaggression.

Macroaggressive exhibiting aggression in a blatant or obvious way.

Macroaggressor an individual who commits a macroaggression.

Microaggression a covert, subtle, or underhanded form of aggression; in this work, it typically refers to manifestations of racial aggression, but it can manifest as other forms of identity-based aggression, such as a class-based microaggression.

Microaggressive exhibiting aggression in a subtle way.

Microaggressor an individual who commits a microaggression.

Microassault a macroaggression or a blatant form of racism.

Microinsult a type of microaggression that disrespects or disparages the target.

Microinvalidation a type of microaggression that undermines the perceptions, feelings, and experiences of targets.

Modern racism a mutation of flagrant racism that manifests through a variety of covert racist attitudes and actions.

Obstructive racism occurs when racists use physical or non-physical barriers to block the progress or agenda of people of color.

Oppression manifestation experiences with oppression are shaped by one's social identity, the social climate, one's physical location, and others in one's environment (depending on these variables, one form of oppression may be more pronounced while another form of oppression may be more recessed).

Overt racism blatant racism; acts that are undeniably racist, discriminatory, or bigoted; macroaggressions; microassaults.

People of color/Person of color non-White people/person.

Post-racial the belief that race is no longer an important social concept.

Post-racism the belief that racism is no longer a major social problem.

Precarious space a space where an individual expects racial aggression to occur.

Predominantly White institution (PWI) (academic) the majority of students are White (greater than 50% of a student body).

Privilege unearned advantages that are given to members of dominant social groups, usually at the expense of targeted social groups.

Processing discussing our experiences with a trusted confidant; taking time to self-care, process our thoughts and feelings, and seek help if necessary.

Protective space a space where an individual expects to be safe and free from aggression.

Racialized gaze when people of color are stared at and objectified.

Racism the mistreatment and harm that people of color experience throughout the social structure on the basis of their race.

Racist belief a view that a particular race is superior or inferior to another.

Racist gaslighting a tactic that racists use to make targets question their own sanity and perception of a racist incident or situation.

Reflective being sincerely contemplative and introspective about a topic or issue.

Reflexive engaging in an in-depth self-analysis about how your identities and social position affect your worldview, speech, and behavior.

Respectability politics the idea that people of color must conform to dominant views or behaviors to earn respect and to be fully accepted into society.

Silenced narratives when people of color and/or marginalized communities are expected or forced to suffer in silence and not name acts of oppression that are directed toward them and their communities.

Social solution a resolution that is attained as a result of people working together to create positive social change.

Targets typically members of underrepresented racial and ethnic groups who are the recipients of racist aggression; people who are the most impacted by individual, institutional, and systemic racism.

Unintentional microaggression/macroaggression an act of aggression that was not premediated or deliberate (although the aggressor is still responsible for the impact of their words or behavior and for making amends to those who were negatively impacted).

Unknown microaggressors/macroaggressors an aggressor the target does not know.

Vertical oppression behavior that reinforces oppression or animosity between targeted group members and dominant group members.

Vicarious racism experiencing the impact of racism because you share the same group membership as the target, or because of your relationship with the target.

Victim worthiness the idea that only some victims (typically not members of targeted groups) are worthy of a basic modicum of respect, care, concern, dignity, and justice after they experience an act of aggression.

Index

C. C. Levchak, *Microaggressions and Modern Racism*,
https://doi.org/10.1007/978-3-319-70332-9

The manufacturer's authorised representative in the EU is Springer Nature Customer Service Centre GmbH, Europaplatz 3, 69115 Heidelberg, Germany. If you have any concerns regarding our products, please contact ProductSafety@springernature.com

Printed and bound by CPI Group (UK) Ltd, Croydon, CR0 4YY
05/10/2026
02228140-0003